Understanding
Shakespeare's England

Understanding Shakespeare's England

A Companion for the American Reader

Jo McMurtry

Archon Books
Hamden, Connecticut

The paper used in this publication meets the
minimum requirements of American National Standard
for Information Sciences—Permanence of Paper for
Printed Library Materials, ANSI Z39.48-1984.

Library of Congress Cataloging-in-Publication Data

McMurtry, Jo
Understanding Shakespeare's England:
a companion for the American reader / Jo McMurtry
p.   cm.   Bibliography: p.   Includes index
1. Shakespeare, William, 1564–1616—Contemporary England.
2. England—Civilization—16th century.
3. England—Social life and customs—16th century.
I. Title
PR2910.M35   1989   942.05′5—dc 20   89–32451

ISBN 0–208–02248–1 (alk. paper)

This book is dedicated to my students, whose interest and curiosity have given me a constant series of new perspectives.

Contents

Acknowledgments

During the preparation of this book, I have been assisted by several research grants from the University of Richmond. I am grateful to Zeddie Bowen, Provost, to Sheldon Wettack, Dean of Arts and Sciences, and to John Bishop, chairman of the Faculty Research Committee, for their help in this matter. I also appreciate the support of my department chairman, Barbara Griffin, in finding ways to juggle my departmental duties and thus create useful blocks of time.

The University of Richmond's academic computer center came to my rescue on several occasions, and I would like to express my thanks to Bob Ducharme, Gilpin Brown, and Bob Littlepage.

I owe a great deal to the librarians of the University of Richmond's Boatwright Library as well as to the staffs of the Library of Congress, the British Library, the London Library, and especially the Folger Shakespeare Library. Jean Miller, Art Curator at the Folger, made my search for illustrations a rewarding excursion.

At The Shoe String Press, the manuscript benefited from the suggestions made by James Thorpe, III, president, whose knowledge of the Shakespearean world helped me improve the book's coherence and usefulness.

Going back a few years to Rice University in the 1960s, I am glad to recall the many ways my attraction to Renaissance literature was strengthened by conversations and classes with Edward Doughtie, John Velz, and the late Kathleen Williams.

My debt to my students is recorded in the dedication. Chaucer's Clerk of Oxenford found learning and teaching a happy combination, and I am lucky enough to enjoy a similar reciprocity in my own daily round.

Introduction

American readers are not without intelligence or imagination, but when we encounter literature which seems to have a great deal in common with the world we live in, as Elizabethan literature does, we naturally tend to think about the connections we can make rather than those we can't. A Shakespeare sonnet, for example, touches on universal human concerns and seems to speak to us quite directly. And yet, especially when we shift our attention to the less lyrical and more realistic writings of the period, we sense certain gaps. It is these gaps that this book has set out to bridge over, though in some cases with a minimal sort of scaffolding. It is, after all, a short book.

Whenever such an approach is useful, we will deal with the quite fundamental and taken-for-granted differences between American and British life. The U.S. Constitution delineates a number of these. Titles of nobility, for example, are forbidden to us, and the separation of church and state is a principle so firmly fixed in our minds that the very existence of a state-sponsored religion may seem a bit scandalous. Aside from our founding fathers' purposeful alterations on the pattern they had inherited, American life has picked up many distinguishing characteristics, chiefly from the other countries that make up our heritage, and has adapted to a quite large chunk of territory, so that we have acquired a set of reflexes not always applicable to the literature of an earlier point in our cultural history.

To make it easier for the reader to decide what he needs to know and what he doesn't, this book is arranged in a nonrigid sequence. That is, basic principles are more fully set out in the earlier chapters, but the reader may feel free to skip the bits in which he has no immediate interest. Chapter 3 provides an example. Shakespeare's history plays are frequently read and staged, and it is assumed that many readers will find useful an analysis of these monarchs' respective pedigrees and claims to

1

the throne. On the other hand, one can spend many happy hours immersed in Elizabethan literature while deferring the history plays to another day, and in such a case missing out chapter 3 will do no harm. With this alternative in mind, the subheadings as well as the chapters are labeled as clearly as possible in order to alert the reader to their intentions.

Some clarification of terminology might be useful. We are concerned here mainly with literature written in the late sixteenth and early seventeenth centuries, a period sometimes called the "golden age" of English literature, comprising the writings of Shakespeare, Spenser, Sidney, Jonson, Marlowe, Donne, and many others. However, the words used for these decades or those surrounding it can vary in their connotations.

The word *Renaissance* brings with it a sense of international influence, especially that of Italy and, more especially, the Italy of the fifteenth century, when this new vitality in arts and letters gained momentum. The movement reached England rather late, often via France or the Low Countries rather than a direct Italian connection; the word *Renaissance* can thus be geographically or chronologically misleading. Another objection occasionally raised to the term is that some segments of the population, whether European or English, did not perceive themselves as being reborn during this era and did not profit from the expansion of human horizons then under way. Nevertheless, the word gets into this book from time to time, particularly in a context of European development. England was looking more and more to the world beyond her insular boundaries, and taking a more and more active part in it.

The term *Tudor* refers specifically to the reigns of the five Tudor monarchs who occupied the English throne from 1485 until 1603 and who are the subject of chapter 2, below. Generally, as used in this book, the word refers to conditions in England rather than in Europe generally. If one takes the year 1485 as a convenient ending point for the Middle Ages in England, the word *Tudor* conveys the sense of a new age, a more centralized government and a greater awareness among Englishmen of England's identity as a unified nation.

Elizabethan and *Jacobean* are fairly self-explanatory from a chronological standpoint, referring respectively to the reigns of Elizabeth I (1558–1603) and James I (1603–25). (*Jacobus* is the Latin form of "James.") *Elizabethan* in particular has the connotation in literary history of a flowering in drama and lyric poetry. This exuberance occurred mainly in the last ten or fifteen years of the queen's reign and continued through roughly the first decade of James's, so that from the perspective simply of literature the word *Elizabethan* often pertains to works dating from, say, 1590 through 1612 or so. The emotional connotation is often upbeat; one thinks of lute songs, happy endings, self-confidence, and general good cheer. Shakespeare's comedies and the aforementioned history plays fall into this period.

When in literary history the term *Jacobean* occurs in opposition to *Elizabethan*, we may be expected to note a contrasting shadow, a tinge of uncertainty, of ambiguous endings and melancholy; examples frequently cited are Shakespeare's tragedies and such unjolly comedies as *Measure for Measure*. (This division is not a tidy one, as the shadows begin to lengthen three or four years before Queen Elizabeth actually died. The date for the composition of *Hamlet*, for example, is generally accepted as 1600. But the discrepancy is then ascribable to a popular consciousness that the Elizabethan glories had begun to lose their luster.)

Whether or not such an Elizabethan/Jacobean mood swing actually existed, the present work does not focus on it, and the word *Elizabethan* is used in the more general sense to mean the late sixteenth and early seventeenth centuries. The life of Shakespeare might serve as an arbitrary but convenient delineation, from 1564 to 1616, the productive years from 1590 to 1612 happening to correspond with the bulk of the other works whose cultural contexts we will examine.

Quotations from Elizabethan works are given here in modern spelling; when faced with a transatlantic choice, I have used the American version unless the word has some appropriate connotation in its British form. Shakespeare quotations and line numbers are taken from G. Blakemore Evans's widely used Riverside edition of the complete works (Boston: Houghton Mifflin, 1974), in which modern spelling coexists with a sensitivity to the rhythm of the lines. Jonson quotations follow the act, scene, and line numbering of the C. H. Herford and Percy Simpson edition (Oxford: Clarendon Press, 1925–52); I have modernized the spelling. Spenser quotations are taken from the Edwin Greenlaw, et al., *Variorum* (Baltimore: Johns Hopkins, 1932–45), and are left in the deliberately archaic form the author intended.

1

Degree and Rank
in Elizabethan England

While Americans often find social distinctions an embarrassing subject of conversation, perhaps on the assumption that nobody is supposed to be better than anyone else, England in former times was less inhibited. Clearly defined and firmly fixed social hierarchies were part of God's harmonious world, wherein one was expected to know one's place and to stay in it.[1] Nobody seemed to mind pointing out the boundaries or, for that matter, attempting to legislate them.

For a quick look at four major divisions of Elizabethan society, we can turn to an eyewitness, William Harrison, a clergyman and topographer whose *Description of England* was published in the 1570s and 1580s as part of Raphael Holinshed's mammoth *Chronicles of England, Scotland, and Ireland*.[2] Harrison lists as separate social categories: 1) gentlemen, 2) citizens or burgesses, 3) yeomen, and 4) artificers or laborers. Not surprisingly, there are numerous subcategories. The category of "gentlemen," for example, includes the king at the top, followed by "dukes, marquises, earls, viscounts, and barons, and these are called gentlemen of the greater sort, or (as our common usage of speech is), lords and noblemen." Next come "knights, esquires, and, last of all, they that are simply called gentlemen."[3]

Harrison at this point still has three social levels to go, and later in this chapter we will turn our attention to them. But as the occupants of the first category figure prominently in literature, we will begin, after a brief digression, at the top.

4

The Status of Women

Women were seen, legally and socially, as wives. Marriage was a permanent state, and within it wives were subservient to their husbands. (See chapter 8, below.) This state of conjunction with another person had legal implications; a wife could not testify against her husband in court, for example.

Women did not have the vote at any level of government. The electorate was quite limited in any case, as will be discussed in chapter 4.

Women were customarily left out of the inheritance of major property; the bulk of an estate went to the eldest son. However, as some families had no sons, there were some wealthy heiresses here and there. Even so, an estate was often entailed upon the nearest male heir, even if he were a distant cousin.

Money left to a daughter was often put in the form of a dowry, to be paid upon her marriage. This dowry was sometimes legally settled so that she could leave it to her children—to her own daughters, for instance. In other cases her husband simply took possession of it. If she never married, she might receive in effect no inheritance at all; the money would remain with the original estate, presumably under the control of her elder brother after her father's death, and she herself would often live as more or less a dependent with her brother's family. (It was sometimes possible, before the Reformation, for a woman in this situation to enter a religious house, her dowry then being paid to that institution.)

In this chapter's survey of society, then, it is useful to remember that women depended for status on that of their husbands. This state of affairs is so taken for granted that Harrison does not trouble to mention it.

Sovereigns: God's Vicars on Earth

In theory, kings ruled by divine right, holding their thrones by the permission (and thus implicitly with the support) of God. Even though the clarity of this principle was sometimes muddied by real life, as we shall see, its importance should not be taken lightly. Shakespeare's Richard II, describing himself as "the deputy elected by the Lord" (3.2.57), was expressing a deeply held tenet of his nation and not, as American readers sometimes assume, demonstrating his unfitness to reign by presumptuously inventing a high rank for himself.

Kings acquired their thrones, at least according to theory, through the principle of primogeniture, or succession by the eldest son. Needless to say, reality could make tangles in this principle, too. A king might have no son to succeed to the throne, or he might die leaving an infant son surrounded by rival caretakers. We will shortly examine some of these complications as demonstrated in Tudor life and literature, but at this point the general idea of primogeniture is useful to bear in mind, as it also governed the succession to titles ranking lower than that of king.

It may be worth noting that a king (or a queen) had no surname. Surnames or family names came into use as a matter of custom, helped along in educated circles by Roman precedent, and proved so handy for record keeping and matters of law that by the fourteenth century everyone was expected to have one, in addition to the given or Christian name that he or she had been baptized by. But by monarchial standards of tradition this custom was both newfangled and unnecessary, as everyone knew who they were anyhow, and kings continued to call themselves by and sign documents with their Christian names, often followed by "R," for "Rex"—or for "Regina," in the case of a queen.

The titles given to sons, daughters, and wives of a reigning monarch present no real problem to present-day American readers, accustomed as we are to monarchial groups in fairy tales. Sons and daughters are princes and princesses; a king's wife is a queen.

A few ambiguities do occasionally present themselves. The term *prince* may be used to mean a sovereign, the ruler of a principality. Thus Machiavelli's political manual, *The Prince,* addresses itself to a hypothetical reader who is already in power, not waiting in the wings.

The title *queen* can be confusing to American readers because one may encounter several queens of England in a literary work, all alive at the same time and talking to each other. Shakespeare's *Richard III* includes Queen Margaret, widow of Henry VI; Queen Elizabeth, wife and then widow of Edward IV; and Queen Anne, wife of Richard III. The clue, of course, is that the title is not taken away when her husband dies, although she may be more accurately described as a "queen dowager" or, assuming one of her children has inherited the crown, a "queen mother."

The Peerage, Beginning with Dukes and Marquesses

All members of the peerage were subservient to the sovereign and thus could be spoken of as "vassals," a word with overtones of hewing wood or herding pigs. This meaning is a correct one in some contexts, but we have here a case of social relativity. A king standing with his vassals on a state occasion would be surrounded by velvet and ermine.

The terms *peer, nobleman,* and *aristocrat* are often used more or less interchangeably, but the connotations differ somewhat. A peer holds one of the five highest-ranking titles and is entitled to sit in the House of Lords. The word *nobleman* may extend beyond the top five ranks and has overtones of chivalrous behavior. The word *aristocrat* is also less specific than the word *peer,* referring usually to a privileged person who has been born into his social status.

The five levels of the peerage are occupied by dukes, marquesses, earls, viscounts, and barons. Historically, the titles of earl and baron originated earlier than those of dukes, marquesses, and viscounts, and, as we shall see, the holders of these titles sometimes had more actual power. But as these five ranks were in place in the sixteenth century, we may as well consider them in their correct order of precedence.

The title of duke was still comparatively new, a European import first utilized by Edward III, who made his eldest son duke of Cornwall in 1337. This son is better known as Edward the Black Prince, and his identity as the first English duke has been overshadowed. The idea of being a duke caught on at once among the elite, however, and several of Edward III's other sons were granted ducal titles in short order.

A duke is addressed as "Your Grace," and spoken of as "his Grace, the duke of Buckingham," or whatever the ducal title may be; he is not called "Lord," this style belonging to the four lower levels of the peerage. With all the other peers, however, a duke is entitled to sit in the House of Lords, the upper house of Parliament, and thus to play a part in the government of the country.

A duke's wife is called a "duchess" and is spoken of as "her Grace, the duchess of Something"; she is not called "Lady" anything, as, again, this style is used farther down the ladder.

As in the case at all levels of the peerage, the family name (surname) of the person holding the title may be quite different from the name of the title itself. The dukedom of Buckingham, for example, is held in *Richard III* by one Henry Stafford, a distant cousin of the king's. (Both are descended from King Edward III.) Stafford is the family name, Buckingham the name of the dukedom.

In literature and in life, a duke is usually close to the throne through kinship or through influence. Since there are not many of them, dukes will generally outrank most of the other characters, although, as we will see, they may not necessarily be the strongest in terms of actual power.

The next rank down from the duke is the marquess, a title which American readers often find confusing, since it looks like a feminine form. In particular it looks like the feminine of *marquis,* which, however, is merely an alternate form of the same word. Both denote a male peer; his wife is called a "marchioness."

The marquess, like the duke, was a comparatively recent innovation, the first in England having been created in 1385. In Elizabethan literature, a marquess often turns out to have been given his title as a mark of the king's favor—a circumstance which is sometimes to his advantage but sometimes not, since other characters may be jealous. *Richard III* includes among its characters the marquess of Dorset, a son by a previous marriage of the queen of Edward IV; as one of the queen's kindred, recently elevated to the peerage, Dorset is resented by the more established nobility.

A marquess, like all peers below a duke, is addressed or spoken about with "Lord" prefixed to the name of the title (not to the family name, if it is different). "Look I so pale, Lord Dorset, as the rest?" asks Buckingham (*Richard III,* 2.1.84).

Earls, Viscounts, and Barons

Moving on to the earl, we arrive at last at a quite long-established English title. Before dukes and marquesses were invented, earls ranked at the top. An earl in literature or in life was likely to be a powerful person with extensive lands, family connections, and interlocking loyalties with other important lords, and for this reason he and the king might eye each other warily. A powerful earl wanted no interference in his way of doing things; a king, no matter how assured he might be of his divine right, nevertheless did well to keep the support of his earls, or a majority of them at least.

The earl of Northumberland, who in *Richard II* supports the king's usurping cousin Bolingbroke and later, in *Henry IV, Part One,* changes his mind, incidentally gives the reader some practice in distinguishing between family names and names of titles. The earl of Northumberland is head of the Percy family, two other members of which are his brother, Thomas Percy, earl of Worcester (often mentioned simply as Worcester), and his son Sir Henry Percy. Sir Henry Percy is referred to by the other characters as "Percy," or, quite often, by his nickname, "Hotspur." Hotspur's wife is called "Lady Percy," the correct style for a knight's wife.

The title of viscount was fairly new to England, the first having been created in 1440. In France, viscounts had once served as assistants to counts, but by the time the title was taken up in England it had become purely honorary and had no duties attached. The wife of a viscount is called a "viscountess."

Technically, the baron occupies the lowest rung of the peerage, but the word *baron* also has a connotation simply of a peer. A reference to "the king and his barons" can denote a quite high-ranking group. Also, "the barony" sometimes means the peerage at large.

Women belonging to noble families took their styles of address from the rank of their husbands or fathers. The wife of a marquess, earl, viscount or baron was called "Lady X," X being the name of the title and not the family name, unless, as occasionally happens, family name and title are the same. (This congruence is particularly likely in the case of barons.) A "Lady" prefixed to a woman's Christian name indicates that she is the daughter of a duke, marquess, or earl. Lady Anne, who undergoes a whirlwind courtship in *Richard III,* is the daughter of the earl of Warwick.

Knights

Strictly speaking, we should next direct our attention to baronets, since a baronet outranks a knight, instead of reversing the sequence. However, the title of baronet only came into existence in the reign of James I, and baronets are seldom mentioned in literature even then. Authors and readers seem to have taken up novelties rather slowly.

The knight, by contrast, has a long history in the annals of honor. A close connection with religion seems to have occurred early on, perhaps through the symbolism of the warfaring Christian who has put on the whole armor of God (Ephesians 6:11). Thus we find King Arthur's fictional knights seeking the Holy Grail, real-life crusading knights wresting the holy city of Jerusalem at least temporarily from the infidel, and a constant coming and going of knights in chapels and priories.

A major distinction between a knight and a member of the peerage, the five ranks of hereditary titles described above, is that a knighthood could not be inherited but had to be earned. Being a knight had more to do with individual effort than with occupying a particular level in the feudal pattern, as was the case with peers. These categories were not mutually exclusive, however, for knights were often of noble family. Many had been knighted quite young, perhaps in their teens, and later inherited (or were granted by their sovereign) a peerage.

William Harrison, our Elizabethan guide to these matters, and by whose analysis of society we are still only in the first category of "gentlemen," explains the situation:

> Knights be not born, neither is any man a knight by succession, no, not the King or prince; but they are made either before the battle, to encourage them the more to adventure and try their manhood, or after the battle ended, as an advancement for their courage and prowess already showed.[4]

By the sixteenth century, one did find knights who were not military types. The Lord Mayor of London, for example, was customarily honored with a knighthood even though he was more likely to be a merchant than a fighting man.

In most Elizabethan literature, knights possess the traditional aura of military prowess and moral uprightness. Chaucer's "verray, parfit gentil knyght," though he precedes the period with which we are concerned, sets a standard. Some variation is possible. The cowardly or bullying knights who turn up in literature appear the more dastardly through contrast to the ideal.

The "Sir" prefixed to the knight's name goes with his Christian name, not his family name, for the institution of knighthood, like that of kingship, originated in an era before surnames came into use. Henry IV speaks of his "true, industrious friend, / Sir Walter Blunt," and, a few lines later, of "Sir Walter"; neither he nor anyone else would say "Sir Blunt." Americans tend to go wrong here, ironically, as we are aware that the British find our first-naming impulse a bit presumptuous, but in the case of knights we are in the right—always remembering the "Sir."

The prefix "Sir" was occasionally used for a clergyman, such as Sir Oliver Martext in *As You Like It*. Instances in literature are self-explanatory.

Knights Who Are Not Necessarily Knights

Usually, a knight encountered in literature fits the pattern given above. But several offices and dignities call their members "knights" even though these members may actually rank below, or in many cases above, the knight as such.

A Knight of the Shire was a member of the House of Commons, the lower house of Parliament, elected to represent a shire, one of England's large territorial divisions such as Lancashire or Derbyshire. A Knight of the Shire might actually be a knight, of course, but it was quite possible that he was not.

Two orders of crusading knights were still known to sixteenth-century

Englishmen, the Knights Hospitalers (also known as the Knights of Malta and as the Knights of St. John) and the Templars. Each had been most active in the eleventh and twelfth centuries, and each had fallen on hard times in England. The Knights Hospitalers, who had cared for sick pilgrims in Jerusalem and later maintained a fortress on the island of Malta, had been among the orders suppressed by the English reformation earlier in the sixteenth century, though they were still active in the Mediterranean. The Knights Templar had been suppressed earlier, in the fourteenth century, and their memory lingered in part because the property they had owned in London, known as the Temple, had been occupied for some time by lawyers.

The Order of the Garter, unlike the two bodies just mentioned, was very much alive in the sixteenth century, as it is today, and appears fairly often in literature. This small and very elite group was specifically English, not international as the much larger crusading orders had been, and it was purely honorary. Knights of the Garter were not expected to go anywhere, fight the infidel, or at all rearrange their lives as a consequence of membership. In addition, being named to such an order did not affect the members' regular titles or styles of address; many of them were already dukes or earls.

According to legend (of which there were numerous variations), the Order of the Garter was founded by Edward III in the fourteenth century on the occasion of his courtiers' laughing when a lady accidentally lost her garter. This bit of personal lingerie, an ornamental blue one, is the insignia of the order, worn below the left knee, with the motto "*Honi soit qui mal y pense*"—"Shame to him who thinks ill of it." The order is dedicated to St. George, patron saint of England, and on ceremonial occasions appears with considerable panoply and takes precedence over the various bodies of honorary knights which have been founded since. (The eighteenth and nineteenth centuries saw several additional honorary orders. Some, such as the Knights of the Bath, claim an ancient tradition.)

In literature, the Knights of the Garter often appear as symbolic of religious and national virtues. Spenser's Redcrosse Knight, in Book I of *The Faerie Queene,* fulfills this function. Redcrosse is in fact not only a Knight of the Garter but St. George himself (1.10.61).

Baronets

The rank of baronet originated as an unabashedly mercenary enterprise. In 1611, King James needed money for a military expedition to Ireland and sold this new dignity for eleven hundred pounds, promising to limit the number of baronets to two hundred. But things got out of hand. Other projects needed funding, and the impulse to raise cash by cutting the price and increasing the number of customers was hard to resist. Under Charles I, son and successor of James I, the price of a baronetcy fell at one point to three hundred pounds.

A baronet, unlike a knight, can pass his title on to his heir. He cannot, however, sit in the House of Lords with the hereditary peers. King James no doubt knew better than to put political influence on sale in so convenient a manner.

A baronet is addressed as "Sir Charles," or whatever his Christian name may be, and his wife is addressed as "Lady Smith," or whatever the family name may be. In this respect he is like a knight.

Coats of Arms and the Gentry

At this point in our broad survey of Elizabethan society we arrive at a level which, though ranking below the nobility and the knights, nevertheless should be seen as solidly respectable, reasonably well educated, and a growing market for literature.

The terms *squire* (or *esquire*) and *gentleman,* often used of persons in this category, had developed considerable overlap, although in earlier times the squire had filled a specific function as attendant to a knight, often being in fact a young knight-in-training.

These members of the gentry shared with the knights, and for that matter with the peerage as well, the right to display a coat of arms and thus to participate to some extent in upper-class pageantry and chivalric nostalgia. Since the late fifteenth century, matters pertaining to heraldry had been supervised by the College of Arms (Herald's College), an incorporated body which kept records of what families were entitled to what arms and granted this right to applicants whom it considered worthy.

Harrison gives us an explanation of who was eligible to apply for a coat of arms:

> Whosoever studieth the laws of the realm, whoso abideth in the university giving his mind to his book, or professeth physic and the liberal sciences, or, besides his service in the room of a captain in the wars or good counsel given at home, whereby his commonwealth is benefitted, can live without manual labor, and thereto is able and will bear the port, charge, and countenance of a gentleman, he shall for money have a coat of arms bestowed on him by heralds.[5]

For the look of the thing, Harrison adds, the heralds would inquire into the past glories of the applicant's family. One might assume that if the fee were properly remitted, some glories would be found.

We might pause here to register a hypothetical objection. Why, if Elizabethan social order is supposed to be so reassuringly stable, is anyone permitted to rise in it? A certain degree of paradox is undeniable. Perhaps human nature has achieved a typical inconsistency; to the Elizabethan mind, it is all those other people who are to remain in place, while one's own merit deserves recognition and reward.

From the perspective of those authorities already high enough on the status ladder to feel unthreatened by an influx at the middle level, an increase in the number of Englishmen acquiring coats of arms and setting themselves up as gentlemen was beneficial to the realm. Gentlemen were easy to tax, being unlikely to hide their wealth or pretend to be less substantial than they really were; their efforts, in fact, usually went in the opposite direction. In addition, they were willing to take on those unpaid civic duties upon which law and order depended heavily—that of justice of the peace, for example.

The moral overtones of the word *gentleman,* quite current today, developed rather gradually. In the sixteenth century, the emphasis was not so much on the person's behavior as on his social rank, although, one gathers, a person of gentlemanly status was expected to treat others courteously, observe self-discipline, and uphold high standards in general, is as the connotation today.

Gentlemen were usually addressed as "Mister," a mark of distinction since those of lesser status were not accorded it. "Master," an earlier usage, persisted through the sixteenth century. Most of the male characters in *The Merry Wives of Windsor,* for example, are addressed as "Master," indicative of this comedy's nonaristocratic though comfortable setting. The style "Master" was also used for a young boy in a gentleman's family.

The word *esquire,* or *squire,* originally meant a knight's attendant, and present-day readers still recognize this figure upon encountering him in literature, as did Elizabethan ones. The word also played a role in defining social boundaries. Appended to a gentleman's name—as in "Davy Gam, Esquire," one of the few English casualties in the Battle of Agincourt (*Henry V,* 4.8.104)—it denoted a gentleman, one who presumably bore a coat of arms and was of an established family.

A gentleman's wife was addressed as "Mistress," despite the fact that she was obviously married. His daughter might be so addressed as well. In *The Merry Wives of Windsor,* Mistress Margaret Page is the mother, quite legitimately and respectably, of Mistress Anne Page. The use of "Mrs." and "Miss" to indicate a married or unmarried woman, as the case might be, was a later development. At this date "Mistress" was used without marital connotations, like today's "Ms."

The word *Madam,* in the sixteenth and seventeenth centuries, was also a form of respectful address, implying some social standing without specific limitations. It was often used by itself, not prefixed or appended to the name of the person spoken to. The tinker Christopher Sly, suddenly lifted to a higher sphere in *The Taming of the Shrew,* is accustomed to women who go by their unadorned Christian names and does not understand this usage; when told to address his supposed wife as "Madam," he responds, "Alice madam, or Joan madam?" (Induction 2.110).

Citizens and Burgesses

The label Harrison gives to the next group down from the gentlemen may benefit from clarification. Today, the word *citizen* is used for any inhabitant of a nation, born into it or naturalized, with an emphasis especially on that person's rights—to the protection of the law, to the ballot if eligible, and so on. In the sixteenth century, the usual meaning was quite different. A citizen was a tradesman possessing certain privileges with regard to carrying on his business; a burgess was a citizen who had reached an eminent height, serving on special councils or even representing his colleagues in Parliament, though of course as a member of the House of Commons rather than the House of Lords. The mercantile world, in short, was a highly organized one, its members usually belonging to guilds which, with their centuries-long traditions, regulated trade and industry by setting standards of workmanship and, one might say, dividing up the turf.

Busy, prosperous, and necessary as the citizenry were, they undeniably worked for their living; and this work, though elegant enough at the top levels so that one could perform it while wearing expensive clothes, still shaded off into manual labor at the lower levels and thus cut the citizenry off from the conspicuously leisured gentlemen. However, should a citizen retire from trade and buy a landed estate, it was possible for him to become a gentleman, or, rather, to attain this status for his children. An interval of a generation or so seemed to help. Harrison, doing his best to deal with these flexible boundaries, notes that merchants "often change estate with gentlemen."[6]

Yeomen and Laborers

Harrison's final two social categories, the "Yeomen" and the "Artificers and Laborers," are decidedly concerned with the world of work, although like the merchants they showed considerable variety and enjoyed the possibility of rising in status.

Yeomen, also called "husbandmen," were tillers of the soil, in a sense; that is, they made sure the soil was tilled, and perhaps did some of it themselves in a pinch, but they might be more accurately seen as supervisors and employers of the laborers at the next level down. Yeomen often held their land on quite long leases, sometimes drawn up not only for the lifetime of the lessee but for those of two or three generations of his heirs. Hardworking and thrifty yeomen, like tradesmen, might eventually rise in the social scale. As Harrison points out, members of the yeomanry

> commonly live wealthily, keep good houses, and travail to get riches
> . . . insomuch that many of them are able and do buy the lands of
> unthrifty gentlemen, and often, setting their sons to the schools, to
> the universities, and to the Inns of Court, or otherwise leaving them
> sufficient lands whereupon they may live without labor, do make
> them by those means to become gentlemen.[7]

Occupants of the fourth and last level, "Artificers and laborers," have, according to Harrison, "neither voice nor authority in the commonwealth, but are to be ruled and not to rule others."[8] Skilled workers such as shoemakers and carpenters are included among the artificers, but, as some of these might by hard work and luck rise to the ranks of citizenry, Harrison may be assumed to mean run-of-the-mill employees, lacking luster, or contented with their present lot, like Bottom and his friends in *A Midsummer Night's Dream*. The farm laborers, on the other hand, are more self-evidently helpless in their political and economic contexts. They worked for wages, and when there was no work, because of crop failure or merely because it was a slow time of year, they and their families might well go hungry.

Styles of address for those below gentlemanly status naturally eschewed the "Mister." Often artificers and laborers were called by their surnames only. At the higher yeoman or husbandman level, "Goodman" or "Goodwife" might be used, sometimes abbreviated to "Goody." "Goodman" could also indicate respect for a person who more strictly would be categorized as an artificer. "Goodman Verges, sir, speaks a little off the matter," Dogberry explains to Leonato (*Much Ado About Nothing*, 3.5.10).

"Sir," incidentally, is usually found as a respectful form of address, used in speaking to a superior, or, in courtesy, to an equal—essentially the same function the word serves today. (This is aside from the knights' and baronets' special usage.) "Sirrah," on the other hand, was used by the Elizabethans in addressing an inferior and may express contempt as well. "Go, sirrah, to my cell," Prospero says to Caliban (*The Tempest*, 5.1.292).

Social Categories, Literacy, and the Population

Any study focusing on literature runs the risk of giving an exaggerated view of the amount of literacy abroad in the land, assuming "literate" here to refer to a reading public—persons who bought books and whose preferences would ultimately determine what was written and published. As always, it is hard to make simple statements. The audiences at playhouses certainly influenced the course of literature, and yet many playgoers may never have bought a book in their lives. At the same time, the aristocracy preserved the courtly tradition of writing for a small audience of personal friends, circulating the manuscripts among themselves, so that a work might achieve great success in this sphere, and have considerable influence on other writers, long before it became available at the booksellers' stalls in St. Paul's churchyard.

A general idea of the number of people exposed to literature, and, for that matter, a general idea of the number of people occupying the various social categories, can be obtained from the figures proposed by Gregory King, a seventeenth-century herald, genealogist, and, in the words of the *Dictionary of National Biography*, "political arithmetician." Although the historical period is a bit late for our purposes, King's figures are generally accepted as more reliable than anything else in the chronological neighborhood, and if we make allowance for some basic changes, the picture that comes through can be adapted, for our rough purposes, to Elizabethan times.[9] (King, for example, gives the population of England as five and a half million in the 1690s, a figure accepted by present-day scholars. Modern estimates of the population in Shakespeare's day, a century earlier, hover around three and a half and four million.[10] It might be added that it was only in the sixteenth century, according to many historians, that England's population fully recovered from the effects of the Black Death in the mid-fourteenth century.)

King's tabulation was intended to display the income and expenses of English households, and King accordingly divides these households into two major groups, those who "increase the wealth of the kingdom" and those who decrease it. The wealth-increasers, perhaps dishearteningly for King, were the smaller group, some 500,586 households comprising 2,675,520 individuals. (King includes as members of a household not only the family but all the live-in servants.) Those who decreased the kingdom's wealth numbered 849,000 households, totaling 2,825,000 individuals.

It is the 500,586 wealth-increasing households whom we might assume to have some connection with the printed word. By making an estimate, probably wildly optimistic, of two readers per potentially educated household, we arrive at some 1,001,172, or between a fifth and a sixth of the total population. As individuals, these hypothetical readers would naturally vary in taste and intensity, but they would also vary according to their social category, and King's figures give us an idea of the relative proportions here.

The highest ranking of the subgroups within the 500,586 wealth-increasing households is that of the "temporal lords," the five levels of the peerage described earlier in this chapter. Only 160 households belong to this group. (They are, however, the largest households, as King gives them an average of forty members each. Most of these may be assumed to be live-in servants.) Twenty-six households of "spiritual lords," or bishops and archbishops, follow. Of households headed by baronets,[11] King gives 800; by knights, 600; by esquires, 3,000; and by "gentlemen," following presumably Harrison's criteria of leisure and coats of arms, 12,000.

These households, where education and the habit of reading had taken root to a greater or lesser extent, may well have sheltered a larger number of readers apiece than my estimated two; some great houses, of course, had built up their own libraries over several generations. Other of King's subcategories may be envisioned as having a fairly positive relationship with the printed word, particularly books related to their special interests. The 10,000 households headed by "persons in the law," the 15,000 headed by "persons in the liberal arts and sciences," the 2,000 headed by "eminent clergymen," and the 8,000 headed by "lesser clergymen" might well be of this number.

Somewhat more debatable with regard to the reading and buying of books would be the 10,000 households headed by persons in greater or lesser "offices and places," including, presumably, aldermen and other municipal authorities; the 2,000 headed by "eminent merchants and traders by sea"; the 8,000 headed by "lesser merchants and traders by sea";

and the 50,000 headed by "shopkeepers and tradesmen." One can probably assume a certain respect for books and, perhaps, the intention of reading and acquiring more of them, as time and funds permitted.

All the households so far enumerated have in common some degree of urban sophistication—a coming and going from London, perhaps, or a familiarity with those who did so, if not actual residence in London or in a large town. They total only 111,586 households, however. In the same general group, those who increase the wealth of the kingdom, King has placed a large number of households which would have been less concerned with the complexities of London and may consequently, since the reading public appears to have been largely centered on the capital, have lived relatively bookless lives. These households include 40,000 headed by "freeholders of the better sort," 120,000 headed by "freeholders of the lesser sort," and 150,000 farmers (presumably copyholders). Of these households, some would correspond to Harrison's description of the comfortably off yeomen, poised to turn themselves or their descendants into gentlemen, and some of these may have established, if not a family library, perhaps a family bookshelf. The total number of households in these three basically rural subcategories is 310,000—almost three times those whom we can imagine with a little more certainty as entering the world of books and readers.[12]

At this point, if not earlier, we can hardly escape noticing a discrepancy between the social and cultural world pictured in or implied by Elizabethan literature, and the world in which this literature actually existed. Making the reasonable assumption that prosperity and literacy had not shrunk in the interval between Shakespeare's or Sidney's writings and King's tabulations, we have to conclude that Elizabethan literature includes a larger proportion of kings, aristocrats, gentlemen, lawyers, merchants, and other courtly, sophisticated, wealthy, and urban types than would be the case if social perspective were more strictly observed. The rural scene, though certainly present, tends to function as a backdrop, often, in fact, seen through the literary tradition of the pastoral.

This discrepancy exists not just between urban and rural settings but even more sharply between the haves and the have-nots, to use a present-day term. The have-nots lacked access to literature and seldom appear in it except as faceless servitors or dangerous mobs. And yet they comprised more than half the population. King's tabulation of the 849,000 households which "decrease the wealth of the kingdom" includes 346,000 headed by "laboring people and out servants," and 400,000 by "cottagers and paupers"—a label that indicates the thin line in effect here, as a cottager when out of work became a pauper. In addition to these two major subcategories, King includes 50,000 households headed by "common seamen" and 35,000 headed by "common soldiers." And, to allow for persons with no households as such, he lists 30,000 individuals under the heading of "Vagrants; as Gipsies, Thieves, Beggars, etc."[13]

As readers of Elizabethan literature, then, we need to recognize and defend ourselves against the temptation to assume that the castles and halls looming so large in song and story are representative of the lives of any hefty fraction of the English population. Literature was, at least in these earlier centuries, an elite pursuit. It is true that many levels of the reading public were less aristocratic than they might have liked to be, and it is possible that one of literature's appeals was its provision for temporary upward mobility through the medium of fantasy. Nevertheless, the ability to concern oneself with the printed word can be seen as a mark of social privilege.

2

The Tudor Dynasty

English literature generally operates on the assumption that the reader already knows quite a lot about any monarch who may be mentioned, be it Bad King John or Good Queen Bess. Americans, however, have pondered other things in their history classrooms than this particular sequence of kings and may find useful a quick review of the Tudor monarchs who reigned from 1485 to 1603.[1]

The reader will remember from the previous chapter that God was assigned a strong role in the sixteenth-century social and political pattern. The sovereign held his kingdom by divine right. God also determined who was to be king in the first place, through His control of who was born to whom, and in what order of birth, so that the principle of primogeniture was thus guaranteed to supply the English throne with a succession of monarchs whom God had intended to sit there.[2] The fact that this rule did not always work—or rather, was not always respected— and that human nature sometimes prevailed and the strong found ways to oust the weak, provides history and literature with much of its dramatic conflict.

It is worth observing that primogeniture, or inheritance by the eldest son, had not always been the English means of transferring power but had developed through the centuries. Before the Norman Conquest and for several generations after it, English kings were chosen by the strongest nobles, the choice sometimes, but not always, happening to fall upon the previous king's eldest son. The reader encounters similar situations in *Hamlet* and *Macbeth*. This method insured that the kingdom was not

put under the nominal leadership of an infant and also that the king had
the support of the majority, at least, of his nobles; otherwise he would
not have been chosen. The decision-making process was not always
peaceful, however. Candidates for the throne might bring armed force
to bear, actual or threatened, and alliances among the nobles might shift
and tilt just when the country was most vulnerable to attack from outside. By contrast, the idea of the crown's descent to a specific and non-
ambiguous person held a deep appeal to the human need for predictable
and immutable order.

The Tudors: An Overview

The family relationships of the five Tudor monarchs are as follows,
with the birth order of Henry VIII's children moving from left to right.
Wives are omitted for the sake of simplicity.

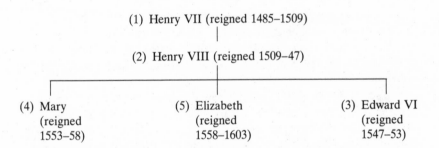

(1) Henry VII (reigned 1485–1509)

(2) Henry VIII (reigned 1509–47)

(4) Mary	(5) Elizabeth	(3) Edward VI
(reigned	(reigned	(reigned
1553–58)	1558–1603)	1547–53)

Henry VII acquired the crown by violent means, to be discussed
below, but his son Henry VIII did succeed to the throne in the standard
hereditary way. Of Henry VIII's three children (by different wives), the
only son, Edward VI, became king on his father's death but did not live
very long thereafter. King Edward's two sisters then came to the throne
in order of their birth. Mary died after only five years, but Elizabeth's
reign is second in length only to that of Queen Victoria, who ruled from
1837 to 1901.

The reign of Henry VII begins with his victory over Richard III at the Battle of Bosworth Field in 1485, ending the Wars of the Roses and the century-long struggle for the crown among the descendants of Edward III. Shakespeare deals with these events in the history plays which we will examine in the following chapter. Meanwhile, a quick look at this century or so of conflict will give us a clearer grasp of the Tudor dynasty's somewhat shaky circumstances.

Edward III and his queen, Philippa of Hainault, had seven sons, but as only four of them are important to the conflict, the diagram below is a simplified one. The order of birth again goes from left to right. The dates indicate life spans, not reigns as in the previous diagram.

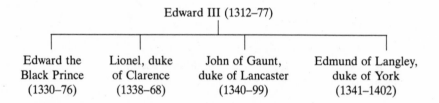

Edward III (1312–77)

| Edward the Black Prince (1330–76) | Lionel, duke of Clarence (1338–68) | John of Gaunt, duke of Lancaster (1340–99) | Edmund of Langley, duke of York (1341–1402) |

Of the remaining three sons, two died young and the third, Thomas of Woodstock, younger than those of his brothers listed here, had descendants whose royal blood sometimes made the occupants of the throne uneasy but of whom none was able to gather enough support for a serious uprising.

No son of Edward III actually reigned. The eldest, Edward the Black Prince, died before his father, but by that time he had a son of his own, Richard, who was crowned in 1377 at the age of ten. In 1399, when he was thirty-six, Richard II was ousted from the throne by his first cousin, Henry of Bolingbroke, a son of the duke of Lancaster, third from the left in the above diagram.

Since Richard II had no children, in the proper course of primogeniture the crown would have descended to the heirs of that son of Edward III who was second in birth order to Edward the Black Prince. This would be the duke of Clarence, not the duke of Lancaster. The duke of Clarence had been dead for thirty years, however, and his only child, his daughter Philippa, had married into a family which, though noble, was not as strong as the usurping branches.

Here, of course, is the point at which theory meets practice, and theory loses. If primogeniture as the will of God is supposed to be so important, one would assume that people would respect it; if not, if instead the throne is to go to whoever can muster the power to grab and hold it, then it seems hypocritical for the contenders to talk about a rightful inheritance. And yet, of course, they did. People then and now long for stability and order, and simultaneously see every reason for a high place for themselves within that stability and order.

Thus the heirs of the duke of Lancaster and the duke of York, respectively, dominated fifteenth-century history as they fought for the crown. The Lancastrians had a theoretical edge in that the duke of Lancaster, even though born after the duke of Clarence, was at any rate born before the Duke of York; but the Yorkists, quite early on, sneakily infused themselves with higher-ranking blood when one of them married a female descendant of the duke of Clarence.

When in 1485 the armies moved into position at Bosworth Field, the crown was worn by a Yorkist, the redoubtable Richard III, a great-grandson of the duke of York in the above diagram; his opponents were led by Henry Tudor, earl of Richmond, a great-great-grandson of the duke of Lancaster. At the end of the battle, Richard III was dead and the earl of Richmond was hailed as king, to reign for over twenty years as Henry VII.

The symbolism of the roses, incidentally, associates a white rose with the Yorkists and a red rose with the Lancastrians. On taking the throne, Henry VII promptly married a Yorkist bride and thus united the two warring factions; the "Tudor rose," then, horticulturally and historically, is streaked red and white.

Henry VII (Reigned 1485–1509)

England's dynastic conflict might now seem to have been resolved with great finality, heraldic flowers and all, and this is naturally the view which Henry Tudor, now Henry VII, hoped everyone would take. But things were not really simple. Henry VII's royal blood, while unquestioned, nevertheless ran at one point through the female line, sometimes an iffy maneuver, and at another point depended upon a third wife who had in fact been merely a mistress when her children were born. Royal blood can distribute itself quite widely during three or four generations, so rivals were many. The ground seemed particularly thick with leftover Yorkists, real or pretended, and, all in all, Henry had his work cut out for him.

Besides ruling competently and managing to accrue more money to the crown than he spent, King Henry succeeded in providing his country with what would seem a sufficient number of heirs. The following children of Henry VII and his queen, Elizabeth of York, survived infancy:

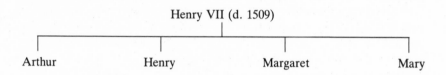

Henry VII (d. 1509)

Arthur   Henry   Margaret   Mary

Arthur, the oldest, is remarkable from our standpoint for three things: his name, his marriage, and his early death.

"Arthur," while not an uncommon name, is not a really common one either, and it seems quite likely that by choosing it for his heir apparent, Henry VII meant to remind his subjects of the legendary King Arthur and to suggest the emergence of a new Camelot. Some of Henry VII's ancestors came from Wales, stronghold of the Arthurian stories, so that the connection had a geographical boost. And tales of King Arthur were popular with the reading public. William Caxton, after setting up England's first printing press in the 1470s, had brought out Malory's *Morte d'Arthur* in 1485—coincidentally, the year that Henry VII defeated his Yorkist rivals and came to the throne. At the other end of the Tudor era, more than a century later, Spenser's *Faerie Queene* includes King Arthur (or, rather, Prince Arthur, as he has not yet become king) among the major characters.

The marriage of this real-life Prince Arthur, to return to the row of siblings with whom we are here concerned, supplies an example of the dynastic manipulations typical of matrimony at these elevated levels. Henry VII desired an alliance with Spain and arranged for Arthur to marry Princess Catherine of Aragon, daughter of the Ferdinand and Isabella who were shortly to enter American history by sponsoring Columbus's voyage across the Atlantic in 1492. In 1488, when the marriage negotiations began, Prince Arthur was two and Princess Catherine three years old. After parents and statesmen had spent some years haggling about the dowry and other matters, the princess arrived in England in 1501 and the couple, then aged fifteen and sixteen, were married in St. Paul's Cathedral.

Shortly thereafter, Prince Arthur died. The king was sorrowful, for he seems to have genuinely loved his children, but he was comforted in that he had a second son. There was also the question of what to do with the widowed Princess Catherine. Since she was already in England and at least one installment of the dowry had been paid, the simplest solution was to espouse her to Prince Henry. A few technicalities had to be worked out. Marriage to one's brother's wife was seen as incest by the Church, so a dispensation was obtained from the pope, Julius II— an investment in future discord, as it turned out.

Henry VII's two daughters, Margaret and Mary, were also expected to do their part in allying the throne of England with the royal houses of Europe. Margaret married, first, King James IV of Scotland, and next, after his death, a Scottish lord, the earl of Angus. Two of her grandchildren by these two marriages, Mary Queen of Scots and Henry, Lord Darnley, married each other in 1565 and produced James VI of Scotland, who succeeded Queen Elizabeth upon her death and ruled as James I of England, founder of the English line of Stuart kings.

Henry VII's younger daughter, Mary, was betrothed to Prince Charles of Castille, who later became Charles V, the Holy Roman emperor, and who was, incidentally, a nephew of Catherine of Aragon; royal families had many interconnections. Negotiations fell through shortly before the marriage was to take place, however, and Mary was sent off to France—under protest as she had meanwhile fallen in love with an English nobleman—to marry King Louis XII, then a widower of fifty-two. Louis died a few months thereafter—danced to death by his eighteen-year-old bride, said rumor; the Englishman in question, the duke of Suffolk, arrived in France on an official mission and Mary promptly married him. Mary's descendants from this marriage include a grand-daughter, Lady Jane Grey, the "nine days' queen" of 1553 (described below in connection with the reign of Edward VI).

Henry VIII (Reigned 1509–47)

Henry VIII is remembered by Americans chiefly for his physical bulk, evidenced by Holbein's portraits and by the suits of royal armor on display at the Tower of London and Windsor Castle, and also for the fact that he had a large number of wives, a total of six. The motive for this marital restlessness was, at least in part, the king's need to leave an heir for the throne—preferably a male heir in sound health. Daughters were looked upon as useful for political alliances, thus forming or strengthening connections between nations, but not as monarch material.

In the late 1520s, after eighteen years of marriage to Queen Catherine, Henry VIII began to suspect that his union with his brother's widow may have been a serious sin after all, despite the pope's permission. After numerous miscarriages and infant deaths, the only surviving child of the marriage was the princess Mary, eleven years old in 1527 when the king's scruples were made public. Catherine was then forty-two, six years older than her husband.

Aside from getting straight with God, the king had an additional motive in the person of twenty-year-old Anne Boleyn, whom he was determined to marry. His powerful minister, Cardinal Wolsey, was given the task of persuading the pope to annul the king's marriage to Catherine—a task which proved impossible. There had been a change of popes; the pontiff was now Clement VII, who had been caught in a struggle among several of the major powers in Europe. He was considerably in awe of the Holy Roman Emperor Charles V, having once been imprisoned by him, and Queen Catherine was the emperor's aunt. Cardinal Wolsey failed in his mission, losing the king's favor in the process, and no help came from the pope.

For the king, only one course remained. England removed itself from the domination of Rome, thus becoming Protestant. Henry VIII could now have his previous marriage annulled and make Anne his queen without need of documents from the pope. He also made himself head of the Church of England, the tumultuous implications of which action will be dealt with in a later chapter.

Queen Catherine remained at the English court. The king, taking the position that his marriage to her had not really existed, claimed to respect her as his brother's widow. She died in January of 1536.

Queen Anne, after all this trouble, produced only one living child, the princess Elizabeth, whose potential was not recognized at the time. Nor did Queen Anne retain her hold on the heart of the king. In May of 1536, only three years after her coronation, she was beheaded on a charge of adultery and treason.

With his next wife, Jane Seymour, Henry finally had a son, Prince Edward, but Queen Jane died a week or so after his birth. Authorities now disagree as to whether the prince was as frail an infant as has been traditionally assumed, but in any case there was only one of him, and his father knew from experience that a back-up heir was a good idea. The king took three more royal brides: Catherine Howard, also beheaded on a charge of adultery; Anne of Cleves, whose union with the king was annulled; and Catherine Parr, a calm widow who outlived the king. None of the king's last three wives had children, and on his deathbed the king ordered that the succession should go in order to his son, Edward, then to his elder daughter, Mary, and finally to his younger daughter, Elizabeth. That is, the succession was so determined in case of need. If Edward had children, as his father no doubt hoped he would, those children would replace their aunts as immediate heirs to the throne. But Edward, only nine when he became king, would not live long enough to extend the dynasty into another generation.

Edward VI (Reigned 1547–53) and Lady Jane Grey (1553)

The six-year reign of Edward VI seems rather uneventful in comparison to the turbulence surrounding the rest of his family. England remained Protestant, and some documents of importance to both literary and church history were drawn up, among them the prayer book of 1549.

. With regard to the succession, the most memorable event of Edward VI's reign occurred at the end of it, as the fifteen-year-old king was dying. One of his guardians, the earl of Northumberland, had contrived a scheme involving the marriage of one of his sons to Lady Jane Grey, a great-granddaughter of Henry VII. King Edward was then pressured into "devising" his throne not to his half-sister Mary but to Lady Jane. This "devise" was a dubious operation; the lawyers ordered to draw up a will according to its terms refused on the grounds that to do so would be treasonous, and yielded only under pressure from the powerful Northumberland. On the king's death, Northumberland brought Lady Jane to London, where she signed a proclamation announcing her accession. Within a matter of days, Princess Mary organized an army, marched to London, captured her rival, and took the throne. Her supporters at this point felt more loyal to this direct descendant of Henry VIII than fearful of a return to Catholicism. Lady Jane, the "Nine Days' Queen," an innocent pawn in the whole affair, was beheaded for treason in 1554.

Mary (Reigned 1553–58)

When Queen Mary came to power, the religious pendulum swung back and England became once again a Catholic country. Mary's two desires were to return her country definitively to the papal fold and, a familiar-sounding ambition, to leave an heir. She was destined to succeed in neither.

The Spanish ruler Philip II, whom Mary married in 1554, was the queen's first cousin once removed. His father was Charles V, emperor of the Holy Roman Empire and the nephew of Mary's late mother, Queen Catherine. He was, of course, a staunch Catholic. But he spent little time in England, where Parliament refused to grant him more than minimal honors as the consort of a reigning queen. There was no child, though Mary wanted one so badly that at least once she deluded herself into thinking herself pregnant when she was not. When she died, Philip did not return for her funeral, or, for that matter, ever again, and thirty years later he sent the Spanish Armada against England, though for reasons having nothing directly to do with the late queen.

The usual view of Queen Mary found in literature is a negative one—not surprisingly, since her plans did not prosper and her enemies won. The Protestant writer John Foxe included in his *Book of Martyrs* vivid and hair-raising descriptions of the burning at the stake of many of Mary's Protestant opponents. Her popular nickname, "Bloody Mary," is still known today, and in fact on this side of the Atlantic the name of this Tudor sovereign would seem to have been permanently linked to a concoction of vodka and tomato juice.

Elizabeth (Reigned 1558–1603)

From a dynastic point of view, Queen Elizabeth seemed made to order. She was young—twenty-five—when she came to the throne, healthy, intelligent, and devoted to her country. Surely she would marry some reliable Protestant, preferably strengthening England's international alliances while so doing, and ensure the future by leaving an heir.

But the queen did not marry. Explanations vary. International diplomacy involved many delicate balances of power, and to conduct tentative negotiations with one suitor after another, keeping everyone in suspense, may have seemed to Elizabeth so advantageous that she delayed making a commitment until her time was up and she could no longer have a child. She may have had an unconscious dread of marriage. The fact that her father had had her mother beheaded might well have put family life in a negative light. Or, possibly, to take up a rather sentimental theory, she was in love with someone should could not marry. Here again there are several candidates—already married, tainted with scandal, of the wrong religion, or just plain undependable.

As the "Virgin Queen," then, Elizabeth reigned for forty-five years as a quite original phenomenon, married, as she said, to her people, and perhaps feeling at some level that the limitations of mortality did not apply to her and that she need not concern herself with dynastic worries. She did, however, with nearly her dying breath, name as her successor James VI of Scotland, a member of the House of Stuart but descended from the Tudors as a great-great-grandson of Henry VII.

James I (Reigned 1603–25)

Despite his Tudor blood, James's family connections might be seen as dubious. He was the son of Mary Queen of Scots, whom Queen

Elizabeth had had beheaded in 1587. James had not taken a permanently hostile stance during this event, however. He had not known his mother; he had been raised a Protestant, though she was Catholic, and he had occupied the Scottish throne in her stead since he was a child.

On James's death in 1625, his oldest surviving son became king as Charles I. It is King Charles who provides the ultimate demonstration that the divine right of kings—that principle so self-evident to generations of crowned English heads, and, indeed, no less self-evident to Charles himself—was no longer accepted as a viable political principle. Representative government in the form of Parliament took an important step, albeit a violent one, toward the supremacy it enjoys today. When the Puritan faction in Parliament took arms against the Royalists, supporters of the king, they eventually captured the latter and beheaded him in 1649. The son of Charles I was restored as king some ten years later, but the situation was different. Parliament was in control, and while the English crown has been passed down ever since in a quite orderly fashion, with the principle of primogeniture observed most of the time, there is now little doubt of where the power really lies.

3

The Genealogies of Shakespeare's Kings

In his history plays, Shakespeare took for granted his audience's familiarity with a complex tangle of family relationships—siblings and half-siblings, offspring of illicit unions, reduced scions of once-powerful houses. It is true that the plays are full of reminders, and family relationships are often emphasized in the dialogue, but some prior acquaintance with the dynastic patterns can greatly strengthen a reader's connection with the plays.[1]

King John *(Written 1594–96)*

King John is set in the early thirteenth century, and the King John of the title (the only King John, as no subsequent English monarch has used that name) is the one who was forced by his noblemen to sign Magna Carta, granting some of his powers to them, in 1215. Shakespeare does not mention this event. Magna Carta did not gain its reputation as a landmark in the subjugation of the monarch to the rule of law until after the Parliamentary victories of the seventeenth century.

The genealogical table governing the play's action is as follows:

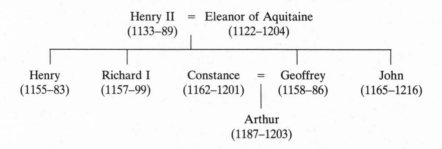

Henry II = Eleanor of Aquitaine
(1133–89)   (1122–1204)

Henry	Richard I	Constance	=	Geoffrey	John
(1155–83)	(1157–99)	(1162–1201)		(1158–86)	(1165–1216)

Arthur
(1187–1203)

   All but four of these people had died by the opening of the play. The survivors are Queen Eleanor; her youngest son, John, now the king; Constance, widow of the third son, Geoffrey; and Arthur, the son of this marriage. The oldest of Henry's and Eleanor's sons, another Henry, died before his father, leaving a son who then died in infancy. Had this child lived, however, there would have been no guarantee of his succeeding to the throne, for the idea of primogeniture had not entirely jelled. Richard did become king when his father died, reigning as Richard I, "the Lion-Hearted," but his success in taking the crown depended not so much on his being next in the birth order as on his being stronger. The brothers' relative strengths had been established during the preceding years when they fought one another in various combinations, rampaging over the then-extensive English holdings in France and occasionally joining forces, with the encouragement of their mother, to rebel against their father.
   Richard left no heir, and John took the throne on Richard's death in 1199, the coast being clear, so to speak. But there was the nephew, Arthur. A faction which not surprisingly included Arthur's mother, Constance, felt he should have dominion, if not over England, at least over the English possessions in France, to which he could claim family rights. The opposition between John and Arthur becomes one of the basic conflicts in the play, although there are others; Shakespeare portrays what seems to have been the real-life King John's talent for antagonizing almost everybody. John's capture and imprisonment of Arthur, followed by Arthur's mysterious disappearance and presumed death, are also historical, though the details are not known. In Shakespeare's version, the king orders first that Arthur be murdered and then, after what might be seen as a softening of heart, that he be blinded instead, neither

of which orders the jailer can bring himself to carry out. Arthur then dies after leaping from a tower in an attempt to escape.

Shakespeare's audience would have remembered that King John was succeeded by his son, who reigned as Henry III for a remarkably long time, considering the uncertainties of the period. Three King Edwards then followed in sequence, each the son of his predecessor, an orderly array at first glance; a few of the family irregularities appear in Marlowe's play *Edward II*. It is the sons of Edward III who, largely by their birth order, provide the dynastic tension in Shakespeare's next plays.

Richard II *(Written 1595)*

By the late fourteenth century, when the events in *Richard II* take place, the concept of inheritance passing down through a sequence of oldest sons, bypassing any later-born uncles or brothers, had gained considerable ground. It simplified the succession of noble titles as well as of property rights. With regard to the throne itself, in which God was assumed to hold an interest since the monarch represented His power on earth, the sovereign who ruled by right of inheritance rather than by strength of arms was seen as reflecting the harmony of the heavens, where the stars followed their courses and all things were subject to divine authority.

This principle, so foreign to present-day Americans, underlies the moral as well as the political conflict in this play and those that follow. No matter how much better suited Bolingbroke may have been for the job, he has committed a grave sin in seizing it. And, as the bishop of Carlisle points out, the consequences will be bloody and prolonged (4.1.134–44).

The genealogy below has already appeared in the previous chapter, but we will now bring it along another generation. Again, the youngest of Edward III's sons, the duke of Gloucester, is omitted; he has died before the play begins, leaving no offspring of immediate importance. He does, however, influence the action from beyond the grave, as a quarrel about the circumstances of his death is central to the first act and recurs thereafter.

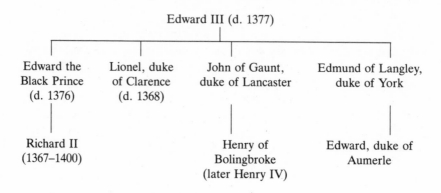

We can see by comparing the dates that Edward the Black Prince died before his father, leaving a son who the following year inherited the throne at the age of ten. This circumstance of course illustrates a potential hazard of primogeniture: the correct person was on the throne, but England still had no reigning monarch. The immediate solution, an ominous one, was the management of the young king's affairs by his strong and able uncles, who competed strenuously with one another and impelled Richard, as he gradually managed to assert himself, to collect a circle of dependents who had no power of their own—that is, no wealth or high titles—and whose loyalty he felt he could depend on.

In Shakespeare's play, Richard II's inadequacies as king are not glossed over; while not a deliberately evil person, he ignores the reciprocal nature of his high position. As God's vicar on earth, the king is obligated to a responsibility for those he rules and to a feeling for his country other than as a sentimental extension of his own ego. It is possible to see Richard as a tyrant, as Robin Headlam Wells suggests.[2] The play does not present easy choices. Shakespeare was, after all, a dramatist, alert for areas of conflict and tension, and traditional theories of kingship, while agreeing on the desirability of order and harmony, were not always unanimous in solving the practical tangles that might arise. Nevertheless, *Richard II* does not condone Bolingbroke's usurpation, and it does not give a simple prescription for what Bolingbroke should have done instead of what he does do. Rather, Bolingbroke's actions appear in an unheroic light. He removes from the throne God's annointed king; he causes that king to be murdered, and regicide is after all a particularly intense category of murder; and he places on the throne a person (himself) who is not the next in line for it. That person would properly be a descendant of Lionel, duke of Clarence, whose daughter had married Edmund Mortimer, earl of March. Neither Clarence nor his descendants are mentioned in *Richard II,* but Shakespeare's audience would have been aware of the situation. And, of course, the Mortimers become more prominent in the plays that follow.

A character whose moral function in the play sometimes goes unappreciated is the duke of York, another of the sons of Edward III and John of Gaunt's younger brother. As Shakespeare portrays him, York is a man of principle, loyal to the concept of a stable throne and a consequently stable state. He reproves Bolingbroke for opposing Richard II and describes his sympathy for the fallen king in a moving passage (5.2.23–40), but once Bolingbroke is crowned, York's loyalty to him causes him to denounce his own son as a traitor. The seeming ambivalence of these actions springs from deeply troubled principles, not from weakness or wishy-washiness, despite the fact that York is sometimes played on today's stage as a comic character who can't make up his mind.

A minor detail for the present-day reader, but possibly a distracting one, has to do with the characters' names. It was customary to nickname the surname-less royalty according to their place of birth; John of Gaunt was born at Ghent, for example. Henry of Bolingbroke was born at a castle of that name in Lincolnshire. In the earlier acts of *Richard II* he is addressed as Hereford, having been made duke of Hereford in 1397. Richard's and Bolingbroke's cousin Aumerle, son of the duke of York, is called by a shortened form of his title as duke of Albemarle. Later in the play this dukedom is taken away from him and he is supposed to be called "Rutland," the name of an earldom he has had all along but has not used since Aumerle is a higher-ranking title.

Henry IV, *Parts One and Two (Written 1596–98)*

In the next play, the first part of *Henry IV,* Bolingbroke is on the throne, and the harvest of unrest and bloodshed so vehemently predicted in *Richard II* is getting under way. Shakespeare emphasizes this theme with a change in Bolingbroke—or King Henry IV, rather. Although he

showed himself a strong and efficient usurper in the previous play, he
now comes onstage shaken with care, practically feeble, corroded with
inward guilt. The apparent fecklessness of his heir, Prince Hal, is seen
by the king as only another bit of divine punishment for his sin. The
audience knows, of course, that Hal will turn out splendidly, but the
usurpation has in fact made the English throne seem dangerously un-
steady; if one king can be got rid of, so can another, and the Percy
family, at first supporters of Bolingbroke against Richard II, now continue their pattern of discontent and start plotting against him.

The Percies, headed by the earl of Northumberland, are a strong and
ancient family, representative of the type of nobility traditionally jealous
of centralized royal power and unwilling to submit to it unless they can
control it. Having lost control of Henry IV, they are eager to start again
with a new candidate—a Mortimer, and a descendant of the duke of
Clarence, next-oldest brother to Edward the Black Prince. Sir Henry
Percy ("Hotspur"), son of the earl of Northumberland, has married into
the Mortimer family and thus into the blood royal. The situation is as
follows:

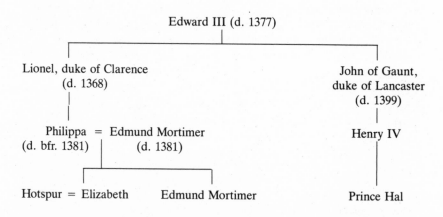

At this point, as we examine events leading to the Battle of Shrewsbury in 1403, two adjustments need to be made between life and literature. First, the Elizabeth who is married to Hotspur goes in *Henry IV*
by the name of Kate—apparently a favorite name with Shakespeare.
Second, her brother, Edmund Mortimer, is entangled in a confusion

which Shakespeare found in his source, Holinshed's *Chronicles*. This Edmund had an older brother, Roger, not shown in the diagram as he is not mentioned in the play. Roger Mortimer inherited his father's title as earl of March and also had a son, confusingly named Edmund, who was twelve years old in 1403. It was this younger Edmund Mortimer whom Richard II, before his death in 1400, had named as his rightful heir.

The Edmund Mortimer of Shakespeare's play, then, was not in fact the earl of March and had not been named heir. He was, however, the brother of Hotspur's wife; he did marry the daughter of the earl of Glendower, as occurs in the play, after having been captured in battle by Glendower; and he certainly did plot against Henry IV, switching sides as he did so, for the king had sent him out to do battle against Glendower and his Welsh rebels. This mutinous element then joined with the Percies, along with some of the rebellious Scots whom the Percies, while still on the King's side, had conveniently captured.

The Battle of Shrewsbury in 1403 ends part one of *Henry IV* with a victory for the king's party. But even though Hotspur was killed, enough rebels are left over to supply the plot for the second part of *Henry IV*. In this next play, a number of rebels are captured by Prince Hal's younger brother, called in this play Prince John of Lancaster (4.2); and as he and the other brothers continue to figure in the plays, we may as well review them here, in order of birth.

1) Prince Hal, later Henry V (d. 1422)

2) Thomas, duke of Clarence (d. 1421)

3) John of Lancaster, later duke of Bedford (d. 1431)

4) Humphrey, duke of Gloucester (d. 1447)

None of Henry IV's younger sons are to leave legitimate heirs. Thomas of Clarence dies before the king; Bedford and Gloucester survive into the era of York-Lancaster struggles.

Henry V *(Written 1599)*

At the beginning of *Henry V,* the former Prince Hal is on the throne, his rapscallion ways miraculously mended, and the play seems poised to

become a pageant of triumphant English nationalism. This is pretty much
what happens. The Battle of Agincourt is, after all, a piece of archetypal
myth come to life; modern historians disagree to some extent with the
numbers Shakespeare cites, but the ratio of Frenchmen to Englishmen
still comes out at approximately five to one, and the victory demands a
celebration.

But the cloud cast by the usurpation has not gone away. The king
prays before the battle that God forget: "Not to-day, O Lord, / O, not
to-day, think not upon the fault / My father made in compassing the
crown" (4.2.292–95), and God complies, for the moment at least. At
the end of the play, however, the audience is told what it already knew;
King Henry will die at the age of thirty-five, leaving his son, "Henry the
Sixt, in infant bands crown'd King." The struggle will begin again.

During the course of *Henry V,* tucked rather inconspicuously into the
heroic panorama, is an event which reminded the original audience of
dynastic complexities to come. Shakespeare does not emphasize the family ties; "Cambridge, Scroop, and Grey," the trio whose would-be treason is exposed and punished before the army leaves for France, seem to
come out of the woodwork as anonymous villains and, in fact, function
mythically as a sort of sacrifice to the gods of war, reminiscent of Iph-
egenia. But one of them, the earl of Cambridge, is quite well connected
indeed:

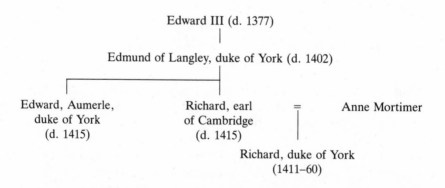

The above diagram omits the older sons of Edward III for the sake
of simplicity, but we will recall that they were: 1) Edward the Black

Prince, whose son Richard II was deposed and then murdered, leaving no heir; 2) Lionel, duke of Clarence, whose daughter married a Mortimer; 3) John of Gaunt, duke of Lancaster, father of the usurping Henry IV and grandfather of Henry V; and 4) Edmund of Langley, duke of York, as shown here, whom we remember as Bolingbroke's uncle, the anguished man of principle in *Richard II*. The duke of York's eldest son, Aumerle, having inherited his father's title, figures in the action of *Henry V.* His role is a gallant one, justifying Henry IV's forgiveness of his incipient treason all those years ago, for he is found under a heap of slain at the Battle of Agincourt, one of the few English casualties.

His younger brother, the earl of Cambridge, is a different story. Cambridge had married a Mortimer, Anne, great-granddaughter of Lionel, duke of Clarence. His treasonous plot with the French was actually more involved than Shakespeare suggests, centering on placing Anne's brother, Edmund—son of Roger Mortimer, earl of March—on the throne. Many members of Shakespeare's audience would have remembered this point and would also have known that the earl of Cambridge left a son, Richard, four years old when his father was executed, who was eventually to gain the family title as duke of York and to lead a series of rebellions against the Lancastrian party.

Henry VI, *Parts One, Two, and Three (Written 1589–91)*

The first of this three-play sequence continues the Hundred Years' War, with the English losing more and more of their French territory. The present-day reader may be startled to encounter a very unholy Joan of Arc—a witch, in fact. The focus then shifts to England's internal affairs, where the family quarrel is about to enter another active phase, and at one point a group of Yorkist and Lancastrian characters enter a garden and pluck a white or red rose, indicative of the party favored by each (*1 Henry VI*, 2.4).

The instigator of Shakespeare's rose-plucking scene is Richard Plantagenet, duke of York, son of the earl of Cambridge who had been executed for treason in 1415. Henry V had not held this blot against the son, and he had inherited his uncle's title as duke of York after the latter's death at Agincourt. This duke of York was in the habit of using the name Plantagenet, strategically reminiscent of the line of English kings going back to the twelfth century; it had been the nickname of Geoffrey, count of Anjou, father of Henry II. York's, or Plantagenet's, claim to the throne draws much of its strength from his father's marriage to Anne Mortimer, sister of the last of the line, Edmund Mortimer. Upon Mortimer's death, Richard Plantagenet becomes the sole conduit of the blood of Lionel, duke of Clarence, and can claim to outrank the Lancastrians descended from the later-born John of Gaunt.

Parts two and three of *Henry VI* follow England's fortunes as internal war breaks out in the 1450s. The king, Henry VI, son of Henry V, remains more or less the pawn of several rival guardians and eventually even of his queen, Margaret of Anjou, a forceful personality. Shakespeare portrays Queen Margaret personally stabbing Richard Plantagenet at the Battle of Wakefield in 1460 (*3 Henry VI,* 1.4), an event which may not have occurred in quite this way. But both the play and more factual history tell us that Richard Plantagenet's head, adorned with a paper crown, was hung by his Lancastrian enemies on the walls of the city of York.

Though now definitely out of the action, Richard Plantagenet had four sons, three of whom carried on the fight. (The earl of Rutland was also slain at Wakefield.)

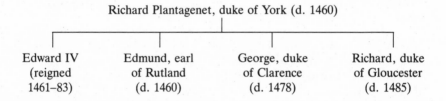

Richard Plantagenet, duke of York (d. 1460)

| Edward IV (reigned 1461–83) | Edmund, earl of Rutland (d. 1460) | George, duke of Clarence (d. 1478) | Richard, duke of Gloucester (d. 1485) |

The eldest son, Edward, took the throne, deposing Henry VI and holding him prisoner. The third son, George, deserted the Yorkist cause for an interval, having married Isabel Neville, daughter of the powerful earl of Warwick, who at first supported the Yorkists but then went over to the Lancastrians. (Warwick then betrothed his other daughter, Anne, to the Lancastrian heir apparent, Edward Prince of Wales, son of Henry VI and Queen Margaret.) George rejoined his brothers in 1471, in time for the battles of Barnet and Tewkesbury, victories for the Yorkists. Richard Plantagenet's youngest son, Richard, duke of Gloucester, fought energetically for his family's side and, at least in Shakespeare's version, stuck at nothing by way of nefarious schemes.

Eventually the Yorkists seemed to prevail. The year 1471 saw the deaths, among many others, of the earl of Warwick, Edward Prince of Wales, and Henry VI himself. Henry VI was slain in the Tower of London, having been imprisoned throughout the later half of the 1460s. Shakespeare shows this murder as undertaken personally by Richard of Gloucester.

Richard III *(Written 1592–93)*

The play begins as Richard of Gloucester tells the audience his plans for making himself king. To do so, he must kill off a number of members of his family who outrank him; and to make sense of Richard's shopping-list of victims, we need to consider not only the two remaining brothers, both older than Richard, but their children as well.

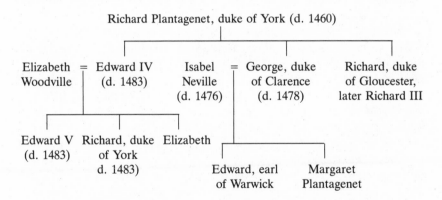

Richard Plantagenet, duke of York (d. 1460)

Elizabeth = Edward IV   Isabel = George, duke   Richard, duke
Woodville   (d. 1483)   Neville   of Clarence   of Gloucester,
                         (d. 1476) (d. 1478)   later Richard III

Edward V Richard, duke Elizabeth
(d. 1483)   of York
            d. 1483)   Edward, earl   Margaret
                                  of Warwick   Plantagenet

Richard of Gloucester and his wife, Anne Neville, also had a child, Edward, who died at the age of eight. Shakespeare omits young Edward, perhaps to streamline the action and perhaps because the demonic Richard, so ferocious in Tudor legend, might appear too sympathetic if shown as a bereaved father. It should be pointed out that much historical evidence supports the view of Richard III as a reasonably good king, at least in the context of his times.

By the time Edward IV dies, Richard has succeeded in getting rid of his brother George, duke of Clarence, and, as the only surviving son of Richard Plantagenet, he manages to bully and hoodwink his way onto the throne. The timing is tricky. The legitimate heir of King Edward is of course the king's elder son, thirteen years old at the time of his father's death, known to history as Edward V; the young prince was never crowned, but the ceremony of coronation merely confirms a monarch's preexisting status, and in theory Edward V was king from the moment of his father's death. Richard of Gloucester gains possession of the young prince's person, on the pretext of protecting him, and has him immured in the Tower of London with his younger brother, the eleven-year-old duke of York.

Richard then makes his move for the throne, issuing to his kinsman and henchman, the duke of Buckingham, a series of dynastic rationalizations which Buckingham is supposed to use for what Americans might call public-relations purposes (3.7.75–94). The two princes, according to this argument, are not legitimate because their father, before marrying Elizabeth Woodville, had been betrothed to two other women, first to Elizabeth Lucy and then to a sister of the king of France; either or both of these entanglements serve theoretically to turn Edward IV's later marriage into "loath'd bigamy," as Buckingham dutifully points out to the mayor and citizens (3.7.177–89). Richard goes even farther; he implies that Edward IV himself was of questionable parentage, his father having been away in France, or so Richard claims, at the time Edward was begotten. Richard hesitates about this one, however. Not only does it seem a bit flimsy, but it slanders the dowager duchess of York, who after all is Richard's mother as well; and Richard advises Buckingham to "touch this sparingly, as 'twere far off" (3.7.93). One suspects that Shakespeare's Richard is sensitive not so much to his mother's reputation as to his own political image, since to cast suspicion on his brother's birth might extend the shadow to his own.

But Richard stands little chance of making these accusations stick permanently. The most effective way to eliminate Edward IV's sons as competitors for the throne is to have them killed, and this Richard does. (Historians are less definite than Shakespeare in postulating Richard's direct involvement in the little princes' disappearance, but he is a prime suspect.)

The children of the late duke of Clarence are also something of a problem, since in theory they outrank Richard, but their case is less pressing. Their parents are dead, and at the moment no party has gathered around them to right their wrongs. Richard deals with them briskly: "The son of Clarence have I pent up close, / His daughter have I meanly matched in marriage" (4.3.36–37), lines which do not quite accord with history with regard to the daughter but which do get both children out of the action for the time being.

These last remaining Yorkists, incidentally, lived on to haunt the Tudor monarchs. Clarence's son Edward, earl of Warwick, spent most of his life in prison and was executed by Henry VII in 1499 on a charge of treason. He had been implicated in the curious plot of Perkin Warbeck, who pretended to be one of the "Little Princes," the duke of York, alive after all. (The case is the subject of John Ford's play *Perkin Warbeck,* produced in the 1630s.) Clarence's daughter Margaret, later countess of Salisbury, had a life of ups and downs, but downs prevailed; Henry VIII executed her eldest son in 1538, and she met the same fate three years later.

King Richard, to return to the play at hand, would thus seem to be sitting pretty. By the fifth act he has got what he wanted, and he has even thought of a new wrinkle; Queen Anne being suddenly and suspiciously dead, Richard plans to marry his own niece, Edward IV's daughter, Elizabeth, and the sister of the late Little Princes. The niceties of primogeniture could be tidily satisfied if his elder brother's descendants were also his own.

But there is a cloud in the sky, one of which Shakespeare's audience would have been aware. The Lancastrian party was not really done for. John of Gaunt, duke of Lancaster, ancestor of the Henrys IV through VI, had another set of descendants as well, the children of his third wife, Catherine Swynford. The picture, greatly simplified, looks like the genealogy on page 46.

This great crowd of Beauforts, pushing John of Gaunt's first wife's descendants off into the left margin, have figured in many of the previous plays. Thomas Beaufort, earl of Exeter, is the "Uncle of Exeter" to whom Henry V speaks with affection before the Battle of Agincourt (*Henry V,* 4.3.53). Exeter, who later becomes one of the guardians and

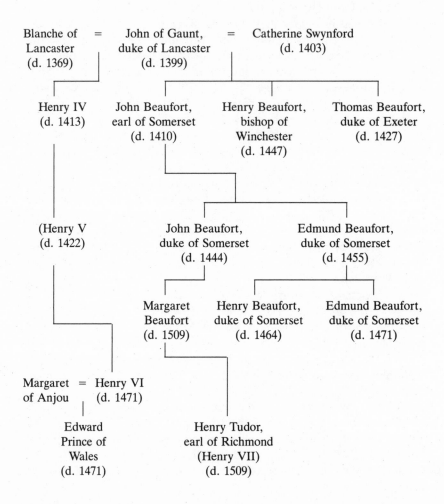

advisers of Henry VI, comments ominously on the quarrel between the duke of Gloucester, one of Henry V's younger brothers, and the bishop of Winchester, his own brother Thomas Beaufort (*1 Henry VI*, 3.1.184–200). Another cluster of Beauforts, the dukes of Somerset, who inherit one another's titles while meeting various violent deaths, are pillars of the Lancastrian cause. It is John Beaufort, third earl of Somerset and then first duke of Somerset, who plucks the first red rose of Lancaster in the garden scene with Richard Plantagenet (*1 Henry VI*, 2.4.31).

The most significant Beaufort for the dynastic pattern of *Richard III* does not appear in the play, although other characters speak of her and send greetings to her. Margaret Beaufort, daughter of the first duke of Somerset, had married Edmund Tudor, who died shortly before the birth of his son, Henry, earl of Richmond. Margaret later married Thomas, Lord Stanley, created earl of Derby after his stepson won the Battle of Bosworth Field and became king. In *Richard III* he is sometimes called Stanley and sometimes Derby, though strictly speaking the "Derby" is anachronistic.

The first four acts of *Richard III* include occasional reminders of the existence of Henry Tudor. The earl of Dorset, for example, is advised to "go cross the seas / And live with Richmond" (4.1.41–42) in Brittany, a northwest region of France, where Richmond had spent the years of Edward IV's reign. Nevertheless, to the present-day reader the sudden appearance of Richmond as savior of the anti-Richard faction can seem quite abrupt, very much the cavalry coming over the hill. Shakespeare's original audience would of course have anticipated this event and would hardly have needed the reminders.

Another matter well known to the original audience would have been the shadow of illegitimacy stretching over Richmond's claim to the throne. Catherine Swynford had been the mistress, not the wife, of John of Gaunt, duke of Lancaster, when her children were born. Lancaster had at that time been married to his second wife, Constance of Castile, a Spanish princess with whom he had a daughter, and had become founder of a line of Spanish nobles of no immediate relevance here. The wife and then the widow of a respectable but not particularly highborn knight, Sir Hugh Swynford, Catherine Swynford had been governess to John of Gaunt's two daughters by his first wife, Blanche of Lancaster, who died in 1369. During the liaison that followed, Catherine Swynford gave birth to the three sons shown on the diagram above, along with a daughter, Joan. Their father acknowledged them and provided for them with both money and advancement, giving them the surname "Beaufort" from his castle in France where they were born. Finally, in 1396, two years after the death of Constance of Castile and three years before his own death, John of Gaunt married his mistress, to the astonishment of the English court. The children, by then in their late teens and early twenties, were promptly legitimized by King Richard II and by Parliament.

Relations between the always-legitimate and the retrospectively-legitimate Lancastrians would seem to have been ambivalent. The Beauforts supported their half-brother, Henry IV, when he took the throne in so irregular a manner, and King Henry was generous with high offices. But the king, upon confirming his half-siblings' patent of legitimacy in 1407, added the reservation that the line was excluded from succession to the English throne. (This detail naturally caused some fast footwork later, when Henry VII, a descendant of the Beauforts, took the throne. It was then claimed that Parliament had ratified the earlier patent, not the amended one.) In the first part of *Henry VI,* some of the characters suggest that discord between the two branches of the family was one of the reasons the English were distracted from properly conducting the war with France. Humphrey, duke of Gloucester, brother of the late Henry V and uncle of Henry VI, quarrels quite fiercely with Henry Beaufort, bishop of Winchester, one of the Beaufort great-uncles, finally calling him "Thou bastard of my grandfather!" (*1 Henry VI,* 3.1.42).

As if this stain were not enough, Henry VII also had a questionable marriage on his father's side of the family, as Shakespeare's audience might have remembered. Owen Tudor, his grandfather, had as a clerk of the wardrobe in the English royal household won the heart of Queen Catherine, widow of Henry V—the charming French princess whom Shakespeare depicted in *Henry V* but whose future is not revealed in the play. Queen Catherine bore Owen Tudor several children, but their marriage was kept secret and there was some doubt of its legality. The legitimacy of the children was not questioned, but the whole matter was not something one would want to shout from the rooftops.

The Tudors, in short, had reason to shore up their sovereignty with all the claims to divine approval they could muster. Richmond's triumph at the Battle of Bosworth Field was, naturally, a great help. The air of resolution which Shakespeare gives to his final scene is just what the descendants of Henry VII would have wished, and while there is no direct evidence that Queen Elizabeth saw this play about her grandfather, it can be assumed that she would have found it acceptable.

Henry VIII *(Written 1612–13)*

By the time Shakespeare's and Fletcher's *Henry VIII* was staged, Queen Elizabeth had herself become history. The audience, in harking back to events early in the previous century, might perhaps have been aware of some drastic shifts in chronological sequence, a rearrangement less likely to disturb present-day American readers; in fact, we might for once have an advantage. The death of Queen Catherine, for example, the first wife of Henry VIII, occurs in the play just before Queen Anne (Boleyn) gives birth to the princess Elizabeth, with which event the play comes to an end. The actual dates are 1533 for the birth of Elizabeth, 1536 for the death of Catherine. The original audience was presumably swept along by the nationalistic emotion which this play, basically a pageant of Tudor virtue triumphing over the schemes of selfish villains such as Cardinal Wolsey, effectively sets out to evoke.

Two background matters with which the original audience would have made quick connections are the pedigree of Edward Stafford, third duke of Buckingham, whose fall occurs in the first and second acts of the play, and the personal history of Cardinal Wolsey, whose fall in its turn occurs in act 3.

The dukes of Buckingham, or so it would seem from literature, were always falling from heights of aristocratic ambition, and the dynastic facts shed some light upon this habit. The Stafford family was descended from Thomas of Woodstock, duke of Gloucester, the youngest son of Edward III to survive to adulthood. This descent is not entirely through the male line, since it was Gloucester's daughter Anne who married a Stafford. However, by the early fifteenth century, all the other royal claimants depended upon a female ancestor somewhere or other.

In addition, the second duke of Buckingham, father of the one in *Henry VIII,* was descended from the Beauforts, the "other family" of Edward III's son John of Gaunt, duke of Lancaster; his mother had been a Margaret Beaufort, not the mother of Henry VII but her first cousin, daughter of Edmund Beaufort, second duke of Somerset. The second duke of Buckingham is the one who first supported and then turned against Richard III, with fatal results for him. His son Edward, our subject here, was restored to ducal dignity by Henry VII.

Although the royal blood here in question was outranked by other samples on display, it was indisputably royal, and it was linked to a good deal of wealth and power. Henry VIII, like Richard III before him, might have felt it too dangerous to have around for long—especially at a time when, as the original audience would have realized, King Henry was becoming desperate for a male heir and feared the vulnerability of the throne to would-be royal supplanters. The evidence produced against Buckingham in *Henry VIII* is based on historical fact, for Buckingham in 1521 was charged with "having listened to prophecies of the king's death and of his own succession to the crown, and of having expressed an intention to kill Henry."[3] A character in the play claims to have heard the duke say "that if the King / Should die without issue, he'll carry it so / To make the sceptre his" (1.2.133–35).

Cardinal Wolsey, on the other hand, annoyed his enemies not so much through the elevation of his birth as through its lowness; one couldn't win. Wolsey, of course, had other traits which made others happy to see his comeuppance. He had risen from humble origins to increasingly responsible positions at King Henry's court, demonstrating, incidentally, the usefulness of the church as a path to power, and he was far from a gracious winner. Many of his contemporaries genuinely hated him. By the time the play *Henry VIII* was produced, Wolsey's real abilities and his accomplishments in international diplomacy had been overshadowed in the mind of the audience by his reputation for arrogance and his association with what had now become not the Church hierarchy but the Roman Catholic hierarchy. The context of Wolsey's ambition, in particular his desire to be pope and his amassing money to that end, automatically condemns him in the eyes of a post-Reformation audience.

Wolsey's bad-guy attributes are quite convenient to the playwrights in distracting attention from the illogic of the play's emotional and ethical pattern. Wolsey becomes something of a lightning rod, gathering villainy from other sources and running it down to the ground without letting it touch those around him. King Henry, for example, is in historical fact trying to annul his marriage to Queen Catherine, who is seen in the play as a sympathetic character. Her dignity on being hauled into court (2.4), and her patient suffering in illness and death (4.2), put the audience firmly on her side. And yet, somehow, the king does not seem to blame; Queen Catherine's misfortunes appear more the result of a personal, vindictive attack by Wolsey. Similarly, since Wolsey is also an enemy of Anne Boleyn, her replacing Queen Catherine becomes a kind of accident, as if she just happened to be there. And Wolsey's disgrace and loss of office, which actually resulted from his failure to persuade the pope to agree to the annulment, seem in the play precipitated by the accidental discovery of a list of Wolsey's assets, "all that world of wealth I have drawn together / For mine own ends (indeed, to gain the popedom, / And fee my friends in Rome)" (3.2.210–13).

Finally, the procession from the christening of Princess Elizabeth ends the play with a sense of ebullient national well-being combined with hints of things to come. Thomas Cranmer, newly made archbishop of Canterbury, has performed the ceremony; the audience knew that his future would include writing much of the Anglican prayer book and then perishing at the stake as one of Queen Mary's martyrs. And the baby Elizabeth receives her share of prophecies. Archbishop Cranmer's closing speech would have been received by the play's audience as a retrospective eulogy of the era they themselves had seen come to an end ten years previous:

> She shall be, to the happiness of England,
> An aged princess; many days shall see her,
> And yet no day without a deed to crown it.
> Would I had known no more! but she must die,
> She must, the saints must have her; yet a virgin,
> A most unspotted lily shall she pass
> To th' ground, and all the world shall mourn her.

(5.4.56–62)

4

Elizabethan Cosmology in Church and Government

The Elizabethans saw God's universe as a harmonious creation wherein the parts fit together and reflected one another, creating a pattern of hierarchies and gradations in which everything had its place.[1] Principles of kingship and social order, as mentioned in previous chapters, were part of the picture. It is true that this model often appeared in literature as an ideal rather than an actuality; a more nearly perfect era, the "golden age," was postulated as having existed in former times, and neoplatonic theology admitted imperfections within those realms of the universe inhabited by man. The geocentric universe placed Earth, after all, the farthest from the outer spheres, the divine empyrean where complete goodness dwelt. Furthermore, the new scientific observations, including those of Copernicus and Kepler, had widened the concept of the physical universe. These innovations and objections, however, did not seriously disturb the popular assumption of a divine cosmic plan demonstrated by the starry heavens.

Although trapped on earth during his mortal life, man could gain access to the higher realms by obeying and furthering God's principles. Thus the task of the Church is to assist the human soul in rising to a higher sphere, while the soul, of course, must cooperate with the Church. Similarly, human society should be governed by the rules of divine justice, as best these might be perceived. Spenser's description of the goddess Justice emphasizes this derivation and also points out the right of the sovereign, now that the Golden Age is past and ethical

52

abstractions are no longer encountered in the flesh, to stand in for Justice (and thus for God):

> *For during Saturnes ancient raigne it's sayd,*
> *That all the world with goodnesse did abound:*
> *All loved vertue, no man was affrayd*
> *Of force, ne fraud in wight was to be found:*
> *No warre was knowne, no dreadfull trompets sound,*
> *Peace universall rayn'd mongst men and beasts,*
> *And all things freely grew out of the ground:*
> *Justice sate high ador'd with solemn feasts,*
> *And to all people did divide her dred beheasts.*

> *Most sacred vertue she of all the rest,*
> *Resembling God in His imperiall might;*
> *Whose soveraine powre is herein most exprest,*
> *That both to good and bad He dealeth right*
> *And all His workes with Justice hath bedight.*
> *That powre He also doth to Princes lend,*
> *And makes them like Himself in glorious sight,*
> *To sit in His owne seate, His cause to end,*
> *And rule His people right, as he doth recommend.*
> (*The Faerie Queene,* 5.Proem.9–10)

The Orderly Hierarchy of the Church

On separating from Rome, the Church of England no longer recognized the two positions which in pre-Reformation times had been situated at the top of the pyramid—the pope, at the apex, and just beneath him the College of Cardinals. (Since the pope, who was chosen by the College of Cardinals from among themselves, in turn appointed cardinals to fill any vacancy that might occur, the two levels could be said to intermingle.) Nevertheless, on encountering these personages in literature, Englishmen still knew who they were. Sometimes, as in Webster's *The White Devil,* such characters are emblematic of lurid Roman Catholic depravity, while Cardinal Wolsey, in Shakespeare's and Fletcher's *Henry VIII*, becomes an archetype of pride. At other times the associations were simpler; English settlers in America, observing the wildlife of their new home, were reminded of the scarlet of a cardinal's robes by a bird and a flower, respectively members of the finch and lobelia families.

Descending down the hierarchy to the archbishop level, we find ourselves in a more nationalistic sphere. Henry VIII, on taking the role of "defender of the faith," had been careful to keep for himself the right to appoint the two Church of England archbishops; previously a special document from the pope, or papal bull, had been needed to confirm the king's nomination. Both the archbishop of Canterbury and the Archbishop of York, in order of precedence, sat, like the bishops, in the House of Lords, where they took part in making the laws of the land.

Bishops, at the next level down, presided over dioceses, or sees, the Church's territorial divisions. The sixteenth century saw considerable rearrangement of the boundaries, but the number of dioceses was generally around twenty. Besides administering their sees and sitting in the House of Lords, the bishops ordained the priests who served in the eight thousand or so parish churches. Ordination was spoken of as "taking holy orders"; the requirements varied, but some level of education was expected. Bishops were to examine the candidates, paying special heed to their Latin. If the bishop found a candidate insufficiently prepared, he might refuse to ordain him or might, according to A. G. Dickens, tell him to study an additional year and try again.[2]

The Church in Daily Life

To ordinary men and women, aware to a greater or lesser extent of the harmonious plan of the cosmos but occupying a fairly humble place in it, religion was primarily experienced as a function of their parish church. This is not to say that everyone took to religion either as a passionate emotion or as an intellectual preoccupation. For many people, church observances were automatic gestures, hardly noticed perhaps, and performed less often than the authorities would have liked. And although most parishes were small enough for the inhabitants to walk to church quite easily, there were exceptions in the thinly populated north, where parishes covered a great deal of ground, and getting oneself to the nearest church might become a major expedition.

But for most of the population the church was always there, in sight of one's door in a typical village, and part of the environment. Attendance at church services was required by law, as was payment of tithes; to be remiss in either could subject one to a fine. The church registers recorded the parishioners' baptisms, marriages, and burials. The church festivals marked the turning year: Easter, Whitsunday, Midsummer Eve, Michaelmas—a late September feast—and Christmas, followed by Twelfth Night or the Feast of the Epiphany. There were many others. The calendar of saints was thinned out from time to time by the Protestant authorities, but numerous special celebrations remained. England could hardly forget her patron, Saint George, for example; his traditional day, April 23, is also celebrated as a reasonably good guess for Shakespeare's birthday, going by the parish register's entry for the latter's baptism.

Church occasions were not always solemn in mood. The "Whitsun ale," a kind of community fair held by the parish church to raise money for various good causes, centered on the sale of that beverage. Another odd and ancient custom was the annual "beating of the bounds," when the whole parish, including the children, walked around the boundary stones which marked the limitations of the parish. As the procession reached each stone, the children were beaten so that they would remember where it was. One assumes that this beating was done in a ritualistic, nonviolent manner, but as contemporary educational theory sometimes ascribed a mnemonic function to physical punishment, one cannot be sure.

Many literary references to the parish church are still self-explanatory for present-day readers, but a review of some of the terminology might be useful. A *living,* for example, was the general term for any ecclesiastical benefice, but in a parochial context it usually included a place for the parish priest and his family to live, a parcel of "glebe land" for him to farm, and the legal right to the parishioners' tithes or some portion thereof.

The tithe was calculated as ten percent of the "increase of the earth"—the rye harvest, say, or the newborn lambs. Tithes might be paid in kind, but often they were commuted to money payments. Should a parishioner refuse to pay his tithes, the priest might bring suit through the ecclesiastical courts. Not all parishioners were subject to tithe payments, of course, since some had either no property or no increase of it.

Various terms more or less synonymous with *priest* were distinguished by the proportion of tithes the incumbent actually received. A rector got all of them, as did a parson; the words mean essentially the same thing. A vicar, on the other hand, served a parish the tithes of which were "impropriated," or handed over to some other body; before the Reformation, this other body had often been a religious house. After the Reformation, the purchaser of monastic property with attached benefices would receive the tithes. The vicar would simply be given a salary.

The words *preacher* and *minister* were not used in the Church of England in the sense current in present-day America, that of the chief occupant of a Protestant congregation's pulpit. A preacher was anyone who preached a sermon, but he might or might not have a church of his own. The word *minister* was more often used in its secular sense, to denote the holder of a high government office.

Lay officials in the parish included the parish clerk, in charge of keeping the register (a duty first required in the time of Henry VIII); the churchwardens, elected members of the congregation who assisted in making parish decisions; the sexton, who cared for the church building and dug graves; and the beadle, who kept order during services. These received a stipend, except for the churchwardens, who were (at least in theory) men of substance who donated their services. The parish's musical resources depended somewhat on circumstance, but often there was a choir of men and boys.

The Ecclesiastical Courts

Besides coherence and ritual, the Church supplied ordinary Englishmen with a quite tangible set of moral restrictions, aimed at improving their chances at a comfortable heavenly home but also regulating their social environment in the world below. These restrictions were enforced through various levels of ecclesiastical courts. The most familiar of these, the archdeacon's court, operated at the parish level; the archdeacon, an administrative assistant to the bishop, had the responsibility of visiting each parish in the diocese at least once a year, although the intervals were sometimes longer.

Upon arriving in a parish, the archdeacon inquired of the church-wardens which persons had been suspected or accused of misdoings; he then held the necessary trials, and prescribed corrective penances—often fairly mild ones, by the standards of the day. Offenses tried at these courts included sexual and procreative misbehavior such as fornication, adultery, making a woman pregnant, giving birth to a bastard, or neglecting to have a child christened. This focus on scandalous doings gave the archdeacons' courts a nickname which Paul Hair has used for his collection of extracts from the official records, *Before the Bawdy Court.*[3] Violent sexual crimes such as rape, like more violent crime generally, were tried by the secular rather than the church courts.

Penalties assigned by the archdeacon, provided he found the accused guilty, typically included some kind of humiliation designed to bring about repentance. The offender might have to make a public confession, walk around the church a certain number of times barefoot, or attend the Sunday service wearing sackcloth and holding a lighted candle. Fines might be exacted in the form of so many pence to be given to the poor. Church courts could not impose the death penalty, though they could go so far as whipping.

Church courts comprised, in fact, a separate part of the legal system. They were based on canon law, the law of the medieval Church which in its turn had been based on the laws of the vanished Roman Empire. Such beginnings predated the rise of English nationalism and were affiliated instead with the older concept of Christendom, of churches and bishoprics scattered through many lands but loyal to the pope.

After the English Reformation, naturally, this connection with the pope was lost, and the higher ecclesiastical courts could no longer appeal to Rome. The system might be said to have been cut off at the top. The archdeacon's courts nevertheless continued to function, perhaps because no other authority wanted the job.

The Elizabethans' Recent Past: Henry VIII and the Monasteries

---

When King Henry dissolved the monasteries in the 1530s, he did not persecute the displaced monks and nuns; they were given pensions, and many of them (monks especially) found niches for themselves in the Church of England. However, a large-scale redistribution of wealth took place, flowing from the monasteries' coffers to the king's, and an institution which had existed in England for centuries came to an end.[4]

In literature, monks and nuns continued to appear and, unlike the popes and cardinals who took on a retrospective moral tarnish, retained for the most part the aura of simple virtue they had always had. (Of course, some flexibility had obtained in earlier times; Chaucer describes conniving monks and lecherous friars, as well as a prioress who is very fond of her comfort.) Figures like Friar Lawrence in *Romeo and Juliet* or Isabella in *Measure for Measure,* whom the other characters trust, remain quite recognizable to Elizabethan readers, who may also of course, have seen these particular characters as plausible because the stories are set in foreign countries.

The words *monastery* and *convent* have by now acquired a gender distinction, and present-day readers think of monks living in the one and nuns in the other. However, during the sixteenth century these terms were often interchangeable. A nunnery, on the other hand, was definitely a feminine habitat, though the word could be used ironically. The *Oxford English Dictionary* cites a 1593 quotation from Thomas Nashe in which *nunnery* means a house of ill fame, a usage which gives Hamlet's instruction to Ophelia a good deal of ambiguity (3.1.120).

An abbey was equivalent to a monastery, although the word sometimes referred to the property and buildings rather than to the people. After the Reformation, the word *abbey* was often applied to the church building only, as in Westminster Abbey.

A monastery, or abbey, was headed by an abbot, often assisted by a prior as next in command. Feminine counterparts were the abbess and the prioress. A priory, continuing the connotation of secondary rank, was a religious house governed by a prior or prioress and established as an offshoot of an abbey, upon which it often remained dependent.

Monks and nuns did not need to have taken holy orders (indeed, nuns could not have done so had they wished) in order to join their religious communities. They simply made vows to live by the rule of their order. Usually, however, the higher positions in a monastery were held by ordained priests.

Religious Tensions during Elizabeth's Reign

Elizabethan readers were naturally aware of the religious upheavals of previous reigns as well as those incipient in their own; one might wonder, in fact, if the tone of cosmic certainty characteristic of much Elizabethan literature represents an effort at self-reassurance. Queen Mary's attempt to undo what her father had done and make England once again a Catholic nation had led to the burning at the stake of some 300 Protestants, among them Archbishop Cranmer, compiler of the Church of England's prayer book. Others escaped to Switzerland, where under the protection of the French theologian John Calvin they waited for better times.

One of the "Marian exiles," as these were called, John Foxe, spent his years in Switzerland preparing a collection of stories about Christian martyrs past and present which became the *Acts and Monuments of These Latter and Perilous Days,* better known as the *Book of Martyrs.* In these pages, the deaths of Cranmer and many other Protestants (including Lady Jane Grey, whose fate Foxe attributes to her religion rather than her pedigree) are described with great immediacy. The book was published shortly after Queen Elizabeth came to the throne and English Protestants were able to regroup; subsequent editions were many. An immense work, illustrated with startling woodcuts, its volumes could be found in parish churches and cathedral libraries, often chained to the shelf for safekeeping, and also in many homes. The *Book of Martyrs* influenced the English view of Catholicism for generations—negatively, needless to say.

The reign of Queen Elizabeth in its turn included some persecution of Catholics, although the intensity was not as great. Approximately 250 were executed or died in prison—close to Queen Mary's total, but then Elizabeth was on the throne for forty-five years to Mary's five. Neither queen deliberately undertook a large-scale retaliation against ordinary people, innocent worshippers as it were; each single martyrdom involved a leader who, in the view of the respective authorities, stubbornly refused to recant although given every opportunity.

Queen Elizabeth's major anti-Catholic actions took place late in her reign. In 1572, papal authorities in Rome had announced that any good

Catholic who assassinated the queen could be assured of having done a worthy deed, a statement which understandably polarized the situation. (The queen's response was to go about in public as usual, without visible protection.) Then, in the 1580s, the Jesuit order undertook the reclamation of England as a special project and sent in missionaries from the Continent, many of whom were captured and executed—not for being Catholic per se but for treason; the intertwining of church and state can be seen dramatically in this instance.

Meanwhile, within the English Church itself, another source of tension had begun to evolve in the form of the various Puritan movements. In the view of many of these, Henry VIII had not gone far enough in removing England from papal authority while preserving the rest of the Church structure more or less intact. Puritans tended to advocate relying on the Bible for organization as well as doctrine, and wished to eliminate the hierarchy of bishops and archbishops along with anything else they felt extraneous—elaborate services, for example, or undue ornamentation in religious art and music.

Cosmology in Government: The Sovereign and the Privy Council

Besides defending the faith, the English monarch from his position at the top of the social hierarchy was responsible for the temporal government, although he was not expected to do everything himself; delegation of authority is implied in the Elizabethan cosmology.

Closest to the sovereign was the Privy (or private) Council, fifteen to twenty ministers whom the sovereign had appointed. Many things about the Privy Council strike a present-day reader, American or English, as ominous. Meetings were secret; individual ministers sometimes set up private spy systems; and the council, unlike bodies operating under the common law, was empowered to use torture when investigating offenses and to obtain forced confessions. The council's special court, the Star Chamber (named, it is said, for the stars painted on the ceiling of its meeting room), could try cases without a jury and had a relatively free hand in assigning punishments.

Later, in the seventeenth century, the Star Chamber was to fulfill its potential as an instrument of tyranny, and it was abolished in the early

1640s. But under the Tudors its influence could be surprisingly benign. It dealt efficiently with cases of riot, for example, and general disorderly behavior. Shakespeare's Justice Shallow, for example, threatens in *The Merry Wives of Windsor* to make a "Star Chamber matter" of Falstaff's having "beaten my men, killed my deer, and broke open my lodge" (1.1.111). This plan might have seemed to the original audience quite appropriate, though Shallow forgets about it and the play goes off in other directions.

The King's Courts in London

The word *court* has two meanings in connection with the sovereign, a state of affairs indicative in itself of the primordial power of kings in early human society. On the one hand, the court is the place where the king or queen lives, characterized in Elizabethan times by panoply, elaborate recreations, courtiers in gorgeous garments, and rumors and intrigue. A court is also, of course, a place where cases are heard and justice meted out. The two meanings overlap in fairy tales and medieval romances, where an adventuring knight who enters a king's court is likely to find the king on his throne, arbitrating his subjects' disputes.

In reality, society had long been so complex that the monarch entrusted the dispensation of justice to specialists, but London, and specifically Westminster Palace, was still the site of the royal courts. These included King's Bench, Common Pleas (also called the Common Bench), Exchequer, and Chancery.

The courts of King's Bench and Common Pleas dealt in statute law— that is to say, laws that had been passed as such and could be found written down on the books—and also in common law, that more abstract entity comprised of the decisions of former courts on cases similar to the one at hand. Originally, King's Bench had tried cases in which the Crown had an interest; Common Pleas, cases between subjects. As centuries passed, the lines of demarcation tended to blur. The Court of Exchequer, also a common-law court, heard pleas which bore on the financial rights of the Crown, or were said to do so. The High Court of Chancery had branched away from common law and had come to specialize in equity, upholding the rights of the individual in cases which had more or less fallen through the net of common law. (An example might be a person who had entered a contract through mistaking the identity of one of the other parties.)

The highest legal figure in the realm was the Lord High Chancellor, who frequently presided over the Court of Chancery and was also speaker of the House of Lords. Second highest was the Lord Chief Justice, presiding over the King's Bench, which was usually ranked highest of the courts dealing in common law. The Lord Chief Justice appears in the second part of *Henry IV* as an embodiment of abstract justice, treating a king's son just as he would anyone else. Prince Hal's acceptance of this principle dramatizes his previously announced intention to reform his ways (5.2.101–6).

County Assizes, Quarter Sessions, and Pie-Powder Courts

Not all Englishmen could conveniently get themselves to London to have divine justice made accessible to human plaintiffs, and quite a lot of law business was taken care of closer to home.

The assizes held twice a year in each county, or shire, tried both civil and criminal cases, usually before a jury. Their cases included the more serious felonies referred to them by the quarter sessions (see below), though cases did not have to go through quarter sessions to get to the assizes. The justices were often Londoners of high rank in the legal profession.

A county's quarter sessions were held more frequently, as the name indicates, and were conducted by local justices of the peace. The *Oxford English Dictionary* observes that the word *sessions,* when used alone, usually denotes the quarter sessions. Shakespeare calls upon them for a metaphor of internal life:

> *When to the sessions of sweet silent thought*
> *I summon up remembrance of things past.*
>
> (Sonnet 30)

The curious name *pie-powder* is derived from the French *pied-pou-*

dreux, "dusty-footed," referring to an itinerant merchant. The pie-powder courts were held at fairs and markets, dealing out justice to the stallholders and customers. Leatherhead, the hobby-horse seller in Jonson's *Bartholomew Fair,* threatens to take Joan Trash the gingerbread woman before "the Pie-powders" for calling away his customers (3.4.93).

The Two Houses of Parliament

From his elevated position in the cosmological hierarchy, the sovereign might nevertheless see himself as in need of advice and concurrence not only from those ministers whom he had chosen for their wisdom and loyalty but from two other groups as well, the hereditary nobility and the more substantial segments of the common people.

The hereditary nobility, persons usually of considerable wealth and power, might or might not be in agreement with the sovereign's policies, and, in fact, often were not, a strong centralized authority putting individual power pockets at a disadvantage. (This seeming paradox, since the nobles were as aware as anyone else of the cosmological ideal of a harmonious state, is perhaps not so baffling in view of human nature. One is somehow able to make large allowances for one's own interests. Historians also point out a slippage in hierarchical loyalty; as actual military service to an overlord was replaced by cash payments, the sense of belonging to an interdependent organic whole grew weaker.)

The king nevertheless needed to call these powers together, however recalcitrant and self-interested they might be, if not for their advice then at least to keep an eye on them and to prevent them from sulking perpetually in their territorial strongholds and forming inconvenient alliances. The House of Lords had evolved through the centuries as the venue of these sometimes uneasy confrontations.

With regard to the House of Commons, Parliament's other body, we might first note that the word *commons* is used in the sense simply of "without a hereditary title." (Knights and baronets could not sit in the House of Lords, but they could and often did find themselves in the Commons.) Members were elected to their seats by a variety of mechanisms, but this practice had originated because the sovereign did not know personally enough nonaristocrats to be able to issue individual summonses, as was done for the House of Lords. The electoral process, in other words, functioned as a means of saving trouble for the king and not as an expression of the power of the people. And the electorate was restricted to persons of substance—country gentry or prosperous merchants, for example, who chose members to represent their own interests.

As a result of Magna Carta in the early thirteenth century, Parliament had the special power of voting taxes. If a sovereign needed money for extraordinary revenue—a military campaign, for example—only Parliament could help out. Thus the king had a strong practical need for Parliament, aside from the fact that any ruler who trampled upon the more powerful of his underlings would sooner or later regret it.

The king nevertheless had the upper hand. Parliaments met only because he had summoned them; they did not follow any set, autonomous timetable. In sending out individual summonses to the nobility to attend the House of Lords, the king was under no obligation to include all of them, and he could always bolster his supporters in that house by creating new peers, first making sure that they were of the right way of thinking. As for the House of Commons, the sovereign could create the "boroughs" which sent elected members to Parliament—or, more accurately, could bestow borough status on a community that already existed. Queen Elizabeth, for example, created some sixty boroughs during her reign.

In Elizabeth's time, Parliament met where it does today, in Westminster Palace, on the banks of the Thames. There was even a clock tower near the site of Big Ben, although Big Ben itself, like much of the present-day palace, dates from the nineteenth century. The House of Lords met in Westminster Hall, now the oldest part of the complex; the House of Commons met in St. Stephen's Chapel, adjacent and at right angles to Westminster Hall. It is now call St. Stephen's Hall and serves as a corridor to the main lobby.

Henry V: *Parliamentary Maneuverings and Social Harmony*

Since bills originating in either house had to be approved by the sovereign before becoming law, considerable scope existed for political trade-offs. Shakespeare in *Henry V* shows his ingenious king manipulating the Church into paying for a war.

The archbishop of Canterbury and the bishop of Ely, early in the play, express their concern about a bill under consideration in the Commons which would let the Crown seize certain Church lands. (This circumstance, which Shakespeare found in Holinshed, incidentally shows the Church's wealth attracting secular attention long before the time of Henry VIII.) The loss of these lands would drink more than deep, says Canterbury; " 'twould drink the cup and all" (1.1.20). The two clerics are uncertain which side the king supports, though Canterbury tries to be optimistic, and both acclaim the Church's decision to make the king a present of "a greater sum / Than ever at one time the clergy yet / Did to his predecessors part withal" (1.1.79–81). The money is not to be directly associated with the pending bill; its declared purpose is to assist the king's military preparations against France, although Canterbury implies that the king will get the connection. The reader is left to speculate on who has bought whom in this case.

Aside from the ins and outs of Parliament, Shakespeare's characters have a great deal to say on the harmony of the ideal state, often drawing images from various parts of the cosmos. The archbishop of Canterbury, shortly after the demonstration of practical politics described above, finds himself in a conversation with the duke of Exeter on the need for government to draw disparate functions into one united whole. Exeter's comparison makes use of an art traditionally aligned with the heavens:

> *For government, though high, and low, and lower,*
> *Put into parts, doth keep in one consent,*
> *Congreeing in a full and natural close,*
> *Like music.*

> (1.2.180–83)

Instead of responding with another image of celestial harmony, Canterbury chooses an example from the ordinary rural scene, finding an analogous society in which each participant is busy about his special task and idlers are summarily dealt with:

> *So work the honey-bees,*
> *Creatures that by a rule in nature teach*

The act of order to a peopled kingdom.
They have a king, and officers of sorts,
Where some, like magistrates, correct at home;
Others, like merchants, venter trade abroad;
Others, like soldiers, armed in their stings,
Make boot upon the summer's velvet buds,
Which pillage they with merry march bring home
To the tent-royal of their emperor;
Who busied in his majesty surveys
The singing masons building roofs of gold,
The civil citizens kneading up the honey,
The poor mechanic porters crowding in
Their heavy burthens at his narrow gate,
The sad-ey'd justice, with his surly hum,
Delivering o'er to executors pale
The lazy yawning drone.

(1.2.187–204)

The fact that these particular creatures are ruled by a queen rather than a king does not affect the image; a sovereign is a sovereign. It might be added, too, that the use of the colony of bees as an emblem of a harmonious society is far-flung; the inscription on a coffin dating from approximately 3600 B.C. includes a hieroglyphic bee, representing the king of Lower Egypt.[5]

5

Elizabethan Money

It is not hard to get our feet on the ground with Elizabethan money.
The basic elements of buying and selling have not changed, and all we
have to do is translate, so to speak. In literature, references to money
have both literal and imagaic functions, and while this chapter will limit
itself to basic facts, the reader will be fairly well equipped to continue
along the literary path. A useful guide can be found in Sandra K. Fischer's
*Econolingua: A Glossary of Coins and Economic Language in Renais-
sance Drama* (Newark, Del.: University of Delaware Press, 1985).[1]

Pounds, Shillings, and Pence

A pound, when encountered in Elizabethan literature, may safely be
considered a biggish chunk of money, a sum to be taken seriously. A
shilling is of less moment; spending a shilling would give a middle-income
buyer some thought, but it would not be a decision to go around brood-
ing about. A penny was an everyday sort of sum, many routine expenses
being reckoned in pennies and such fractions thereof as halfpence and
farthings. (As we will see, the Elizabethan penny was worth considerably
more in buying power than any of its present-day namesakes.) Very
roughly, and ignoring all the real-life variables, we can think of a penny
as the price of a chicken (live in the farmyard, not dressed to cook), the

67

shilling as the price of a pig, and the pound as the price of a cow. A more detailed look at buying-power equivalents appears below, following a quick survey of the coins' values relative to one another.

In the early 1970s, just before Great Britain shifted to its present decimal currency after centuries of inflicting impossible arithmetic problems upon the young, the following ratio was in effect:

One pound (£) = twenty shillings

One shilling (s) = twelve pence (d)

The old pound thus consisted of 240 old pence. The currency in use in the sixteenth century was close enough to this ratio for us to consider it a ballpark norm, though there was some fluctuation.

Since paper currency as we understand it, issued by a government (or by a bank) and backed by gold or silver reserves, did not exist in these earlier times, *money* meant coins. These coins were, or were supposed to be, the real thing, a certain weight of silver or gold corresponding to the face value stamped on the coins. It was possible for a government to issue debased coinage, but the consequences usually were not good.

Some amounts of money were talked about, or used in calculations, but did not actually exist as a coin—as an American might speak of "two bits." Oddly, the pound was one of these; no coin existed to cover precisely this amount until some centuries later. (One thinks of the sovereign, mentioned below, as the equivalent of a pound, but some sovereigns were larger and were worth more.) Again, the mark was basically a measure of weight but was sometimes used to indicate an amount of money, usually a little over thirteen shillings. Scotland, whose coinage differed from the English in many respects, did have an actual coin called the mark.

The following list includes coins most likely to be mentioned in Elizabethan literature and runs from the most valuable down to the least.

The *sovereign* was an impressive gold piece worth, usually, a pound or slightly more. Some extra-large sovereigns were issued at a value of thirty shillings, or a pound and a half. The earliest English sovereigns, issued by Henry VII, weighed, according to James Mackay,

240 grains of almost pure gold and, since there would be 240 pence to the pound, "is a reminder of a time when a grain or pennyweight of gold was worth just that—a penny."[2] The coin bore the image of the sovereign in whose reign it had been made, hence the name.

The *royal,* also spelt *ryal* or *rial,* was a gold coin usually issued at a weight valued at ten to fourteen shillings.

The *angel,* also gold, bore the figure of the archangel Michael treading on a dragon. Angels were coined at various weights but usually were worth between seven and ten shillings, or half a pound.

The *noble* was originally issued by Henry VIII at a value of a third of a pound, but by the end of the century it had been issued at various weights of gold, and its value was often the same as that assigned to the angel.

Gold coins such as the ones just described were the elite of the English currency. They were used in foreign trade and thus were somewhat protected against debasement; a monarch tempted to use this expedient knew that foreign merchants might refuse to accept debased coinage, having plenty of alternatives, while Englishmen at home were more helpless in this regard.

In theory, the ratio between the value of gold and that of silver was ten to one. William Harrison makes this claim;[3] and Shakespeare's prince of Morocco, choosing between gold, silver, and lead in *The Merchant of Venice,* refuses to compare Portia to silver, this metal "being ten times undervalued to tried gold" (2.7.53). The ratio varied in practice, however, since the values of gold and silver fluctuated and did not always do so in tandem.

The following silver coins are often mentioned in literature:

The *crown* was usually valued at five shillings; four of them added up to a pound.

The *half-crown,* naturally, was worth two and a half shillings, or two shillings sixpence.

The *shilling* was worth twelve pence.

The *sixpence* was worth half a shilling.

The *groat* was worth four pence, a third of a shilling.

The *threepenny piece,* the *half groat* (twopence), *penny, half-penny, three-farthings piece* and *farthing* (worth a fourth of a penny) are self-explanatory.

Lower denominations were badly needed in the Elizabethan economy, and the lack of them caused many problems, but it was hard to see a solution as long as gold and silver remained the only metals that could be made into money. The lesser coins were already inconveniently tiny. The silver penny was the size of one's thumbnail, the silver halfpenny only slightly larger than a present-day shirt button. The farthing was so small it was not even coined during Elizabeth's reign; to buy something worth a farthing, one had to pay with a penny and get back a three-farthing piece in change.

The suggestion that the authorities solve the small-change problem by using a less valuable metal for small denominations, or by alloying the correct amount of silver with enough base metal to make the coin large enough to handle, evoked negative reactions; it was argued, for instance, that this recourse would make it harder to tell good coins from counterfeits. Some base metal coins were made for use in Ireland, and some English merchants issued lead or tin tokens redeemable in their own goods, but the problem continued until copper coins were finally introduced later in the seventeenth century.

Sixteenth-Century Pounds and Present-Day Dollars

Equating the money of one era to that of another is impossible, of course, since the kinds of things available for purchase are so different. Consequently, with the inexactitude of this process firmly in mind, we might as well go ahead and take a stab at it, thus coming up with an approximate notion of the buying power of Elizabethan money which will be useful as we continue to adjust our literary responses.

The suggested ratio is a fairly staggering 400 to 1, dollars to pounds. The shilling, a twentieth of a pound, then translates to $20.00, and the penny, a twelfth of a shilling, becomes $1.66, or $1.50 in more psychologically immediate round numbers. Or, if we prefer to visualize the penny at $1.66, the halfpence becomes $.80 and the farthing $.40.

Alternately, Elizabethan money can be turned into present-day British pounds at a ratio of 225 to 1; this figure assumes the approximate pounds-to-dollars rate which has prevailed throughout the 1980s, though with many fluctuations. Inflation, too, has risen in a nonsynchronized pattern; transatlantic visitors to either country usually find on going shopping that some purchases are good value and others are either shocking or out of sight, depending on the national idiom.

For some quick practice in adjusting our economic emotions, we will look briefly at books, foodstuffs, and horses, all goods bought and sold by both present-day Americans and sixteenth-century Englishmen, with, of course, many variations in type and quality.

The first-folio edition of Shakespeare, to choose a well-known literary item, is said to have cost a shilling in 1623.[4] This works out to twenty dollars in our money, which seems a bit low for such a large and impressive book. It would have been sold without a binding, however; the purchaser merely bought the printed and gathered sheets and took them to the binder of his choice, much as we take a picture to be framed.

Some years earlier, in 1609, the quarto edition of *Troilus and Cressida* is said to have sold for sixpence,[5] or ten dollars. A quarto was much smaller than a folio, the pages being a fourth as large if we assume the printing was done on the same size sheets. Naturally, with smaller pages, the quarto could not be very thick, and in fact quarto editions of plays often resembled pamphlets. *Troilus and Cressida* had just under fifty pages. Quartos were usually sold in a vellum covering, ready to read.

Moving on to food, we find that a loaf of wheat bread weighing one avoirdupois pound (sixteen ounces or 7000 grains, that is, the weight that is still with us)[6] usually cost a penny in the sixteenth century, or, say, $1.60. This is higher than the present-day price for a loaf of American bread, $.89 in the fall of 1988. Rye bread, incidentally, once cheaper than wheat, is now often more expensive.

A pound of butter, according to the accounts kept by a London bachelor in 1589,[7] cost five pence, or around $8.00. The present-day equivalent has definitely come down in price, to $2.29 in 1988.

Milk, like many Elizabethan foodstuffs and some of our own, varied in price according to the season, being more plentiful and therefore cheaper in summer. John Stow includes in his *Survey of London* a childhood memory of buying "three ale pints for a half-penny in summer, and . . . one ale quart for a half penny in winter, always hot from the kine [cows], as the same was milked and strained."[8] The sixteenth-century quart was larger than ours, but the price of a quart of American milk was $.74 in 1988, fairly close to that of Stow's boyhood. There are differences in the product, since our milk is pasteurized, homogenized, and elaborately packaged; nevertheless, there is something very appealing in buying one's milk straight from the cow. In view of the dearth of small change in the economy, incidentally, it is interesting that the customer was not allowed to pay more or less money according to the season; he paid the same halfpenny and took home more or less milk.

Fruit was much enjoyed, the price varying, as does our own, according to season and availability as well as quality. Oranges were imported and found an eager market; seven oranges for two pence, fifty cents each in present-day money, is a fairly typical price,[9] not out of line for today (except in Florida).

Another luxurious item of produce in the early seventeenth century was the Irish potato, then called the "Virginia potato," imported from the New World and sold at two shillings a pound, or $40.00.[10] The price today is around $.25 a pound, in ten-pound sacks.

For examples of a large-scale purchase, one that would ordinarily require careful thought and some comparison shopping, we move on to the horse. There have, of course, been some changes. Trained warhorses are seldom offered for sale these days, and we do not have much use for the packhorses that moved such a large proportion of Elizabethan goods from place to place. Conversely, the hunters and show jumpers seen today, figuring in the Olympic Games for example, would have perplexed the Elizabethans. Fox hunting in its present form did not develop until the eighteenth century, after the old open-field cultivation had been replaced by enclosure, and jumping was not a standard skill for horse or rider.

Nevertheless, pleasant riding horses have retained their appeal through the centuries. The Elizabethans were used to paying from two to four pounds for an outstanding horse,[11] and we can find a rough equivalent in today's advertisements. A "Quarter horse—Registered bay gelding, seven years old, quiet, trail and western pleasure, $1250"[12] might have seemed to an Elizabethan, given the chance, worth paying three pounds for. Similarly, a "Morgan mare—registered eight year old upheaded chestnut, $1800"[13] might have been worth four and a half pounds to a wealthy merchant in search of a horse that would stand out in a crowd. If style and elite lineage were not required, the Elizabethans could buy a quite adequate riding horse for a pound or two, as can we: "Paint mare, six years old, $600," or "Pony—large chestnut, blaze face, three white stockings, rode Western on trails, asking $550."[14]

Racehorses, then as now, were something else again. King James was the first English monarch to pay much attention to fast horses; from the perspective of pedigree, it is interesting that the present-day royal family is descended from him. Shortly after coming to the English throne, King James paid five hundred guineas, well over a million present-day dollars by the computation we are using (a guinea was worth twenty-one shillings), for an Arab stallion brought from Constantinople by Gervase Markham.[15] Nothing much came of this horse, but King James had the right idea; the three great Arab stallions who founded the English stud book were imported in the eighteenth century. And paying a million dollars for a horse which does not fulfill his potential is not an unusual fate in racing today.

Money in Shakespeare

The following examples are intended to shed light on these particular Shakespearean moments and also further to help the reader develop a sense of what sums, approximately, would buy what sorts of goods or services.

The gold coins most often mentioned in Shakespeare are the angel and the noble; these usually appear in a context not so much of purchasing power as simply of wealth. They are irresistibly the subject of puns. Benedick in *Much Ado About Nothing* describes his ideal woman, who must be "Mild, or come not near me; noble, or not I for an angel" (2.3.33). King John, planning to transfer some of the Church's wealth to himself, orders a henchman to "Shake the bags / Of hoarding abbots; imprisoned angels / Set at liberty" (3.3.8).

Unlike the golden angels, Shakespeare's silver coins are of this workaday world, a medium of exchange; silver, in *The Merchant of Venice,* is in fact described as a "pale and common drudge / 'Tween man and man"

(3.2.103–4). The Boar's Head Tavern is alive with silver. Francis the drawer, says Prince Hal, "never spake other English in his life than 'eight shillings and sixpence'" (*1 Henry IV,* 2.4.27). Falstaff's itemized bill for sack (sherry), capon (chicken), sauce, and bread is made out in shillings and pence, and Prince Hal professes to be shocked at the ratio of sack to bread, five shillings eightpence for the one and a halfpenny for the other (2.4.534–41). "Quoit him down, Bardolph, like a shove-groat shilling," Falstaff says at a later point, ordering Pistol thrown down the stairs (*2 Henry IV,* 2.4.192); the analogy is to a game in which coins were thrown at a target. And Nym demands of Pistol, "You'll pay me the eight shillings I won of you at betting?" (*Henry V,* 2.1.94), starting another fracas.

In a less disreputable context, presumably, a shilling is the price of admission to a theater, as described in the prologue to *Henry VIII:*

> *Those that come to see*
> *Only a show or two, and so agree*
> *The play may pass, if they be still and willing,*
> *I'll undertake to see away their shilling*
> *Richly in two short hours.*
>
> (9–13)

Usually one could get into a theater for considerably less—a penny, even—but the price depended on where one sat, or stood, in the case of a cheaper admission. At the rate of twenty present-day American dollars, a shilling for a comfortable seat does not seem exorbitant.

The sixpence, to Shakespeare's characters, was definitely worth getting, and it often appears as a tip for good service. "There is sixpence for you. Let's have a song," Sir Toby says to Feste (*Twelfth Night,* 2.3.32). The song is 'O mistress mine, where are you roaming?" and the sixpence, one suspects, was originally Sir Andrew's. Sir Andrew's generosity continues on the present occasion as he gives Feste a "testril" or "teston"—one of Henry VIII's coins, carrying a shilling's face value but made of debased metal and thus accepted at sixpence or lower. The teston had been officially recalled in 1548,[16] but some were still circulating at the turn of the century.

Sixpence is also the daily stipend which Flute assumes Bottom would have received for his performance in *Pyramus and Thisby.* "O sweet bully Bottom! Thus hath he lost sixpence a day during his life. . . . And the Duke had not given him sixpence a day for playing Pyramus, I'll be hang'd" (*A Midsummer Night's Dream*, 4.2.20–22). Bottom reappears and plays Pyramus to great effect, but the duke's reward is not specified.

The groat was usually valued at fourpence; in literature, it often has the connotation simply of a small sum, relatively speaking. Fluellen in *Henry V* insults Pistol first by forcing him to eat a leek (a vegetable something like an onion and a symbol of Wales) and then by giving him a groat, threatening to make him eat another leek if he refuses to accept it (5.1.58). Pistol, who may be harder to insult in this way than Fluellen thinks, accepts the groat—"in earnest of revenge," he says, saving face.

Threepence, in today's buying power five dollars, is the value of a dish containing stewed prunes which figures in the remarkably obscure dispute between Elbow and Pompey in *Measure for Measure*: "A fruit-dish, a dish of some threepence—your honors have seen such dishes; they are not china dishes, but very good dishes" (2.1.92–94).

The penny, though a perfectly realistic unit of exchange, often appears in Shakespeare in the same symbolic phrase that we use today— "not a penny." Juliet's nurse says this when Romeo offers her a tip, but as she does not deny the offer when it is repeated, one assumes that she accepts it and that the sum was probably a bit more than a penny (1.4.183–84).

The three-farthing coin, worth three-fourths of a penny, was distinguished by a rose placed behind the queen's profile head. In *King John,* one character mocks another by saying that if he had such a thin face, he would not dare put a rose behind his ear "Lest men should say, look where three farthings goes!" (1.1.143).

The half-penny, as mentioned above, was quite a small coin, and a purse intended to hold several of them quite a small object. In *The Merry Wives of Windsor,* Master Ford, determined to find Falstaff no matter where he may be hiding, says, "He cannot escape me; 'tis impossible he should; he cannot creep into a halfpenny purse, nor into a pepper-box" (4.1.144–46).

A knowledge of the names of coins plus some simple arithmetic are needed to get the point of one of the social-status jokes in *Love's Labor's Lost.* The rustic Costard is asked by two characters in turn to carry love letters to the characters' respective ladies, and each gives him a tip. The first, the pretentious Armado, says grandiosely, "There is remuneration, for the best ward of mine honor is rewarding my dependents." Costard, eager to enlarge his vocabulary, discovers that "remuneration" is obviously "the Latin word for three farthings" (3.1.137). Berowne, a nobleman higher on the social scale, hands over his letter with the words, "There's thy guerdon; go." Costard is delighted to find that this new word is better even than "remuneration"—in fact, "eleven-pence-farthing better"—and we deduce that Berowne has given him a shilling, quite a generous amount.

Shakespeare mentions numerous foreign coins, usually in the context of a foreign setting. The crown comes into this category, even though England had a crown, a silver coin worth five shillings. It was not minted between 1553 and 1601, however, and to Shakespeare's audience the coin had a connotation of exotic wealth—particularly since many of the crowns coined in other countries were made of gold.

Baptista in *The Taming of the Shrew* offers a dowry of "twenty thousand crowns" with his daughter Katherina (2.1.122), and later doubles the amount, on Katherina's amazing transformation. Helena in *All's Well That Ends Well* offers the Widow of Florence a purse of gold, the exact contents unspecified, and an additional 3,000 crowns for the use of the Widow's daughter, Diana, as bait in Helena's scheme to sleep with Bertram (3.7.35). And in *As You Like It,* Orlando complains that his father's will left him "but poor a thousand crowns" (1.1.3), a sum withheld by Orlando's brother. The aged servant Adam promptly offers Orlando his own life savings, 500 crowns (2.3.38). Like the other sums expressed in crowns, these amounts are essentially symbolic. Orlando does not incur specific expenses which must be subtracted from Adam's contribution, and the main point is that Adam is willing to give it.

The ducat, a gold Italian coin, had a value in England of something over four shillings, but Shakespeare uses the word for its effect of foreign and, sometimes, morally dubious wealth. Ten thousand ducats is the wager for which Jachimo sets out to undermine Imogene's honor in *Cymbeline* (1.4.127). Borachio, in *Much Ado About Nothing,* boasts that his part in the plot against Hero, another attempt upon a lady's honor, has netted him a thousand ducats (3.4.109). In *The Merchant of Venice,* Shylock's loan to Bassanio is for 3,000 ducats; and two bags of "double ducats" leave Shylock's house along with Jessica and evoke the reaction, "My daughter! O my ducats! O my daughter! . . . Would she were hears'd at my foot, and the ducats in her coffin" (2.8.15; 3.1.90).

American readers encountering the "dollar" in Shakespeare feel suddenly at home, although to the original audience the dollar would have had a connotation of foreignness. The word was derived from the *riksdaler* or *rigsdaler* (Swedish and Danish forms) or from the German *thaler.* The Scandinavian flavor is appropriate to the episode in *Macbeth* when a Norwegian king, on being defeated by the Scottish army, agrees to pay "ten thousand dollars to our general" use (1.2.63). The word becomes a pun in *King Lear,* when the Fool says, "Thou shalt have as many dolors for thy daughters as thou canst tell [count] in a year" (2.4.54).

The "doit" was a small Dutch coin of copper, worth half a farthing, or an eighth of a penny. Doits sometimes circulated in England to relieve the perennial small-change shortage. Trinculo, plotting in *The Tempest* to take Caliban to England as a freak-show exhibition, says of the English, "When they will not give a doit to relieve a lame beggar, they will lay out ten to see a dead Indian" (2.2.30–32).

Money in Jonson's The Alchemist

Greed on every scale, large and small, high and low, and often illegal, is the subject of *The Alchemist.* Appropriately, the money accrued is itself quite a miscellaneous heap.

One of the more lavishly duped victims, Sir Epicure Mammon, has been taken in by his own vanity, his love of thinking himself an expert on alchemical mumbo-jumbo. According to his own reckoning, he has given the impostors Face, Subtle, and Doll "eight score and ten pounds within these five weeks" (5.3.88), quite a large amount. And he has even brought in an assortment of his own household goods—andirons, pots, and pans—on the assumption that they can be turned into gold, once the formula is just right.

Other victims are milked for whatever they have. Abel Drugger, the tobacconist who seeks astrological advice in setting up his shop, is induced to part with "a portague, I have kept this half year" (1.1.542). This was a famous Portuguese coin, the gold *crusado,* bearing the design of a cross and worth around four pounds during the sixteenth century. It was often kept as a good-luck piece.

Tribulation Wholesome and Ananias, two Puritans on a visit from

Amsterdam, not only expend considerable sums for coals and other alchemical supplies but also buy up Sir Epicure's pots and andirons under
the impression that the owners are deserving orphans who should get a
good price. Once again, the dupes think this ware is to be turned into
gold and silver, but in this case it is to be further modified into "as good
Dutch dollars / As any are in Holland" (3.2.179). Any doubts as to the
legality of this last process are soothed by Subtle: "It is no coining, sir. /
It is but casting." The change in nomenclature reassures everyone.

Poor Dapper, the lawyer's clerk, is perhaps the most thoroughly and
ludicrously cleaned out. His original errand is merely to buy a small-
scale familiar spirit, a little something to help his luck at the gaming
table. However, having been identified by secret signs as the nephew of
the Queen of Fairies, Dapper is dazzled by this prospect and is eager
for an interview with Her Grace. He must make gifts to the queen's
servants, a tribute which includes "six score Edward shillings . . . an old
Harry's sovereign . . . three James shillings, and an Elizabeth groat,"
(3.3.424–26). The "James shillings" are of fairly recent coinage, but the
"Harry's sovereign" would go back to the reign of Henry VIII. The
Edward shillings of which Dapper has so many were not worth their face
value, Edward VI's reign having been characterized by a debased coinage. (In fairness to King Edward, it must be pointed out that it was his
father who debased the country's coinage as a hasty fix for his financial
problems. Returning England to a trustworthy coinage was begun by
Queen Mary and continued by Queen Elizabeth.)

In addition, Dapper must prove his trust in the Fairy Queen by
throwing away his purse, handkerchiefs, rings, and any other bits of
money he might have about him; during this part of the process, he is
blindfolded and pinched by the supposed fairies. Sure enough, two gold
coins come to light. One of these, the "spur-ryal," or "royal," was an
up-to-date coin with a value of around fifteen shillings. The name apparently came from the design of a sun, which looked something like
the rowel of a spur, but there may have been a connection with the
earlier coin called the "royal" (or "ryal" or "real"), coined from time
to time since the early sixteenth century.

The second gold piece provides a moment of poignancy, despite the
fact that Dapper has brought his fate on himself through gullibility and
greed. Dapper confesses to having "a half-crown / Of gold about my
wrist, that my love gave me; / And a leaden heart I wore since she

forsook me" (3.2.520–22). Most half-crowns were silver; the smaller gold ones would have been an appropriate keepsake. Face, quite unmoved, takes the coin but allows Dapper to continue wearing his metaphorical leaden heart.

Counterfeiting and Clipping

To counterfeit money, one simply made a mold of the real thing, filled the mold with melted copper or tin, and then covered the resulting facsimile with a thin coat of silver or gold. Alternatively, one could imitate the method used in the royal mint, striking a metal blank with a die in order to impress the design.

By whatever method the coin had been made, getting rid of it was something of a problem. The deception would become apparent fairly soon, and if a number of counterfeit coins were traced to one's possession, things would look bad. One might give the coin in change to a traveling tradesman who would not go to the trouble of coming back, or if one happened to be a traveling tradesman oneself, one might pass counterfeit coins to the customers.

An easier road to illicit riches was simply to snip off little bits of the genuine coins that came one's way. One then passed the coin on, at its original value, and eventually the snippets would pile up sufficiently to make it worthwhile to melt them into an anonymous but quite valuable lump. The trick, of course, was to make one's inroads into the coin of the realm as inconspicuous as possible. The most foolproof method— the perfect crime, in fact—was to put a number of coins in a bag and shake them; gold or silver dust would accrue, and the damage done to the coins would look like normal wear. Unfortunately, like most perfect crimes, this one had a hitch. The number of coins one would need, and the amount of time spent in shaking them, made the enterprise inefficient. Generally, people simply shaved off a more or less greedy crescent. Apparently many coins circulated in this gibbous state, at or near their face value, especially in remote parts of the country where coins were scarce.

Penalties for counterfeiting or clipping, as the latter process was called, were quite harsh. Both were classified as treason, an attack on

the king and his sovereign power, and the proper punishment for those
found guilty was to be hanged, drawn, and quartered—a procedure to
be described in chapter 11 below. Some offenders, especially young ones,
were given milder sentences.

Moneylending and the Question of Usury

England, or for that matter western Europe, did not have in the
sixteenth century banks of the sort we know today. No central banks
offered customers the convenience of savings plans or personal loans.
Banking functions were evolving in various parts of the economy, but
one could not go to one place and conduct one's financial business with
the kind of assistance we know today.

With regard to the ease with which monetary operations could take
place, a considerable difference existed between large-scale and small-
scale transactions. A small businessman had no means of transferring
money easily. With no paper currency and no regular systems of credit,
he had to carry around bags of coins. A large trading company had more
scope. It might, for example, set up a system of agents and pay its
accounts through bills of exchange, thus keeping the wheels of commerce
turning. Since these bills were drawn on a specific mercantile house, the
necessary element of faith was easy to achieve.

On this comparatively large scale, and particularly when the business
was being done abroad, loans could be arranged, usually at a reasonable
rate of interest because the borrower was not helpless and might seek
better terms elsewhere. Nations as well as companies were involved here.
The financial wizard Sir Thomas Gresham, for example, spent much of
his career in Antwerp negotiating loans for the Tudor sovereigns.

International finance owed a considerable amount of its growth to
the Jewish moneylenders who in many countries of Europe had become
an important part of the picture. Holland particularly welcomed refugees
fleeing persecution elsewhere, in contrast to England's continuing medieval bias.

The association between Jews and lending money on interest, or
usury, had been mandated, in the view of many Englishmen, by the
Bible itself, which appeared to say that Jews might charge interest from

Christians and that Christians should not charge interest from each other. Upon examination one finds that this interpretation depends on a somewhat twisted logic. In Exodus 22:25 and Deuteronomy 23:19, Jews are forbidden to lend money "upon usury" to fellow Jews but are allowed (in Deuteronomy) to enter such transactions with "strangers"—interpreted as Christians, although an Old Testament text could hardly be specific about this particular type of stranger. Neither passage goes into the question of what kind of loans strangers are allowed to make to each other.

The theme of both biblical passages is that of charity to one's friends and neighbors, and in the context of a simple agricultural society such charity is very appropriate. A prospective borrower was unlikely to be a wealthy entrepreneur, on the lookout for enterprises to develop the economy as well as line his own pockets, and much more likely to be a desperate peasant whose crops had failed. Since interest rates in such societies were usually unregulated and often ruinous, a bad harvest might put much of the population into the clutches of moneylenders, never to return to solvency. (A similar situation has existed in India, for example, until quite recent times.)

Gradually, during the sixteenth century, England's official attitude toward the charging of interest, whether by Jews or Christians, shifted. The view of capital as a commodity like any other—warehouse space, for example—to be made available for lease on certain terms, began to win practical acceptance, and the notion that money might "breed" other money no longer seemed an offense against nature. Between 1545 and 1552, Parliament allowed certain types of interest-bearing loans to be made, provided the interest charged was no higher than ten percent. (This stipulation referred to transactions within England. Loans arranged in foreign countries, even if English merchants or the English government were involved, had never come under Parliament's authority.) The ban on usury was renewed in 1552 but was finally lifted in 1571, the same year that Gresham opened the London Royal Exchange—a handsome, four-story building modeled after the bourse at Antwerp, with a central court surrounded by arcaded walkways where merchants might discuss business matters without having to stand in the rain. The building served as a quite practical symbol of England's increasing prominence in the world's economy.

6

London

In the sixteenth and seventeenth centuries, London was England's only city. There was simply no competition; no other community had grown beyond the status of a large town.

By contemporary standards of size, London started the sixteenth century impressively enough and then grew larger with a speed that astonished and sometimes dismayed both the inhabitants and the city officials. London's population, estimated by today's historians at 60,000 in the 1520s, had by the end of the century risen to roughly 200,000.[1]

These bustling inhabitants were crammed into a few square miles bounded by the city walls that surrounded London on three sides. On the fourth side was the River Thames, its current flowing east or west according to the tide and its broad expanse dotted with every sort of craft that could be propelled by sail or oar. The one bridge connecting the city proper with the equally busy south bank could not be raised to permit large ships to pass—the bridge, in fact, had houses built on it—and oceangoing vessels by necessity stayed downstream, but for human passengers and smaller cargoes the river served as a major highway.

London was not aristocratic in its power structure, a point that perhaps should be stressed, because the earlier chapters of this book have had so much to do with kings and nobles. Londoners of course owed allegiance to the Crown, but the city government was not directly controlled by the sovereign. On ceremonial occasions, the queen might visit the mayor and aldermen as they sat in the Guildhall, and the mayor and aldermen might visit the queen as she sat in Westminster Palace. (All of Westminster, including the Abbey, was then a quite separate community from London.) These meetings, when they occurred, would be filled with the panoply suitable to an interaction between two ancient and mutually respectful institutions which spent most of their time in separate spheres.

Inside and Outside the City Wall

Although municipal authority was here and there extended for a short distance outside the city wall, for the most part the City of London was defined by this ancient structure. The word *city* in this limited territorial sense is still used in London today, where it refers to what has now become the financial district. Here, neither the plan of the streets nor their names have undergone major change since Elizabethan times. The buildings have shot upward, all but a few segments of the wall have disappeared, and the urban area has expanded for miles around, swallowing up what were once fields, orchards, and separate villages, but "the City"—customarily capitalized when speaking of this particular territory—still has an atmosphere of its own.

The southeast corner of the wall was held down, so to speak, by the Tower of London, an ancient fortress which today's visitor is quite likely to go to see. One side of the tower, the southern one, touches the river. From here the wall ran northward, curved to the west, and eventually bent down to the river again, meeting it at Blackfriars, about a mile upstream from the tower. Blackfriars had been a monastery before the Reformation; its secular modifications included the conversion of the refectory, or dining hall, to the Blackfriars' Theatre, which Shakespeare's company used for indoor productions.

One of the major landmarks within the city walls was St. Paul's Cathedral, a spot known to Americans both personally and by way of television, as it is a favorite venue for royal weddings. St. Paul's was in Elizabethan times a gothic edifice; its present domed and neoclassical incarnation dates from the rebuilding that followed the great fire of 1666.

The city wall naturally had gates in it. John Stow in his *Survey of London* describes six principal ones and several "postern gates,"[2] small openings which would let in a man afoot but not a mounted party, and so might be more safely opened when the identity of the person requesting admission was not known. In the sixteenth century, the closing of the main gates at night was still a traditional routine, from time to time officially justified by the proclaimed possibility that Spain or France might secretly land troops and invade the city, but as life was generally peaceable the gate-closers were sometimes remiss.

The larger gates were substantial structures, resembling triumphal arches in a bristly, medieval-Tudor way. None has survived, but their memory lingers as names of streets and even of underground stations; today's visitor will find Moorgate and Aldgate on the Circle Line.

Outside the walls (or, from the Latin derivation of the word, below the walls) were the suburbs, a term that has remained with us and now connotes, in the United States, well-kept lawns and a certain amount of affluence. The suburbs of sixteenth-century London fit this picture to some extent, as they included aristocratic mansions and rural retreats. The site of present-day Hyde Park, now surrounded by present-day London, was in Tudor times a royal hunting preserve famous for its deer, and Whitehall Palace, a chief royal residence at the time, stood west of the city wall, near Westminster. Other parts of the suburbs were less elegant. Beyond the reach of city authorities, suburbanites could slaughter cows, put up public theaters and bull-baiting arenas, roof their houses with thatch (forbidden inside the city as a fire hazard), smelt copper, entertain sailors in low dives, and operate bawdy houses.

The word *suburb* in Elizabethan literature frequently has the connotation not just of distance from the center of things, as we use the word, but of low rent and shabbiness. Portia in *Julius Caesar,* persuading her husband, Brutus, to confide in her, asks him, "Dwell I but in the suburbs / Of your good pleasure?" (2.1.285–86); she implies not only that Brutus is keeping her a long way from his main concerns but that he does not value her.

The Aldermen and the Lord Mayor

London was governed by twenty-six aldermen, representing each of the twenty-six wards into which the city was divided. The electorate consisted not of all the inhabitants generally but of the leading busi-

A sketch of the Queen made by one Thomas Trevelyan, thought to have been a London craftsman, for the "commonplace book" or personal notebook he compiled for his own recreation. Though Trevelyan was not a professional artist, he catches the spirit of emblematic authority that was central to Elizabeth's person and reign. (*Courtesy of the Folger Shakespeare Library.*)

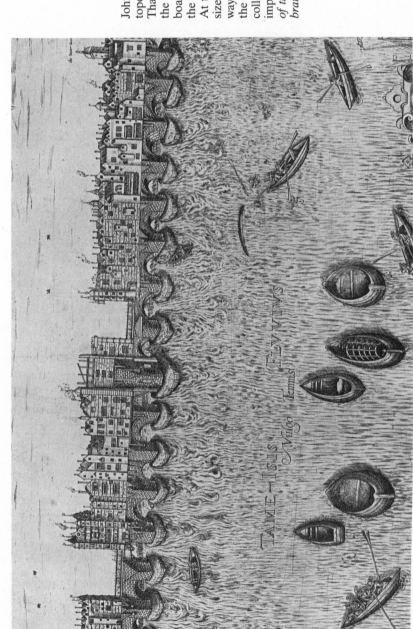

John Norden, surveyor and topographer, depicts the Thames in a turbulent state as the tide rushes out. Several boats can be seen shooting the arches of London Bridge. At the right a boat has capsized, and rescuers are on the way. The arched gateway to the left displays an impressive collection of traitor's heads, impaled on pikes. (*Courtesy of the Folger Shakespeare Library.*)

GRACE · CHVRCHE · MARKET ·

Grace Church Market in London.
Vendors offer fruit and cabbages,
along with pigs' heads and other
ready-butchered meat, while passing
traffic shows a metropolitan brisk-
ness. Stalls are arranged according
to the goods' place of origin; the
pillar to the right displays a variant
spelling of Surrey. The drawing appears in Hugh Alley's *Caveat for the
City of London* (1598), dealing with
the regulations that governed the
city's markets. (*Courtesy of the Folger Shakespeare Library.*)

The plowman

A plowman goes about his business amid signs of spring. His team of two oxen is smaller than the usual eight-ox team, but it gets the idea across. The spiky rectangular frame at lower left is a harrow, to be dragged over the newly-plowed field to break up the clods. At upper left, a row of houses demonstrates the English countryman's habit of living in villages instead of in isolated farmhouses, the pattern that developed in America. (*Courtesy of the Folger Shakespeare Library.*)

Thomas Cranmer, a leader of the Protestant Reformation in England, burns at the stake during the reign of Queen Mary. Cranmer had previously recanted his Protestant faith; when he changed back again, according to the story, and consequently faced execution, he declared that he would put his right hand first into the flames, as punishment for having signed the recantation. From John Foxe's *Actes and Monuments*, better known as the *Book of Martyrs*. (*Courtesy of the Folger Shakespeare Library.*)

An English wedding scene. The couple hold hands as the service is read; the wedding party waits decorously. A woodcut border from the printer Richard Day's *A Book of Christian Prayers* (1578), sometimes called "Queen Elizabeth's Prayer Book." Day's heart was in his work; he later took holy orders and became a vicar. (*Courtesy of the Folger Shakespeare Library.*)

School days in Elizabethan England. A reward of some sort, perhaps an apple, seems to be on offer; a dish of them can be seen beneath the master's chair, along with a bundle of switches. Other pupils await their turn to recite. Title page of Alexander Nowell's *Catechism* (1593) for beginning Latin students. Nowell, a former master of Westminster School, became dean of St. Paul's but kept his interest in education. (*Courtesy of the Folger Shakespeare Library.*)

nessmen, or burgesses—*citizens*, in this use of the term. Aldermen served for life and thus became quite established fixtures.

The Lord Mayor of London was chosen annually by the aldermen from among themselves and spent his year as the chief officer of the City, distinguished by his gold chain of office. While within the boundaries, he took precedence over every other person except the sovereign, should the sovereign happen to be visiting. The "Lord" in his title, however, was simply a perquisite of his office; it did not admit him to the hereditary aristocracy.

Most of the Lord Mayor's special duties were ceremonial, but he continued functioning as an alderman, and after his year was up he resumed this permanent role. The seventeenth-century churchman and essayist John Earle describes the alderman as a picture of dignity in his beard and scarlet gown; "he oversees the commonwealth [the City] as his shop" and, having served as Lord Mayor in a year long past, "his discourse is commonly the annals of his mayoralty, and what good government there was in the days of his gold chain."[3]

Besides the Lord Mayor, the aldermen chose two sheriffs for an annual term of office. A sheriff might or might not be an alderman as well; there was room for a newcomer. This post was largely ceremonial, as the administrative duties could be done by deputies. It was expected that sheriffs, like aldermen and Lord Mayors, were to be of a generous and what we would call civic-minded disposition, contributing to charity and sponsoring new projects for the general good.

The Lord Mayor and the aldermen sat on the two most important decision-making bodies in London. The higher, the Court of Aldermen, controlled City finances, appointed chief officials, and generally held the reins. The second, the Court of Common Council, consisted not only of the aldermen but of around 200 citizens, serving one-year terms. This body passed City regulations on a great variety of concerns, including water supplies, street repairs, the treatment of apprentices, and much else.

Involved as the City was with money and power, it naturally attracted the attention of the sovereign, and a mutually beneficial relationship usually obtained. The Crown attempted to protect London's mercantile interests, sometimes finding itself opposed to the nobility and to the more national constituencies represented in Parliament. And the City was often in a position to lend funds to the Crown, doing so more or less graciously and with an eye to benefits received or promised. This reliance on private capital was not limited to the English government; before the development of more thoroughgoing tax systems, such as the income tax, this type of transaction was a common governmental recourse.

The Lord Mayor's Show and Other London Spectacles

As he began his term of office, the Lord Mayor played a starring role in the ceremonial procession from the City to Westminster Palace and back again, an annual extravaganza as familiar to Londoners as the Rose Bowl parade is to us. In the late sixteenth and early seventeenth centuries, the route was partly by water and partly by land. The Lord Mayor, the two sheriffs who were also beginning their one-year terms, and all the aldermen, in decorated barges accompanied by musicians, traveled upriver to Westminster, where the mayor took his oath of office. On the return journey, the barges landed near St. Paul's Cathedral and the dignitaries rode through the City with banners and panoply, accompanied by numerous bodies of officials. At the Guildhall, the center of civic government, a feast was served to the thousand or so participants—at the charge of the Lord Mayor and the two sheriffs. Prosperity was, after all, an understood prerequisite for these offices.

An important part in the Lord Mayor's show was played by the various trade guilds, whose elaborate pageants might be called the ancestors of the floats in today's parades. That is, the mobile ones might; the word *pageant* could be applied either to a wheeled vehicle moving along with the procession, or to a stage-like platform erected on scaffolding. In the latter case, the procession would halt so that the Lord Mayor and other dignitaries might admire the effect and even listen to poetic addresses—take in a brief performance, in short. The themes were often allegorical, with costumed figures representing such favorite abstractions as Honor, Industry, and Britannia. Among the writers who supplied the scripts were George Peele, Thomas Middleton, and Thomas Dekker.

Other occasions besides the Lord Mayor's processions might call out displays of emblematic tableaux, related to literature in that they illustrated some of the traditional ways in which Elizabethan and Jacobean readers visualized abstract concepts. Queen Elizabeth's annual summer progresses, during which she visited the far-flung mansions of her wealthier subjects, usually ended with a festive return to London and a parade through the City. The queen's reign had, in fact, begun with a particularly splendid example. Her coronation procession in 1558 traveled from the Tower of London, where the queen had been staying in the state apartments, through the City and on to Whitehall Palace, halting for symbolic pageants and tableaux. In one of these, the figure of Time emerged from a cave, leading by the hand his daughter Truth, who carried a Bible.[4] This depiction of Queen Elizabeth's and the late Queen Mary's religious persuasions—needless to say, from the Protestant point of view—foreshadows the kind of allegorical imagery Spenser would use in the *Faerie Queene,* with regard to his method as well as his subjects.

The London Guilds

The guild system had developed in other towns besides London, but so much of London life was structured by the guilds that considering them here seems a natural course. Most guilds, wherever situated, began in medieval times as loosely organized fellowships and passed through a sort of evolution, often over several centuries, before achieving the full dignity of a royal charter.

London's guilds were called "livery companies," a term which sounds as if they hired out horses but which in fact refers to the regalia, or "livery," worn for special occasions—silk gowns trimmed with fur, for example. Special occasions were quite numerous. Guildsmen marched or rode in processions, as described above; they held ceremonial dinners, met to discuss matters pertaining to their respective trades, and in short spent many hours in elaborately dressed dignity.

The twelve "great" guilds in London, the largest and most prosperous of the varied assortment, included the Goldsmiths' Company, the Mercers' and Drapers' Companies (representing various branches of the textile industry), and the Grocers' Company, with others.[5] The sixty-odd smaller guilds (some of which were still in a pre-charter phase) included barbers, musicians, saddlers, glaziers, wheelwrights, and two separate guilds for candle makers, depending on whether the material used was beeswax or tallow. The Stationers' Company, chartered in the 1550s, controlled the printing trade; its register, listing books licensed for publication and many other matters, sheds considerable light on the literary scene.

New guilds might be formed in the wake of new technologies or products. A clock-makers' company, for example, was chartered in the seventeenth century to oversee the production of fine indoor clocks, even though large church clocks were still made by blacksmiths, who had their own guild. Guilds occasionally merged but were more likely with increasing specialization to divide themselves up. The makers of bows (bowyers) had separated from the makers of arrows (fletchers) in the late fourteenth century. And the Grocers' Company, one of the top twelve, lost the drug business when the apothecaries broke away in 1617 to form their own company, a few years after Jonson's Abel Drugger, in *The Alchemist,* had been identified as a "free of the Grocers" (1.3.4)— that is, a member in good standing.

Membership in a guild could be acquired in three ways—by being born into it, if one's father were a member; by serving an apprenticeship; or by "redemption," making a direct cash payment. The last was quite expensive. Most guild members entered by the apprenticeship route, bound by legal articles to a specific "master" for a period usually of seven years. At the proper time, the apprentice appeared before the court of the guild and proved his proficiency by whatever method the guild specified. In order actually to practice his trade, the newly accredited guildsman had to gain the "freedom of the city," a procedure which involved a separate oath and a separate fee.

Once "free" of both the guild and the city, the new member was technically a "journeyman" and could work for wages while contemplating his next step up the ladder, that of becoming a master. After filling these requirements, differing from guild to guild but sometimes including the submission of a "masterpiece" to demonstrate the quality of his work, he might go into business for himself and eventually take apprentices of his own.

Masters and Apprentices: The Shoemakers' Holiday

Dekker's *The Shoemakers' Holiday* gives a lively picture of the master-apprentice relationship. Masters were expected to provide a family atmosphere, encouraging moral development as well as technical proficiency in their charges, and this the master Eyre does, despite his bounding tongue and amazing choice of epithets. His charges, who live in his house and take their meals at his table, learn responsibility and right behavior and have considerable pride in their craft. The workday in Eyre's shop begins early, just before seven, but, provided his men show the right spirit (as they all do), Eyre has no objection to stopping work to celebrate special occasions, such as welcoming a new employee. Besides his apprentices, Eyre employs several journeymen, as he is required to do; the authorities did not want the graduates of the system to be edged out of work by apprentices who, if less skilled, were nonetheless cheaper.

The play's last scene puts apprentices into a pattern of reciprocal social responsibility. Simon Eyre, having become Lord Mayor through a stroke of good luck quite unrelated to shoemaking, gives a vast breakfast for all the apprentices in the City. Eyre explains that he is fulfilling a vow; when he was young and so poor that he was working as a water carrier, some "mad boys"—apprentices, in Eyre's personal idiom—gave him his breakfast, and he swore that "if ever I came to be Lord Mayor of London, I would feast all the prentices" (5.5.179–80). One of Eyre's journeymen describes the menu: "Fritters and pancakes comes trowling in in wheelbarrows; hens and oranges hopping in porters' baskets; collops [bacon] and eggs in scuttles; and tarts and custards comes quavering in in malt-shovels" (5.2.191–94). The day Eyre chooses for his breakfast is Shrove Tuesday, just before the beginning of Lent, better known to Americans by its French nickname of Mardi Gras and a traditional time for merrymaking.

Not all apprentices enjoyed so jolly a master, but most of them seem to have been reasonably well treated and to have learned their trades. Regulations passed by the Court of Common Council prevented rampant exploitation by the masters. And, though working hours were long—from dawn to dusk in some shops—Sundays were work-free and the many traditional holidays and saints' days gave extra leisure, either for a whole day or for an afternoon. Apprentices might walk to the open fields just outside the city walls and hold what Americans would call a track meet, competing in running and jumping. Or they might go to a theater, indulging in ale and oranges while they watched the play, or hire a boat for a trip on the river.

A more frowned-upon form of recreation was brawling, to which apprentices were stereotypically given. The rallying cry was "Prentices and clubs!" when, at least according to the stereotype, the streets would immediately fill with young men so armed. Sometimes the opponents were rival apprentices, sometimes constables and other municipal peace-keeping authorities.

City regulations forbade apprentices to carry edged weapons other than a short knife for utilitarian purposes. The restriction was intended partly to restrain violence, since it was felt that an apprentice could do quite enough damage with a club, but the matter of social status was involved as well. Swords were supposed to be worn only by gentlemen. With the same object of maintaining the distinctions upon which it was felt that social harmony depended, regulations prescribed or attempted to prescribe an apprentice's dress and forms of recreation. An apprentice could not indulge in embroidered shirts or starched ruffs; he might go bowling but was not supposed to play tennis. (Both these games were then at earlier stages of their evolution. Bowling was played outdoors and had an everyday, village-green connotation; tennis courts were built indoors and represented a more expensive pastime.)

In *Eastward, Ho!* by Ben Jonson, George Chapman, and John Marston (1605), the bad apprentice, Quicksilver, enters with a sword and dagger hidden under his cloak, along with a tennis racket, and is reprimanded when his master discovers these gentlemanly appurtenances. (The good apprentice, Golding, does everything right.) Quicksilver defends himself on grounds of heredity. He was born into the gentry, he explains, but only as a younger son (1.1.23–26); and because he could not inherit the family estate he has become a goldsmith's apprentice. Quicksilver's aspirations bring him to debtors' prison and repentance, but his case illustrates the fact, acknowledged by observers at the time, that the landowning gentry did sometimes put their younger sons into trade, especially into the more respectable or less grimy industries. This exchange could also go the other way; merchants on gaining wealth often bought land and set themselves up in the style of long-established country families.

The Merchant Classes in Literature

Dekker, portraying merchants and tradesmen in a sympathetic light, is in a minority, for these classes were regularly the victims of literary stereotypes. Citizens—using the word in its special sense as inhabitants of the City—were shown as narrow in their interests, competitive rather than supportive in their relationships with one another, comically unacquainted with genteel recreations, and sometimes scheming quite deliberately to invade the turf of the landed gentry. A sexual element is sometimes present as well. Perhaps because of his one-track concentration on making money, the tradesman is seen as a less than adequate husband, and the citizen's wife becomes fair game for dashing young gentlemen.

Shakespeare's Jaques, meditating in *As You Like It* on the plight of a wounded deer in the forest, invokes the idea of the tradesman as a competitive automaton. The deer is languishing alone when

> *Anon a careless herd,*
> *Full of the pasture, jumps along by him*
> *And never stays to greet him. "Ay," quoth Jaques,*
> *"Sweep on, you fat and greasy citizens,*
> *'Tis just the fashion. Wherefore do you look*
> *Upon that poor and broken bankrupt there?"*
>
> (2.1.52–57)

In Beaumont's *The Knight of the Burning Pestle,* the citizen, who happens to be a grocer, and his wife are portrayed as uneducated in the sense that they are unaccustomed to theatrical conventions. After interrupting the player who tries to speak the prologue, the couple climbs onto the stage, rearranges the cast, and dictates the action, adding an appropriate dimension of naïveté to the *Don Quixote*-like plot.

A quite open conflict between the gentry and the merchants appears in Middleton's *Michaelmas Term,* with the merchant as guileful villain. Quomodo, a wealthy draper, schemes to become a landed gentleman by marrying the sister of a young heir and then making sure the heir is disinherited. Quomodo's machinations are aided by his shop assistants Shortyard and Falselight, their names indicative of the kind of thing that apparently goes on in his place of business.

In Jonson's *Every Man In His Humour,* the operative "humour" for the merchant Kitely is his jealous assumption that his wife may be seduced at any moment by the fashionable gentlemen-about-town who visit his house. Kitely has in a sense brought this jealousy on himself by marrying into the gentry class to begin with; the visitors he so fears are friends of his wife's brother, one Wellbred. But respectable morality prevails. Kitely's suspicions turn out to be unfounded, and it is his own unmarried sister Bridget who is the object of one of the gentlemen's attentions—and quite honorable attentions at that, object matrimony.

John Donne's "Elegie XIV: A Tale of a Citizen and His Wife" creates in seventy lines of verse a vignette of the dashing young narrator, the curmudgeonly old tradesman, and the delicious young wife who in true Ovidian fashion signals her prospective surrender to the narrator. The three meet on the road to London—the Great North Road, in fact, judging from their eventual arrival at the Angel Inn at Islington. As they ride, the narrator tries to engage the husband in conversation and eventually, with a succession of business-page topics—the reputation of the London Exchange, the number of recent bankruptcies, tradesmen's profits as compared to those of the previous decade—succeeds in doing so. The conversation is punctuated by secret smiles between the narrator and the wife, who, seated on a pillion behind her husband's saddle, is out of his line of vision. On parting, the husband grudgingly complies with the narrator's wish to know where he lives—at which information another glance between the narrator and the wife ends the story, or what we are told of it.

Courtiers and Gallants

A large contingent of young men-about-town is encountered in literature, particularly in such lively descriptions of London's kaleidoscopic hurly-burly as Dekker's *The Gull's Horne-booke,* Greene's *Conny Catching* pamphlets, and the character sketches of Thomas Overbury and John Earle. These works and many like them[6] are easily accessible to present-day American readers because they are written in an explanatory fashion, warning innocent newcomers of the perils of the big city or, perhaps, giving tongue-in-cheek advice on how to be fashionable. A few background details might nevertheless be helpful in clarifying the social distinctions which the original audience would have picked up automatically.

The courtier, often portrayed in literature as a superficial social climber, was technically an habitué of the royal court, a person who was admitted to the presence of the sovereign at Whitehall and at the several other royal palaces in the vicinity of London. This group was a fairly large one, for anyone in the company of a person already known to the court could get past the attendants at the doors (provided the new-comer's dress and manner blended in); he might then be presented to the sovereign and gradually work his way toward being accepted, rec-ognized, and welcomed on his own. The process was, of course, not automatic, for if he annoyed anyone of importance he might be forbidden to return.

A prospective courtier also had to face the question of expense. One was expected to wear costly clothing. Courtly amusements such as hunt-ing and hawking required the right equipment. Finally, the courtiers' collective addiction to gambling served to screen out the impecunious. In theory, at least, a reasonably good player's winnings would balance his losses over time, if nobody cheated, but one had to be able to stand the heat in the meantime, and the variables were too many to count on.

On these rocks and shoals, needless to say, the careers of numerous would-be courtiers foundered, and any hopes they might have had of some splendid advancement, of being given a commission to explore the New World, appointment to some high office or a lucrative monopoly, came to grief. It is this figure, secretly disappointed but outwardly still bluffing away, who often appears in literature. His desperation for funds may lead him to desert the court, at least temporarily, and search the City for gullible newcomers to dazzle into standing him a meal, lending him a few shillings, or playing a hand or so of cards with him.

Continuing down the social scale a notch or two, we find the literary figure of the courtier blending with that of the city gallant, a character who would not object to large-scale fame and fortune should it come his way but whose ambitions are usually somewhat lower, perhaps focused on marriage to a wealthy City widow. He likes to indulge in fashionable dress, conspicuous seats at the theater (where his behavior is the subject of a particularly vivid sketch in Dekker's *The Gull's Horne-booke*), and the pleasures of alehouse and tavern. His status as "gentleman" derives, like the courtier's, from his not being seen to work for a living, and he may have some kind of family connection with the landed gentry.

The comedy potential of the courtier, the gallant, and, of course, the would-be fashionables who admire and try to imitate them, hinges on this built-in discrepancy between appearance and reality—a process of image building, as we might put it today, or "impression management," to use a sociologist's term. Thus the right clothes, the correct use of the toothpick (not a disposable sliver of wood but a major accessory of gold or ivory, with a jeweled head), and a fashionably pugnacious attitude were accomplishments to be worked on.

The art of quarreling, often mentioned in literature, was an assertion of status, for only gentlemen were supposed to understand the fine art of reciprocal insult leading up to a challenge. Shakespeare's Touchstone satirizes this idea when he gives a lecture on "the quarrel on the seventh cause" in *As You Like It* (5.4.68–82). In *The Alchemist,* Kastrill, "a gentleman newly warm in his land"—that is, just old enough to claim his inheritance—is described as having come to London to learn to "carry quarrels / As gallants do; to manage them by line" (2.6.57, 63–64). Subtle, of course, being an expert in every other branch of knowledge, promises to tutor this subject as well.

London as a Habitat

These literary characters and their real-life readers moved about a city which everyone, particularly the old inhabitants, perceived as changing almost faster than the mind of man could grasp. John Stow (c. 1525–1605), writing his *Survey of London,* did his best to record the reality of both past and present as he worked his way through the city's history street by street and building by building, reading documents, interviewing officials and old-timers, and often consulting his own memory. Among these recollections, some of the most poignant describe the vanished orchards and gardens of Stow's childhood, lost as the city grew.

Buildings in London might be as tall as five or six stories, but most of them stopped at two or three. Often a shop occupied the ground floor, with lodgings above. In such a house, the main vertical beams were connected by a sort of woven wickerwork, over and around which plaster, or sometimes durable types of mud, was daubed. The walls were thick and remarkably tough, and, when the beams were painted black and the plasterwork white, the result was the familiar "Tudor" facade still used today when the builder wants something a little different, although construction methods have changed. The tiny windowpanes were made by blowing the molten glass in bubbles, then pressing it flat; circular ripples often remained.

Many of London's houses were soundly designed and built, but others were little more than shanties squeezed into any available space, even between the buttresses of St. Paul's Cathedral. As the population grew, buildings were divided into smaller and smaller rental tenements, and open spaces were transformed into mazes of narrow streets and rows of new houses. This explosion of growth distressed the City authorities, who from time to time issued ordinances, clearly ineffective, forbidding new construction inside the walls.

Many of London's streets were narrow and crooked, having evolved from footpaths in the medieval town. Others, among them a few laid out by the Romans, were more carefully directed, but even these were not particularly wide; with space in such demand, the houses tended to grab it. Often the upper stories overhung the streets and put them into constant shadow. At night the streets could be murky indeed. Street lighting was the responsibility of the individual householder, not of the municipality; the Court of Common Council passed regulations requiring that a lantern with a candle be hung outside every house. (This attempt failed in some quarters because, even though householders might install their candle, the regulations could not force them to keep it lighted.)

Londoners might get their drinking water from the river, a dubious idea since most of the privies emptied into it. Besides, since the Thames was a tidal river, the water was salty. Other sources were springs and wells in the surrounding villages, particularly those in the hilly environs of present-day Hampstead Heath, north of the City. Conduits, some made of lead (another dubious idea) and others of hollowed logs, carried the water to central points in the city. Here horses could drink, and there water carriers filled their bottles and delivered water to their customers' houses. Cobb, in Jonson's *Every Man in His Humour,* follows this trade and plausibly interacts with a varied collection of characters.

In the early decades of the seventeenth century, the New River Company succeeded in bringing large quantities of water into London by the process implied by its name, that of engineering a new river. The channel, almost forty miles long, delivered its water into a series of reservoirs north of London. The usual wooden or lead pipes took the water on to the city, and a few houses along the route were hooked directly into this supply. It was to be some time, however, before Cobb and his fellows disappeared from the streets of London.

Even though Londoners did not drink from the Thames if they could help it, they spent a great deal of time on it. It was often easier to go from point to point by water than to find one's way through the dark and muddy streets. The "watermen," the equivalent of today's taxi drivers, took fares across the river; many passengers preferred this method to crossing by foot on London Bridge. For longer journeys upstream or downstream, the watermen called out "Eastward ho!" or "Westward ho!" according to their destination, thus incidentally providing playwrights with titles. Since the direction of the current changed with the tide, a passenger might time his journeys to catch the shortest travel time. The watermen prided themselves especially on their skill in shooting the arches of London Bridge, where the rushing water made a five-foot fall if the tide were strong—an early form of white-water sport.

John Taylor, best known of the watermen, lived an extraordinarily busy life, diverting his career from his earlier occupation (after the new-fangled coaches stole the customers, or so he claimed) to that of journalist, traveler, and impresario. His works, in both rhyme and prose, describe his wanderings over various parts of Europe and the British Isles, and he often wrote scripts for the Lord Mayor's shows. Taylor also had a most appropriate hand in arranging water pageants, including one in honor of the marriage of King James's daughter Elizabeth, later queen of Bohemia.

The watermen were not the only Londoners to dislike the new coaches. Everyone complained about them except the passengers, who enjoyed not only private and mud-free transportation but the instant superiority still noticeable among occupants of high-status vehicles. The market for this product had developed rather quickly in the early seventeenth century following some technical improvements in comfort; earlier carriages, including those used by Queen Elizabeth on state occasions, had jolted uncomfortably, but now springs were used to absorb the shock. (These were not spiral bedspring-type contrivances but more on the order of a graceful curve.)

The English view of vehicle-riding as effeminate remained in force for some time, and the coaches were associated in popular stereotype with women and vanity. Michael Drayton, assuring his lady of the lasting fame his poetry will bring her, compares her to her less fortunate colleagues:

How many paltry, foolish, painted things,
That now in coaches trouble every street,
Shall be forgotten, whom no poet sings.

(from *Idea*, 1619)

Theater in London

Then as now, the theaters of London were a unique part of life in the capital, a treat which a visitor would not want to leave without tasting. No city on the Continent had anything quite like them. Permanent theaters included specially built open-air structures as well as the smaller indoor houses, and plays continued to be put on, as they had been before the first of the theaters were built in the 1570s, in inn yards.

The open-air theaters such as the Globe, circular in shape or having a sufficient number of sides to give the effect of being circular, held as many as 3,000 persons,[7] some standing in the unroofed pit but most seated in the galleries around the sides. Wherever they might be seated, the audience seems to have been a lively lot, talking and eating and sometimes giving only intermittent attention to whatever was transpiring onstage. Some of the audience might even be seated on the stage itself, a practice that some present-day plays are reviving (Peter Shaffer's *Equus* supplies an example), with results less distracting than one might think.

Though some of the public theaters had been built to the north of the City, the Globe and several others stood on the south bank of the Thames. Either way, north or south, the public theaters were outside the jurisdiction of the City authorities. The Bankside area in particular became a center for various forms of recreation, some of it dubious. Prostitution seems to have become a major local industry, and several of the taverns had the reputation of thieves' dens.

The theaters also competed for customers with the bull- and bear-baiting establishments, where crowds watched a bull or bear, as the case might be, fend off attacks by mastiffs; the number of dogs, and the chains or other restraints applied to the bull or bear, were carefully adjusted to permit maximum suspense and gore. Dogs seem to have been considered expendable, but the star attractions were seldom killed

outright, partly because they were expensive, and bears in particular
sometimes enjoyed individual fame and a following among the clientele.
As a commercial enterprise, bull- and bear-baiting had a good deal in
common with the theater and were sometimes promoted by the same
managers. Philip Henslowe, for example, seems to have spent as much
energy on the bears of the Paris Garden as on the actors of the Fortune
Theater. Since the same type of building was required for either pastime,
it is not surprising that at least one theater, the Hope, was designed to
do double duty, with the stage set up on trestles so that it could be
moved out of the arena.

The audience for the public theaters covered a wide social spectrum.[8]
This willingness of the audience to mingle may have resulted partly from
the buildings' design, which allowed playgoers to maintain status distinctions according to where they sat. Wealthy citizens might thus be
found in the upper and more comfortable galleries, while tradesmen and
gallants crowded the lower ones and apprentices stood in the pit; admission to the pit generally cost a penny, and one paid more as one
ascended. The aristocracy does not seem to have frequented the public
theaters, and respectable women did so only in the company either of
their husbands or of equally respectable women friends; these precautions served to distinguish them from the prostitutes who infiltrated the
audience to further their trade—and, quite possibly, to enjoy the play
as well.

The public theaters were not the only place where one might see a
play. Shakespeare's company, the King's Men (earlier, during Queen
Elizabeth's reign, the Lord Chamberlain's Men), performed plays not
only at the Globe but, during the winter months especially, at the Blackfriars' Theater, an indoor space which before the Reformation had been
part of a Dominican monastery. Blackfriars, though within the City, was
legally a "liberty," or area exempt from City regulations, including those
forbidding theatrical enterprises. (Trouble on this head arose from time
to time nevertheless.) Here, with a proscenium-type stage and considerable control over the lighting, players could indulge in elaborate scen-
ery and what we might call special effects. Audiences at the private
theaters were smaller, the Blackfriars holding approximately 600 persons. (The term *private* simply referred to the small size of the establishment; one did not have to join a club to attend.) Admission prices
were higher, typically a shilling. It is true that many playgoers paid this

much for admission to the galleries at the Globe and other public theaters, but in this instance cheaper options were available.

London's theaters began to lose their popularity in the 1620s, as fashions changed and the Puritan influence grew. By 1642, when Parliament closed the theaters, the great days had passed. Those of the public theaters still standing (including the Globe, rebuilt after the fire of 1613) were pulled down, to be replaced by tenements or other buildings of more immediate commercial value.

London in Crisis: The Plague

Periodically, London was struck by recurrences of the blight which in the mid-fourteenth century had killed from a fourth to a third of England's population. These recurrences were never quite so bad as the Black Death, as the first visitation was called, but they were bad enough. Particularly severe epidemics occurred in 1563–64, 1592, 1599, and 1603; and plague was seldom or never entirely absent from London, usually intensifying during the summer.

City authorities kept a running tally of victims, the "bills of mortality" or "plague bills," taken each week from the records of one hundred or so parishes in and near London. When the numbers were sufficiently alarming, the aldermen ordered the public theaters closed and other steps taken. Some regulations were in the nature of a quarantine. Any house where a plague victim lived was to be shut up, inhabitants and all, and a cross painted on the door; provision was made for food to be brought in, but circumstances hardly favored the hapless housemates. Those dying of plague could be conveniently disposed of by hailing one of the carts which during times of severe visitations traveled the streets collecting bodies and taking them outside the city walls to be buried in large pits.

The two main types of plague, now known to be caused by the bacillus *Pastuerella pestis,* are the pneumonic form, affecting the lungs and speedily fatal, and the bubonic form, more common in Elizabethan times, affecting the lymph glands and producing great swellings. From the second type patients sometimes recovered. The Elizabethans, unaware of bacilli, assumed that plague was caused by an unfavorable judgment from God and recommended as a remedy the repentance of sin. Other precautions included eating onions roasted with molasses and pepper, carrying cakes of arsenic under one's armpits, and wearing charms and amulets of all sorts. (Our own popular press, of course, supplies us with frequent evidence that belief in outlandish cures and bizarre preventative measures is not limited to previous centuries.)

Londoners who could afford to do so went to the country and waited for conditions to improve. Jonson's Lovewit, in *The Alchemist,* follows this custom, quite plausible to the original audience, leaving his house in the care of his butler, Face. This means of escape was generally successful, for by leaving London the traveler also left the rats that carried the fleas that carried the plague—a connection that would not be suspected for centuries.

7

Village and Countryside

Magnetic as London had become, living in a city was far from the usual thing in sixteenth-century England.[1] D. M. Palliser cites statistics indicating that by the year 1600 only 8 percent of the population lived in towns of over 5,000 people. And more than half of this urban 8 percent lived in London.[2]

Town-dwellers, furthermore, were more likely to know about country life than is the case today; for us, urban reality often becomes all-encompassing. Sixteenth-century towns and their surrounding farmlands were closely linked, economically and socially. Even sophisticated Londoners often had come from someplace else and went home from time to time. Shakespeare, buying property in and around Stratford and eventually retiring there, is an example.

The Look of the Land

The traditional American farm is a family enterprise, often self-contained and somewhat isolated. The American farmhouse sits surrounded by its own acres of cropland and pasture; other households or the nearest town are generally to be found at some distance, not a few steps from the door.

Sixteenth-century England, by contrast, had had its rural landscape organized by the feudal system centuries earlier. The lord of the manor held a large chunk of land; his serfs, and any freemen who had put themselves under his protection in those dangerous times, worked fields that were divided into strips—some strips for themselves, some for the lord of the manor. (The term *lord* in this case simply denotes the authority that comes from ownership; a lord of the manor was not necessarily a member of the titled nobility.)

These tenants lived in a village, usually a single street with houses on both sides, and commuted, so to speak, to their work in the fields. The arrangement was efficient because so much of this work was done cooperatively. Besides field workers, the village housed a few specialists—blacksmiths and bakers, for example—and their shops. There was also the parish church, with its churchyard where the dead were buried, and perhaps a village green, a bit of open space used, at least according to literary tradition, for dancing around maypoles. Thus village life might be quite self-contained, all the essentials within walking distance.

If the parish and the manor were coterminous, as was often the case, the lord of the manor was something of a microcosmic monarch, in charge of all he surveyed. He had his own desmesne, or private farm, which he might oversee himself or might lease to a farmer—an illustration, incidentally, of the link between the word *farmer* and the phrase "to farm out."

The village houses and shops also belonged to the lord of the manor, and the parish church, along with the parsonage and the glebe land for the rector's use, was ordinarily "in his gift"; that is, he had the power of appointing the rector. One might add that the rents paid by manorial tenants were not enormously large, nothing like the proportion of one's living expenses that is usual for rents today. Nevertheless, land was considered a reassuringly reliable source of wealth.

Some changes in the older feudal picture had taken place by the sixteenth century. Serfdom, or villeinage, had ceased to exist. Tenants no longer owed military service to their overlord; they were not tied to the land and might move away if they liked. This flexibility can be traced to the aftermath of the Black Death in the fourteenth century, when workers were so scarce that landholders found themselves making concessions.

The lords of manors, too, had undergone some changes since the old system began to break up. Some still followed the traditional pattern—

a resident squire, belonging very definitely to the landed gentry, living in his ancestral manor house a short distance from the village, serving as justice of the peace, attending the parish church, and knowing personally the tenants from whom he—or one of his agents, rather—collected the rents.

There were exceptions to the tradition of the resident squire, however. Some manors were owned by the nobility—say, by a wealthy earl whose family had built up its own holdings through marriage; in such a case, unless the manor happened to be near the earl's castle or other seat, it would be managed by an agent. Other manors were bought as investments by City merchants; sometimes ownership of a manor was split up and sold in fractions. And occasionally the traditional country squire rebelled against his tradition, got tired of living in the country, bought a house in London, and spent most of his time there.

The absentee landlord was seen by many observers in the sixteenth century as a major cause of rural troubles. Instead of belonging to the land and seeing it and its human inhabitants as an organic unity, the absentee was envisioned sitting in London and crunching numbers, as we might put it—concerned only with the profit the land would bring him. In *As You Like It,* Shakespeare alludes in passing to this state of things when Rosalind and Celia arrive in the Forest of Arden. The old shepherd, Colin, apologizes for the poor cheer to be found in his house, for, he says,

> *I am shepherd to another man,*
> *And do not shear the fleeces that I graze.*
> *My master is of churlish disposition,*
> *And little reaks to find the way to heaven*
> *By doing deeds of hospitality.*
> *Besides, his cote, his flocks, and bounds of feed*
> *Are now on sale, and at our sheep-cote now*
> *By reason of his absence there is nothing*
> *That you will feed on.*

(2.4.78–86)

Rosalind inquires as to who the prospective buyer might be, and on finding that it is Silvius, a young swain too preoccupied by love for any other thought, she declares her intention to buy the property herself.

Celia's addition to this plan aligns the two with the right kind of land-holder. Colin will not only get to keep his job, but, says Celia, "we will mend thy wages."

The Village Fields and the Manorial Court

An English village still following the feudal model at, say, the beginning of the sixteenth century, would typically cultivate three very large fields, two of them under crops and the third lying unused, or fallow. Rotation each year kept the fields from losing their fertility. Sheep were folded, or kept at night, on the fallow field, to ensure a supply of manure, and the fallow was also one of several sources of pasturage for oxen and horses.

Each of these fields was subdivided into strips, holdings of approximately a half acre or so, though of course there was a great deal of variation. The length of a single strip was described as a furlong, a measurement eventually standardized at 220 yards. The term originally referred to the distance an ox team could pull a plough without stopping to rest; while they were resting, one might as well get them turned around. The strips were separated from one another by unplowed grassy paths known as balks. These served as boundaries and also as footways, so that people might travel "through the fields"—or, in the song, "through the rye"—without having to push through a mass of standing grain. Nicholas Breton in the early seventeenth century describes

> *the merry country lad*
> *Who upon a fair green balk*
> *May at pleasure sit and walk.*

("The Passionate Shepherd")

R. E. Prothero suggests eighteen acres of arable (cultivated) land as an average holding.[3] If strips averaged about half an acre, this would be thirty-six separate strips, not necessarily adjacent or even very close together. The vicissitudes of marriage and inheritance usually resulted in a miscellaneous collection of holdings.

In earlier times, these strips had been allotted by the lord of the manor to his serfs; now they were more likely to be held from the lord "in copyhold," on long leases for a cash rent. By the sixteenth century, also, an increasing amount of land was held "in freehold"—in practice, owned outright. Theoretically, English common law did not allow for absolute ownership of land; nevertheless, a freeholder held his land "in fee simple," for himself and his heirs forever, unless he should choose to dispose of it.

Freeholders ranked as yeomen, just below gentlemen in the recognized social hierarchy. They might become quite prosperous, leasing out some of their land and collecting rents, and many yeoman families, after several generations of prosperity, petitioned for a coat of arms and gained gentlemanly status.

Villagers who owned an ox or two would combine them to make up a plough team, usually consisting of eight animals, which then ploughed their owners' strips. Often the man who actually held the plough was a day laborer, or cottager, employed by the landholders for the grubbier and lonelier jobs. Harvesting, however, was a group effort, with work of various intensities for everyone. Even little children could carry drinking water out to the fields.

One of the most picturesque of village occupations, often mentioned in literature, was the making of hay. Hay had to be cut, then left lying in the field to dry out before it was gathered up and stored. To hasten the drying phase and prevent mold, the villagers came out with rakes and turned the cut hay over—a job for all hands, and a dramatic one if rain threatened.

Decisions about what crops to plant, when to plant them, and agricultural matters in general were made at the manorial court, a body consisting of those who held lands from the lord of the manor. Usually the lord's steward, or manager, presided. Freeholders attended the manorial court as well, since their farming operations were meshed with those of the manorial tenants. To coordinate work in the fields, one of the villagers was annually elected *reeve,* a word which can denote various types of supervisory jobs. This particular responsibility was apparently considered more a chore than an honor, for Rowland Parker notes that one could be fined if one declined the office after being chosen for it.[4]

The Village Common and the Enclosure Question

Besides the cultivated fields, landholders were entitled to use pas-turelands, often streamside meadows which were cut from time to time for hay, and woodlands; many parts of England still had heavy forests, oak in particular, busily growing acorns to nourish the villagers' pigs. The poorest land, good for practically nothing, was called the common waste, or simply the common. The word can be confusing. The fields we have just examined were called the common fields, the pastures were called common pastures, and so on. The term simply meant that these resources might be used by anyone, provided the user has a right to do so—has paid rent for a certain amount of land, for example.

The common waste, by contrast, was land which even a cottager, a person who managed to pay rent on a dwelling (often a ramshackle one) but who did not hold strips in the cultivated fields, might use to pasture a cow or gather wood. This asset was often of crucial importance to a poor household, as wages for day labor were both small and seasonal. If the cottager were not a laborer but, say, an elderly widow, her cow and the bit of garden beside her cottage might be all she had.

This was the class most visibly hit by the changes in agricultural patterns typical of the sixteenth century. Efficiency as well as greed was the motive, for the increasing population put pressure on the land to grow more food. The lure of trade, however, and the profits to be made from wool undoubtedly had some influence on landholders' decisions.

Enclosure was a key concept, referring basically to consolidating one's holdings and fencing them off to be managed separately rather than as part of the village co-op. Thus a landholder, whether copyholder or freeholder but especially the latter, might try to get all his field strips in one place, trading with his neighbors until he did so. He would then enclose his fields with walls or hedges, plough up the balks along with the old strips, and increase his yield. Similarly, pastureland when estab-lished as the property of a single landholder might be fenced off, to the improvement of stock breeding since one could shut out one's neighbor's inferior bull—or try to do so, at least. Another option open to land-holders with consolidated holdings was to stop growing field crops and convert the land to pasture instead. This is the choice which had an immediate impact on the human side of village economics. Sheep-raising was much less labor intensive; even shearing, busy as it is, only lasts a few days. Ploughmen and field workers who depended on day wages faced hard times.

Loss of wages was bad enough for the cottagers, but another blow might fall should the lord of the manor begin to eye the common waste. Even though this land might be rocky and poor compared to the manor's other holdings, it might support a few sheep. Landowners might have to go to court to prove their right to the common waste, but often such attempts were successful.

One sixteenth-century voice enthusiastically in favor of enclosure belongs to Thomas Tusser, whose *Five Hundred Pointes of Good Husbandrie* went into many editions from the 1570s through the seventeenth century. Tusser claims that farmers will improve their land and use efficient methods only if they foresee an immediate profit, a more likely result with enclosed fields than with the communally worked fields. (Tusser was talking about the consolidation and enclosure of individual strips in the fields already used for growing crops, not necessarily about the more emotional issue of enclosing common wastes.) According to Tusser, one acre of an enclosed field would give triple the yield of an acre under the old arrangement.[5]

Field Crops: What "Corn" Wasn't

To Americans, the mention of corn brings to mind Indian corn, maize, with its sturdy stalks and large leaves. But Indian corn was unknown to the Elizabethans except as a curiosity brought back from the New World; it does not grow in England because the climate is too cool. The word *corn* continued to mean what it always had; cereal crops generally, and especially wheat, rye, and barley.

The choice of what grain to grow depended largely on the region's climate and type of soil. Most villages (and most self-contained farmers, as the shift to enclosure got under way) grew wheat or rye, sown in early winter and harvested in the spring, and also oats or barley, sown in early spring and harvested in late summer or autumn. This method allowed some variety in what was grown, spread the labor out over the year, and hedged the agricultural bet if disaster overtook one of the harvests. In the old-fashioned three-fold rotation system, one field might be under wheat and another under barley, while the third lay fallow. This sequence might be varied by putting a field into beans or peas, to the nourishment of the soil since legumes have the ability to fix nitrogen.

Wheat was comparatively temperamental as a crop, requiring warmer temperatures and richer soil than, for example, rye. Thus it was often scarcer and more expensive. Since refined wheat flour baked up into the lightest and most elegant bread, it tended to be associated with the community's elite. There were, of course, different grades of wheat flour, the less expensive ones ground with a larger proportion of bran, or mixed with rye flour.

Barley was made into bread of a coarse, everyday sort, but it was also important for brewing ale, the principal English drink. Oats could be made into bread or cakes—cakes in the older sense of a flat pan-bread, turned so as to cook on both sides and not expected to rise into a loaf.

Harvests were local and crucial. A bad one could mean intense hardship. England's roads were passable by foot or on horseback, but transporting wagonloads of grain for long distances was something else again, so that importing food from another part of the country was often infeasible. This lack of options made a local population helpless in the face of price rises and increased the volatility of the local farm economy. Farmers and corn factors, or grain agents, sometimes hoarded grain early in the season, on the chance that the main harvest would be poor and prices would go up; if, instead, the harvest were a good one, they would lose their gamble, though the people would gain. The porter in *Macbeth,* welcoming damned souls into hell, finds among the group such a speculator whose plans had gone awry: "Here's a farmer, that hang'd himself on th' expectation of plenty" (2.3.4).

Poor harvests might be caused by drought, the kind of farm crisis Americans are accustomed to, but they could also be caused by too much rain; England has, after all, a very wet climate. Shakespeare's picture of rural distress in *A Midsummer Night's Dream* is based, some scholars feel, on the abysmal summer of 1595. Titania tells Oberon how the winds have sucked up from the sea

Contagious fogs; which, falling in the land,
Hath every pelting river made so proud
That they have overborne their continents.
The ox hath therefore stretch'd his yoke in vain,
The ploughman lost his sweat, and the green corn
Hath rotted ere his youth attain'd a beard.

(2.1.90–95)

The "beard" which the "green corn" (wheat) has not attained is the awn, or tufty growth surrounding the grains at the head of the stalk. Unfortunately, the reconciliation of Titania and Oberon at the end of the play did not have the real-life effect of improving the weather, as Titania implies that it might; grain continued to drown in the fields for the following three summers, and great hardship resulted.

Oxen, Horses, and Sheep

The word *ox* had varying denotations. Today it means a steer, potentially a bull but castrated in youth, used as a draft animal. (To Americans, the mention of oxen often brings to mind the relatively large and powerful beasts that pulled covered wagons across the plains.) In the sixteenth century this was the usual meaning, but in some parts of England any member of the cattle family might be referred to as an ox if used for traction, including heifers (young females), mature cows temporarily or permanently uninvolved in motherhood, and even bulls.

Oxen could supply pulling power quite economically, as they ate less than horses. Eight oxen made up the usual team, more or fewer being used depending on the heaviness of the soil. The ploughs broke up the soil and made it easier for seeds to put down roots, but they did not turn the soil over in the scooping, curving action that the ploughs invented in the eighteenth century were to do.

Cattle were slaughtered for beef, though they were not raised in herds for this purpose, except in a few areas of western England. The typical ox or cow killed for beef on an Elizabethan farm was one that had worn out its usefulness as a draft animal or a milker.

The question of horses versus oxen as draft animals was frequently debated by Elizabethan landholders. Oxen were cheaper to buy and feed and were also more resolute, one might say, as they will keep on pulling at a seemingly impossible job when horses get discouraged after a lunge or two. The usual recourse for the driver of a horse-drawn wagon when mired in mud was to go and find a team of oxen to pull it out again. But horses were faster and thus a better choice for the wagon, provided the mud holes were manageable. As roads improved, a slow process during the seventeenth century, horses took the ascendant. Oxen did not disappear, however, as there were plenty of jobs in which speed did not matter.

Until roads improved, riding a horse was virtually the only way to cover a long distance with any kind of dispatch. William Harrison, whose *Description of England* includes a survey of the nation's animals, makes a point of praising the comfortable gait of English horses and adds a detail which might not occur to today's mechanized travelers: "It is moreover very pleasant and delectable in his [the rider's] ears, in that the noise of their well-proportioned pace doth yield comfortable sound as he traveleth by the way."[6]

For sheep, the qualities most valued were thick fleeces and a genetic tendency for twinning. Sheep provided mutton, but their owners did not seem systematically concerned about breeding for efficient weight gain. Sheep were also valued as a source of milk; six good ewes were said to give as much milk as a cow. Shakespeare's Perdita, unaware of her own royal blood, says after the apparent disruption of her romance with Prince Florizel:

> *This dream of mine*
> *Being now awake, I'll queen it no inch farther,*
> *But milk my ewes, and weep.*
> (*The Winter's Tale*, 4.4.448–49)

In literature, sheep naturally hold a prominent place in the pastoral, that long-lived genre which from the third century B.C. to the present has celebrated (sometimes with irony) the joys of rustic life. Elizabethan readers familiar with the country realities in general and sheep-raising in particular would be well equipped to appreciate pastoral pieces pointing out the discrepancy between the ideal and the actual. Christopher Marlowe's passionate shepherd, urging the object of his affections to "come live with me and be my love" in an eternal May morning, is countered by Sir Walter Raleigh's nymph, who points out that sooner or later "wayward winter reckoning yields."

Spenser's *Shepheardes Calendar* combines traditional subjects and forms in a way that leaves room for the reader's memories of real-life scenes. Here Cuddie describes the feeble condition of a flock at the end of winter:

> *So lustlesse bene they, so weake, so wan,*
> *Clothed with cold, and hoary wyth frost.*
> *Thy flocks father his corage hath lost:*
> *Thy ewes, that wont to have blowen bags,*
> *Like wailefull widdowes hangen their crags:*
> *The rather lambes bene starved with cold . . .*
>
> ("Februarie," 78–83)

The "flock's father" is the ram; "corage," a cognate of "courage," has a sexual connotation. The ewes, instead of healthily nursing their young, are hanging their necks. The "rather" lambs are those born early in the year.

Market Towns and Fairs

Towns, communities larger than villages and possessing, say, five or six streets and a thousand or so people, were organized differently from the villages. In comparatively few cases was all the land of a town owned by a single landlord who collected all the rents. Some farming land-holders might live in the town, but many of the inhabitants kept shops and ran other urban enterprises on a larger scale than could be done in a village.

Towns were governed not by a manorial court but by a more complex system of municipal bodies and councils. Often the town had aldermen, something like the London model though not identical. Usually there was a large variety of town officers, from clerk to constable. Tradesmen's guilds also played a role in town life.

The right to hold a market, a highly valued asset, was granted to towns by the sovereign. Stratford-upon-Avon, for example, had held a weekly market (on Thursdays, in Shakespeare's time) since the early fourteenth century. Winchester, to choose another town known to many American visitors, had two market days, Wednesday and Saturday, thanks to a charter granted by Queen Elizabeth. The regulation of market days, like that of so many other aspects of commerce, meant that competition was evenly spread. Towns within twenty or so miles of each other would not ordinarily hold their markets on the same day of the week. If one town's market were on Tuesday and the other's on Friday, for instance, farmers might take produce to each, with butter freshly churned the day before. In *As You Like It,* Rosalind tells Phoebe that her (Phoebe's) feminine charm is of limited appeal and durability and that the more quickly she trades on it the better:

> For I must tell you friendly in your ear,
> Sell when you can, you are not for all markets.

(3.5.59–60)

Fairs were a more elaborate enterprise, usually taking place once a year and attracting merchants and customers from a wide area. As was the case with markets, the right to hold a fair was eagerly sought, as a town could levy dues of stallholders and could also expect, of course, to see their economy perk up from lodging and feeding the participants. Sovereigns accordingly granted the right with discretion. Ben Jonson's *Bartholomew Fair* is set at the annual fair held in Smithfield, at that time a suburb of London, on St. Bartholomew's Day (August 24) since the early twelfth century. Scarborough Fair, memorialized in a haunting ballad, dates from a grant given by Henry III in the mid-thirteenth century. This fair ran for an unusually long period of time, from the Feast of the Assumption, on August 15, to Michaelmas, on September 29. Scarborough's remote Yorkshire location and the difficulty of traveling may have had something to do with this leisurely pace.

8

Marriage Arrangements and Customs

As far as romance and marriage are concerned, present-day American readers find few immediate differences between the conventions of Elizabethan literature and those to which we are accustomed. Hero and heroine fall in love, overcome obstacles of various kinds, and are married (or headed for marriage) at the end.

What is different is the extent to which this pattern reflects the everyday life of the readers. Elizabethans seldom married for love alone and took into consideration many other factors. The prospect of marrying a person with whom they were not totally bedazzled, or even a person they hardly knew, did not fill them with horror.

The Court of Wards: Forced Marriages

Although parental affection usually guaranteed some concern for the preferences of the bride and groom in an arranged marriage, it was nevertheless taken for granted that parents had absolute control of their offspring. Parents who forced their children to marry despite the latter's objections were represented in literature as wrong; the wrong did not reside in the power itself, however, but in the parents' misuse of it. They had, in a sense, failed to observe the principle of noblesse oblige, of the responsibility the holders of high place should feel toward those below them in the accepted hierarchy, and misfortune generally resulted.

113

If parents could not always be relied on to resist the temptation of using their children as pawns to further some plan of their own, one would hardly expect more of any other authority holding a similar control over the child. Elizabethan readers would have recognized references to the institution of wardship, for example, as a category of exploitation familiar in everyday life.

The Court of Wards was invented by Henry VIII and was not abolished until 1660. By this time, many of those likely to become enmeshed in wardship tangles had found ways of legally protecting themselves, but earlier victims were many. The idea behind this court goes back to feudal times, when a tenant owed military service to his lord. Should the tenant die, his heir, even if a small child, would still owe this service, and the lord was in a strong position to demand something else instead. What he did demand was control over the child—his vassal, after all—with regard to decisions on the child's education and also the child's marriage.

In earlier times, it might be presumed that the lord's need for well-educated and advantageously married vassals would cause him to act for the child's well-being. However, when Henry VIII set up his system in the 1540s, the object was quite baldly to make money for the Crown, despite claims that the court was founded on ancient tradition. In selling off the lands he had confiscated from the monasteries, the king stipulated that the buyer must hold these lands through knight-service.[1] Thus, any heir to these lands who was under age when the owner died became a ward of the Crown.

In an age of high parent mortality, the Crown could thus be assured of a steady supply of orphans, or half-orphans at least; even if only the father had died, the child still went into wardship. The Crown might then dispose of the child's hand in marriage and also had the power to manage the land until the child came of age. If all these negotiations were too much trouble, the Crown could simply sell the wardship to someone else, as was usually done, the Court of Wards serving as a sort of auction block.

Should the hapless ward refuse to go along with the guardian's plans for his or her marriage, a fine would be charged against the estate. The guardian, in short, could hardly lose. Buying up a good wardship could be seen as quite an attractive investment. With regard to marriage, the legal age of consent was quite low, fourteen for men and twelve for women, so wards might be married (or threatened with marriage) when mere children.

It was possible, incidentally, for a widow to buy the wardship of her child, thus presumably assuring some regard for the child's well-being. Such an outcome was not usual, however. The widow had little or no access to her late husband's estate, so unless she had some money of her own it was easy for someone else to outbid her. Wards were sometimes removed from their homes and taken to those of their guardians; others were allowed to continue their lives much as before.

Lord Burghley, Queen Elizabeth's chief statesman, was Master of the Queen's Wards and took a number of them into his house, where they formed a sort of courtiers' academy, with masters for instruction in Latin, dancing, riding, and other subjects. Roger Ascham, tutor of Queen Elizabeth and author of *The Schoolmaster,* was one of the instructors.

In literature, references to wardships have a variety of connotations, sometimes simply that of a character's age. In *Romeo and Juliet,* old Capulet and one of his guests try to recall the last time they danced as maskers. They agree on the occasion, the wedding of one Lucentio, but disagree on how long ago that event took place. Thirty years and more, insists the guest; Lucentio's son is that age. Capulet cannot believe it: "His son was but a ward two years ago" (1.5.40)—that is, under twenty-one. An unspoken note of poignancy is added by the implication that their friend Lucentio has died; his wedding, and the speakers' youth, become even more remote.

In *Bartholomew Fair,* Grace Wellborn manages to outwit her guardian's attempt to marry her to a man she does not like and to gain his approval of the suitor she prefers. The play implies that Grace has done the right and sensible thing.

The Miseries of Enforced Marriage, a play by George Wilkins, takes straight aim at the institution of wardship. Young Scarborrow, a ward with three years still to go, falls in love with, and promises to marry, a young lady of good but not aristocratic family. Since he has made this promise before her father, the exchange would count as a plighting of troth, the implications of which we will examine below. At this point Scarborrow receives a summons from his guardian, who has found a wife for him, and complications ensue. The play raises but does not settle the question of whether a marriage contracted after one of the participants has been betrothed to someone else is bigamous. The betrayed lady short-circuits the conflict by dying, whereupon Scarborrow abandons his wife and behaves with considerable violence. None of these misfortunes would have come about, the play makes clear, were it not for the tyrannies of the wardship system.

Age at Marriage: Juliet versus the Statistics

Judging from the low age of consent which made wardship so profitable, marriage at quite a young age would seem to have been the usual thing in the sixteenth and seventeenth centuries, and in fact many people today seem to have that impression. It is not correct, however, with regard to the majority of Englishmen, who, after all, did not stand to inherit vast estates and would not have been subjected to the diplomatic negotiations characteristic of the upper classes.

In the middle stations of life, a couple normally had to wait until some slot opened up for them—a copyhold lease becoming available, say, so that the new family would have some land and could support itself. Apprentices tended to marry late because guild regulations typically forbade their becoming "free" of their craft or trade before the age of twenty-four, and they would usually work for a few more years as journeymen before setting up on their own.

The ages of brides and grooms were not recorded in the parish registers, but couples applying for marriage by license rather than by banns (see below for this distinction) were often required to give this information. Peter Laslett cites statistics derived from over a thousand applicants for licenses in the diocese of Canterbury during the seventeenth century, concluding that the mean age for brides was just under twenty-four years and that for bridegrooms just under twenty-seven.[2] Within this group there was some variation according to social class. Aristocrats tended to marry younger, as we might guess; Laslett gives a mean of just over nineteen years for brides and just over twenty-four for grooms. The mean age of brides from the gentry class was twenty-two, which would put them in between, but grooms from this class stayed at about the general mean, twenty-seven.

Shakespeare's Juliet remains a puzzle. The source of the play, Arthur Brooke's *The Tragical History of Romeus and Juliet,* specifies Juliet's age as sixteen—quite young. But Shakespeare takes off another two years.

Juliet's father, during his more indulgent phase at the beginning of the play, feels that fourteen is too young for marriage and that her suitor, Paris, will have to wait. He later changes his mind and orders her to the altar. Meanwhile, Juliet's mother is adamant that fourteen is quite old enough and tells her daughter:

> *younger than you,*
> *Here in Verona, ladies of esteem,*
> *Are made already mothers. By my count,*
> *I was your mother much upon these years*
> *That you are now a maid.*

(1.3.69–73)

Lady Capulet's sense of time is hardly trustworthy, as her dialogue with the Nurse on the question of Juliet's age might demonstrate. Nevertheless, she speaks with such assurance, and the Capulet household, despite its Italian setting, seems so closely aligned with everyday English life, that generations of readers have assumed that these lines are a transcription of reality.

Perhaps Shakespeare made his Juliet very young in order to intensify the play's tragedy. Perhaps, since youthful marriages were more frequent in the English aristocracy than in the middle classes, he wanted to emphasize her high birth. Perhaps the boy actor he had in mind for the part was more convincing as a fourteen-year-old than as a sixteen-year-old. Or perhaps precocity in marriage was one of the exotic characteristics his audience associated with Italy. Whatever the reason may have been, Juliet was a statistical anomaly in the context of the lives of most of Shakespeare's original audience.

Marriage Preliminaries: The Espousal

The middle-class Elizabethan bride and groom may have come quite close to the ideal of marrying for love. Often they had grown up together and had a great deal in common. The decision to marry might well have been their own, after making which they would seek their parents' approval. These authorities might, of course, disapprove and thus bar the marriage, but usually a negative response would be carefully considered and would not represent a blind whim. What each of the parties sought, after all, was a harmonious consensus.

A sufficient degree of good will having been achieved, the process of getting married was begun. There were several phases. First, and quite important, the couple vowed their intent to marry, before witnesses. This espousal, or betrothal, was considered quite binding, and in many cases it appears to have legitimized, as far as society was concerned, the young couple's sex life; the fact that a large proportion of Elizabethan brides were pregnant at the time they actually said their vows in church can be documented from the parish registers, which give the dates of marriages and baptisms. No real stigma seems to have attached itself to these cases; as long as a marriage took place, a child born shortly thereafter would not be considered cause for the parents to be hauled into the archdeacon's court.

This rather comfortable ambiguity concerning betrothal vows may account for the fact that Elizabethan society seemed to have comparatively few illegitimate children—few, certainly, in comparison to our own age. It would be difficult to determine whether, in the majority of cases, the vows came first and the sex shortly thereafter, or the sex (and perhaps the early signs of pregnancy) first and the vows thereafter. Only the couple need know for sure.

Premarital carryings-on are not suggested in the case of Prince Florizel and his shepherdess love in *The Winter's Tale*, but the original audience would have understood the importance of the espousal vow in one of the play's more dramatic moments. Florizel asks a pleasant elderly gentleman whom he has just met at the sheep-shearing feast to "mark our contract"—to serve as a witness to his vow to marry the beautiful Perdita. The gentleman replies, as he removes his false beard and reveals himself as Florizel's father, "Mark your divorce, young sir!" (4.4.417).

The sexual aspect of the marriage contract plays a part in Claudio's problems in *Measure for Measure*. As he explains to his friend Lucio,

> *upon a true contract*
> *I got possession of Julietta's bed.*

You know the lady; she is fast my wife,
Save that we do the denunciation lack
Of outward order.

(1.2.144–49)

The reason the marriage ceremony has not taken place, Claudio adds, has to do with a disagreement about Julietta's dowry, and this snag is apparently of such difficulty that it continues to prevent the simple solution that occurs immediately to Isabella—"O, let him marry her" (1.4.48). Nobody pays any attention to this suggestion, and of course the plot must somehow be got under way. The original audience may have been reassured by the fact that the harsh laws so suddenly being enforced, condemning Claudio to death for having got Julietta with child, are presented not as English laws but as those of faraway Vienna.

Shakespeare's Marriage

The circumstances of Shakespeare's own marriage are shrouded in the mists of slender evidence and conflicting interpretations, but Stratford's parish register does indicate that Anne Hathaway, whom Shakespeare married in 1582, when he was eighteen and she twenty-six,[3] was one of the large number of Elizabethan brides who went pregnant to the altar. A daughter was born six months afterward. The custom of betrothal vows, along with the complicated church calendar of seasons when marriages might and might not take place, makes it possible to claim the whole matter was perfectly aboveboard and no cause for scandal. That is, one might postulate that Anne Hathaway had to get married, all right, but she didn't necessarily have to get betrothed.

In the same way, it is impossible to speculate with any accuracy on whether or not Shakespeare's marriage was a happy one. Records indicate that for most of his career he occupied lodgings in London while his wife and family lived in Stratford, but there is no way to tell how often he traveled back and forth. Commuter marriages have succeeded before the present age. Certainly Shakespeare kept up with events in Stratford, bought property there, including a quite comfortable house for his family, and spent the last years of his life there, a prosperous gentleman enjoying his hearth and home.

The fact that Shakespeare bequeathed to his wife the "second best bed" has been given all sorts of dire interpretations. (Among those pondering this question are a fictional group, Stephen Daedalus and his friends in James Joyce's *Ulysses.*) The facts were probably quite ordinary. As a widow, Mrs. Shakespeare would have been granted the use of the house during her life, and the best bed, whichever it was, would have gone with it; the second-best bed was simply an additional bed. It may have come from the Hathaways' old home, or have had some other connection, and her husband simply wanted to make sure she got it.

Banns and Licenses

Marriages had to take place in church, and in Elizabethan and Jacobean times the church had to be the Church of England, where the words of the service were set forth in the prayer book. There were no Roman Catholic churches as such, and most of the Protestant denominations and sects so familiar today had not yet evolved. When they did, they would be spoken of as "dissenting religions," having dissented from the Church of England, and it would be several centuries before marriage services might be held under their authority rather than that of what was, after all, the official state church.

The ceremony itself fell under a good deal of regulation. Marriages could not take place during certain seasons of the liturgical year, and must be celebrated during the "canonical hours" of the day, even in the right season. The church chosen for the ceremony must be that of the parish where either the bride or the bridegroom was living at the time. And the banns, or the announcement that the couple intends to marry, must be proclaimed from the pulpit of that church for three successive Sundays before the wedding. Quite dramatically, anyone who knew of any reason why the marriage should not take place—either party's being married to someone else, for example—might make his or her objection known at that point, thus "forbidding the banns."

Some of these requirements might be dropped if the participants obtained a special license from the ecclesiastical authorities. The number of times the banns must be "cried," for example, might be reduced in this way. A fee was charged for the license, allowing the Church to benefit from what it would otherwise be obliged to consider undue haste.

Wedding Customs

Elizabethan newlyweds did not go away on a honeymoon; instead, they were ceremonially put to bed in the house where the wedding feast had taken place. Bridesmaids had the additional duty of helping the bride off with her wedding gown and on with her nightgown, and the pair were brought a cup of spiced wine before their well-wishers finally left them together.

Brides might be married in white, but only because they liked it; the connection between white and virginity had not yet become customary. A popular color was russet, a brownish pink; the fabric might be velvet, damask, or a less expensive linen or wool. Sewn with a stitch or two to the dress would be an assortment of "favors," ornamental knots of ribbon in various colors; after the ceremony, the bachelors of the party rushed the bride and snatched off the favors, which they wore in their hats for several days thereafter.

The feast which followed the wedding varied according to the social class and financial abilities of the participants, with a major effort being made whatever the circumstances. William Harrison describes the wedding feast of a rural village as a kind of potluck, "where it is incredible to tell what meat is consumed and spent, each one bringing such a dish or so many with him."[4] The "bride-ale," another village custom, called for the bride to sell ale at her own feast, the guests buying their refreshments for whatever sums they cared to contribute to the newlyweds' purse. At the other end of the scale, aristocratic and royal weddings knew few limits in expense or imagination; music, masques, fireworks, and days of entertainment were the usual thing.

In general, literary references to Elizabethan and Jacobean weddings present few difficulties for present-day readers. Our own culture contains so many variations in wedding customs that most of us are quite used to adjusting to them, and the basic idea of joyous celebration has not changed.

Marriage and Cosmology in Elizabethan Literature

Needless to say, the concept of marriage fit quite centrally into the Elizabethan's view of the universe. Marriage took its place as an emblem of harmony, concord, and the reconciliation of disparate elements into a perfected whole.

Canon law recognized marriage as a sacrament, not merely a civil contract. This distinction had evolved in the early days of the Church and set Christian practice apart from that of the Roman Empire. As a holy institution, with the relation between husband and wife analogically compared to that between Christ and the Church (Ephesians 5:25–28), and with Christ's words on the subject (Mark 10:9) echoed in the Church of England's marriage service, marriage was considered in its essence indissoluble.

Divorce, consequently, was not part of the Elizabethan experience of marriage, despite the prominent example of Henry VIII. This case was, after all, most exceptional, a matter of agitation for all Europe, and was technically not a divorce as such but an annulment of the king's previous marriage. A very few instances occurred of a form of divorce (*a mensa et thoro*) that took effect as a judicial separation, allowing a couple to live apart but not permitting either party to remarry. A society as replete as is our own with divorced and remarried ex-spouses would have been unimaginable in sixteenth-century England. Attempts to imagine it would no doubt have bogged down in visions of social chaos.

The permanence of the matrimonial alliance naturally enhanced the Elizabethans' view of marriage as a reflection of Christ's union with the Church and also as a reflection of the divinely created cosmos. Order, priority, and place naturally were part of the picture. In the passage from Ephesians cited above, St. Paul goes on to clarify his analogy: "For the husband is the head of the wife, even as Christ is the head of the Church." In line with the principles of noblesse oblige and the duties pertaining to high place, St. Paul recommends that husbandly power be administered in a gracious and reciprocal context: "Husbands, love your wives, even as Christ also loved the Church . . . let every one of you in particular so love his wife even as himself; and the wife see that she reverence her husband."

Appropriately, then, the bridegroom in Spenser's "Epithalamion" celebrates his bride for her beauty, honor, and modesty, and she is the focus and centerpiece of the poem; yet she meets the groom, when night brings an end to revelry and the couple are alone, "in proud humility" (306). But a more immediate aspect of Spenser's poem is its placing of marriage in general, and this one in particular, into the setting of a brilliant, orderly cosmos. The moon peeps in the window ("Is it not Cinthia, she that never sleepes?"); the "high heavens," in which "a thousand torches flaming bright / Doe burne," are asked to:

> *Poure out your blessing on us plentiously,*
> *And happy influence upon us raine,*
> *That we may raise a large posterity,*
> *Which from the earth, which they may long possesse,*
> *With lasting happinesse,*
> *Up to your haughty pallaces may mount.*
> *And for the guerdon of theyr glorious merit,*
> *May heavenly tabernacles there inherit.*

(415–22)

John Donne's epithalamions (the word means "nuptial song") incorporate time in its various divisions, heavenly objects (especially the sun), and earthly creatures. In his poem to the princess Elizabeth, daughter of James I, who married the Count Palatine on February 14, 1613, Donne begins with the tradition of the birds' pairing off, two by two, on Valentine's Day:

> *Haile, Bishop Valentine, whose day this is,*
> *All the Aire is thy Diocis,*
> *And all the chirping Choiristers*
> *And other birds are thy Parishioners.*

This same real-life wedding included among its festivities a production of *The Tempest*, in which several heavenly deities descend to bring the young couple the blessings of the wider universe to which this new marriage will, by analogy, belong.

> *Honor, riches, marriage-blessing,*
> *Long continuance, and increasing,*
> *Hourly joys be still upon you!*
>   (4.1.106–8)

Obedient and Disobedient Wives in Shakespeare

In Shakespeare's tragedy, where reality is confronted in a head-on fashion, the subservience of wives to husbands is for the most part observed. The result is not always at one with harmony and justice, however. Desdemona protects her husband with her dying breath; asked who killed her, she replied, "Nobody; I myself" (5.2.124). Emilia has earlier supplied her own husband, Iago, with a key piece of false evidence when, obeying Iago's request, she steals the handkerchief that Othello once gave Desdemona. When Emilia chooses truth over loyalty, revealing Iago's villainy to the officials gathered in Othello's chamber, she apologizes for, in effect, breaking out of her proper place:

> *Good gentlemen, let me have leave to speak.*
> *'Tis proper I obey him, but not now.*
>   (5.2.195–96)

Wifely disobedience, on the other hand, is fittingly punished in *King Lear* when Goneril, who has jeered at her husband's kind-hearted nature and has schemed to replace him with the opportunistic bastard Edmund, kills herself when her plans go awry, leaving her husband as one of the play's few survivors.

Comedy operates on a different wavelength. Here reality can be turned inside out, as part of the game, and here wives dominate husbands in shenanigans aimed, finally, at the greater good of all. Mistress Ford, quite in control of her part of the plot in *The Merry Wives of Windsor,* pretends to succumb to Falstaff's blandishments and leads both him and her jealous husband into one ludicrous tangle after another, proving, as her friend Mistress Page puts it, that "wives may be merry, and yet honest, too" (4.2.105).

In *The Taming of the Shrew,* Katherina's reluctance to take up her traditional subservient role provides much of the play's fun. Opinion having shifted during the last few centuries, it seems probable that today's audiences are more enthusiastically on Katherina's side than were the original ones. Certainly Katherina's closing speech poses a problem for present-day actresses, and it is sometimes spoken with a conspiratorial wink. But to the original audience Katherina is expressing a manifest truth about harmonious social institutions; knowing and keeping one's place is simply the only answer.

> *Such duty as the subject owes the prince,*
> *Even such a woman oweth to her husband;*
> *And when she is froward, peevish, sullen, sour,*
> *And not obedient to his honest will,*
> *What is she but a foul contending rebel,*
> *And graceless traitor to her loving lord?*

> (5.2.155–60)

In-Laws, Cousins, and Grandparents

Having become spiritually one flesh and thus acquired, along with the cosmological connotations, a new set of relatives in this world below, the bride and groom needed to call them something, and the results can be confusing to the present-day reader. "In law" terminology was part of the Elizabethan vocabulary, but like other kinship nomenclature, it was often more loosely applied than is our own custom. A father-in-law might, in fact, turn out to be what we would call a stepfather. The reader must stay alert. In Jonson's *Every Man in His Humour,* Wellbred's references to Mistress Bridget as his "sister," though she is actually the sister of his real sister's husband, can make his courtship of the lady seem a bit scandalous.

Another source of ambiguity is the Elizabethan habit of using the word *cousin* to denote many kinds of family relationships. Mortimer, in the first part of *Henry IV,* says to Hotspur, "Fie, cousin Percy, how you cross [contradict] my father" (3.1.145); he means his father-in-law, Glendower, whose daughter he has just married. And Hotspur is not literally

Mortimer's cousin but his brother-in-law, having married Mortimer's sister.

Grandparents were called "Grandmother" or "Grandfather," as they are today, but "Granddam" and "Grandsire" were also frequent. "Gammer" and the masculine form, "Gaffer," had a more rustic connotation and were often applied to elderly people who were not relatives. The title character in *Gammer Gurton's Needle* is an example.

Cuckoldry Jokes

The inevitability with which on the Elizabethan stage any reference to horns, whether deer's antlers or musical instruments, elicits a joke on cuckoldry makes one wonder if perhaps the inevitability were part of the joke. It is easy to picture the actor standing quietly, a smile spreading on his face, while the audience begins to laugh before the line is delivered.

The horns of the cuckold denoted an unfaithful wife and were visible, by the terms of the joke, to everyone except the unsuspecting husband himself. Benedick, in *Much Ado About Nothing,* appears to associate marriage primarily with the potential humiliation of cuckoldry; should he ever go to the altar, he says, "pluck off the bull's horns, and set them in my forehead, and let me be vildly painted, and in such great letters as they write, 'Here is a good horse to hire,' let them signify under my sign, 'Here you may see Benedick the married man'" (1.1.262–67). Benedick, needless to say, changes his mind about marriage and decides to take the risk.

In a less comic mode, both Othello and Leontes refer to the cuckold and his horns in the light of a profound betrayal, quite understandable in the circumstances each (wrongly) thinks himself in. Possibly, of course, even the more casual horn jokes found in the plays hide a deeper anxiety than is immediately apparent. Allusions to the frequency of this form of decoration may comprise a kind of "misery loves company" consolation. Often, however, cuckoldry jokes occur in a context of high spirits and may have no real connection to the plot. In *As You Like It,* for example, Jaques suggests setting the horns of a freshly killed deer on his master the duke's head "for a branch of victory" (4.2.5), without implying any scandal about the absent duchess, who, in fact, is never mentioned in the play and is presumably deceased. The courtiers then go off with a cheery song aimed at no one in particular:

> *Take thou no scorn to wear the horn,*
> *It was a crest ere thou wert born;*
> *Thy father's father wore it,*
> *And thy father bore it.*

(4.2.13–16)

Similarly, Christopher Marlowe's *Dr. Faustus* includes a joke on one Benvolio, who has made fun of the doctor and must pay the penalty, during which episode Benvolio discovers that he is wearing a stag's antlers and everybody is laughing at him (4.1.71ff.). The adolescent tone of the prank, something like pinning a "kick me" sign on someone's back, might add to the audience's suspicion that Dr. Faustus does not really get much power, or even much fun, in exchange for his soul.

Jonson's Corvino, in *Volpone,* contributes to his own near-cuckoldry so gullibly that he becomes a quite unsympathetic figure of fun. At the end he is sentenced to be rowed down the Grand Canal "wearing a cap, with fair long ass's ears / Instead of horns" (5.12.137–38). Similarly, Spenser's Malbecco, while jealous of his wife for quite good reason, comes off worse than she does. Dame Hellenore betrays Malbecco first with Paridell and then with a whole herd of satyrs, but she continues her wanton ways quite cheerily while Malbecco is appropriately buffeted by the satyrs' horns and ends up alone in a cave, having metamorphosed into the allegorical figure of "Gelosy" (*The Faerie Queene,* 3.10).

9

Education

If we imagine a group of Elizabethan children learning their ABCs, the picture will not be very different in its essentials from a classroom scene today—or, for an even closer analogy, from a classroom scene of seventy-five or so years ago. The one-room schoolhouse so familiar to Americans has many similarities to its Elizabethan predecessor. The one-room schoolhouse, however, gathered within its walls a much larger proportion of the young population than was the case earlier. In America, as well as in England and other parts of the world, the nineteenth and early twentieth centuries saw the rise of a new social concept, that of universal education.

For the Elizabethans, all schooling was voluntary. No laws required parents to send their children to school or imposed a penalty if they did not. The idea that a nation would benefit if the entire population were able to read was still far in the future, although the importance of reading the Scriptures as an aid to salvation had impressed itself upon many people, and parishes increasingly sponsored schools for instruction in the rudiments of English letters.

With regard to higher rather than primary education, the basic similarity between our own times and the sixteenth and seventeenth centuries needs little qualification as we, too, continue to see college as a voluntary enterprise which a student may or may not be moved to undertake. Also, we are accustomed to so many variations among our own institutions of higher learning—in size, purpose, location, sponsorship, plan, and conduct, among other things—that taking in a few more will not involve a major stretch.

Basic Literacy: Reading and Writing

D. M. Palliser cites the large proportion of parishes which set up so-called petty schools to further basic literacy, as well as the attempts made by the parishes and by local benefactors to pay the tuition fees of poor children. In the diocese of Canterbury, for example, 113 out of a total of 266 parishes had a schoolmaster at some time (though not necessarily continuously) between 1561 and 1600.[1]

These schoolmasters were required to have a license to teach, obtainable from the bishop of the diocese, though the licensing procedure sometimes had more to do with the applicant's religious orthodoxy than with his intellectual ability or talent for teaching. Fees were kept as low as possible; amenities were quite basic. The school sometimes met in the church, or in the house of the schoolmaster. Few parish schools had their own buildings at this point, though grammar schools often did—a separate category of institution dealing with the Latin rather than the English language, to be examined below.

Another type of elementary schoolmaster was not directly connected to the parish but functioned as an entrepreneur, charging a fee of his pupils (or of their parents, rather), sometimes though not always a bit higher than the fee charged by the parish schools, and instructing as best he could. He did not need to be accredited in any way, but a schoolmaster usually tried to give as pedantic a public impression as possible, since he had to act as his own advertisement.

The dame school, kept by an elderly woman of uncertain accomplishments for the rudimentary instruction of children, apparently did not evolve until the latter part of the seventeenth century, though it was to become a familiar institution. The Elizabethan equivalent was more of a child-minding enterprise and might be seen as roughly equivalent to what present-day Americans call day care.

Whether the petty school, as distinct from the dame school, was attached to the parish or functioned as a private enterprise, it was more

likely to attract boys than girls. Girls were usually accepted should they
appear, however. Reading was, after all, a useful skill, and from the
schoolmaster's viewpoint a tuition fee was a tuition fee.

Pupils' ages usually varied from five years old to seven or so. Not all
attended for two years; some could be spared for only a few months.
Village and farm life had many jobs for little children—frightening birds
from newly sown fields, gathering sticks for firewood, looking after their
younger brothers and sisters—and as the children grew older and
stronger their lives held less room for such luxuries as schooling.

At the basic level, which was all that most petty school pupils ever
attained, reading and writing were treated as quite separate skills. Reading, at least reading the Scriptures, was an aid to living a pious life;
writing had about it no religious necessity and was useful in some walks
of life but by no means all. Another reason for the division was economic, as David Cressy points out in his study of Tudor and Stuart
literacy.[2] Paper and ink cost money, as did quill pens and knives for
sharpening them. The type of desk at which a pupil might deal with
these fearsome appliances was more expensive and more space-consum-
ing than a simple bench; supervision of writing exercises had to be closer;
and the time required for achieving a presentable result was discourag-
ingly long. Unlike present-day children, who spend hours with paper and
crayons, both in school and at home, developing the small-muscle co-
ordination which we take for granted, Elizabethan writing pupils were
likely to make a considerably less adroit beginning.

But if writing was seen as an onerous undertaking, reading might be
more quickly and more tidily attained, and received a much greater
emphasis. Pupils began with the alphabet, assisted by a highly popular
instructional device, the horn book, named for the thin sheet of trans-
lucent horn which covered the letters and words on display. The horn
book, incidentally, is exceptional in that it does not seem to have elicited
automatic cuckoldry jokes; in *Love's Labor's Lost,* the schoolmaster,
Holofernes, is the subject of a complex joke involving horn books and
sheep, but it is not a primarily sexual joke (4.1.46ff.).

Holding this "book," a short-handled wooden paddle onto which a
leaf of vellum or paper had been fixed, the pupil recited along with his
schoolmates; then, more frighteningly, he might be called on to recite
alone. A horn book usually presented on its single page the alphabet,
perhaps in several type faces—Old English, or "black letter," italic, and

Roman, the last being the kind of lettering which has become the norm today. It might also contain the Lord's Prayer and other short scriptural verses.

After the horn book, the petty-school pupil would progress to the primer, a small book containing a set of prayers and the catechism, questions and answers summarizing Church of England doctrine and explaining the way to salvation.

The fact that many more Elizabethans apparently learned to read than learned to write should perhaps be emphasized in view of our present-day tendency to equate literacy with the ability to sign one's name. Reading may have been more widespread, in other words, than seems to be the case if one allows an "X" in a parish register to stand as evidence that the man or woman who made it must have been completely removed from the world of letters.

It is easy to see how this option, the "X" or sometimes an individual doodle or an emblem of the signer's trade, might be preferred even by a person who at one time had learned to write. The pen feels awkward, one has forgotten the art of dipping up just enough ink to make a smooth line but not an embarrassing blot, and everybody else—one's wedding party, for example, if one has just been married—is waiting to get on with things.

The Reading Public

Aside from the writing question, there would also be considerable variation in the extent to which the petty-school pupil, going on to other things at the age of seven or so, retained the bit of reading he or she had learned. If he seldom came into contact with books or had any reason to puzzle them out, even his familiarity with the alphabet would probably fade. But if he liked reading and had opportunity to go on with it, he might take a few more steps up the ladder.

Many masters taught their apprentices as part of their training. One of a number of Elizabethan books on the teaching of reading was intended for this purpose, and promised tailors, weavers, and shopkeepers that their work would not suffer if they took on this extra project: "thou

mayst sit on thy shop board, at thy looms or at thy needle, and never
hinder thy work to hear thy scholars."[3]

Certainly an increasing number of people were able to read, and
authors and printers catered to a wide spectrum of needs and tastes. A
tradesman's household, which a generation or so earlier had been quite
innocent of the printed word, might now own a Bible, a devotional book
or two, an almanac with its lurid astrological predictions, and perhaps
a jest book or a few ballads. This last term, incidentally, was used in
Elizabethan times in reference not to orally transmitted folk songs, a
connotation that has since taken over, but to printed verses on contemporary events—a form of journalism, one might say, though frequently
of a quite imaginative order.

Printed ballads appear in *The Winter's Tale* as a hobby of the shep-
herdesses Mopsa and Dorcas, who, though perhaps somewhat idealized
in this pastoral environment, nevertheless retain the air of real-life village girls. Both can read, and they sing their parts in the ballad Auto-
lycus offers for sale. (They know the tune already, as Dorcas points out.
Many Elizabethans could read music at sight, but presumably so height-
ened a degree of education would have been implausible for this social
milieu.) Mopsa is intrigued by the sensational subjects of some of the
ballads—a singing fish, for example, and a usurer's wife who gave birth
to a litter of moneybags; Americans might suspect that the descendants
of this genre live on in the tabloids available at supermarket checkout
counters. Mopsa demonstrates the naïveté of this new class of readers,
still in awe of the authority of the page, and no doubt amused the more
sophisticated members of Shakespeare's audience. She loves a ballad in
print, she says, "for then we are sure they are true" (4.4.261).

Grammar Schools

To us, the term *grammar school* is synonymous with elementary education, a first step. The connotation was the same for Elizabethans,
except that the language in which these first steps were taken was Latin.
It was assumed that the pupil beginning grammar school, at age seven
or thereabouts, had already made a beginning in English. There were,

of course, exceptions to this statement, and some grammar schools accepted pupils without previous preparation and started at the beginning.

Unlike the typically somewhat haphazard petty schools, the grammar schools often had deep roots and embodied a carefully thought-out system of education. The scholar and humanist William Lily, a friend of Erasmus, wrote a Latin grammar which held sway through the sixteenth century and for several centuries thereafter. The question of how a boy might become not only proficient in Latin but fond of learning was pondered by theorists such as Roger Ascham, whose book *The Schoolmaster* shows a warm awareness of students as real people.

It might be pointed out that, although only boys were regularly admitted to grammar schools, girls in affluent circumstances often learned similar lessons at home, with tutors. One thinks of Shakespeare's Bianca, reading Ovid with her tutor in *The Taming of the Shrew.* In *The Schoolmaster,* just mentioned, Ascham praises the accomplishments not only of Queen Elizabeth, whose tutor he had been, but of Lady Jane Grey, executed some fifteen years before the publication of *The Schoolmaster* but still remembered by Ascham as a noble and learned lady.

Horace and Ovid, especially the *Metamorphoses,* were favorite grammar-school texts. Latin plays were sometimes added, especially the tragedies of Seneca and the comedies of Plautus. These seem to have made an impression on Shakespeare's Polonius, for he mentions them in introducing the players (*Hamlet,* 2.2.400) and also remembers having once acted the part of Julius Caesar (3.2.103), presumably in a Latin play done as a school exercise.

Besides literature (which was often invoked for linguistic or rhetorical illustrations rather than for its own sake), the boys studied composition, putting sentences together in a variety of ways and arranging effective speeches and letters, with appropriate decorations from mythology—all, of course, in Latin. By the time they were in the upper forms, or advanced levels of study, when they were eleven or twelve years old, they were expected to use Latin in everyday schoolroom conversation.

Many schools also taught Greek, though less intensely, with readings from Homer and Plato. Modern foreign languages did not usually appear in the regular curriculum, though some schools offered them as an extra. Other subjects which we now consider a standard part of academia—geography and history, for instance, along with higher mathematics—were also seen as options.

The origins of the grammar schools varied. Many had been attached to monasteries before the Reformation; Westminster School, where the headmaster Nicholas Udall wrote the comedy *Ralph Royster Doyster* for his pupils to perform, was originally under the auspices of the Benedictines. Others were founded by trade guilds, such as Merchant Taylors School, where Spenser began his education before going on to Cambridge and where Thomas Kyd was inspired by Seneca to adapt, in his later career, the classical revenge-play characteristics for his *Spanish Tragedy*. Still other grammar schools had individual founders. Eton College, for example, was founded by King Henry VI. (Here, confusingly, the word *college* does not mean an institution for older students, although it usually did.)

Shakespeare and his classmates received quite good schooling in the King's New School at Stratford-upon-Avon, to judge by the schoolmasters' qualifications and salary. Oxford University, only some forty miles away, provided a supply of young men who held master's as well as bachelor's degrees, and the school paid a competitive salary—twenty pounds a year in addition to a rent-free house. Samuel Schoenbaum lists the five schoolmasters who held the post during Shakespeare's youth, with their qualifications and later careers.[4]

Many grammar schools took boarding pupils, while others, if they lived nearby, attended by the day. Shakespeare's

> *whining schoolboy, with his satchel*
> *And shining morning face, creeping like snail*
> *Unwillingly to school*
>
> (*As You Like It*, 2.7.145–47)

would seem to be a day student, but boarders might display a similar reluctance. This attitude is understandable; the school day was long and hard, usually beginning at seven in the morning and continuing until five in the afternoon. The Elizabethans had no compunctions about corporal punishment in the schools, though enlightened thinkers such as Ascham advised against it, and many school-day memories seem to have centered on physical pain. Holidays were few, typically two weeks or so at Christmas and again at Easter, with no equivalent of the long summer vacation to which Americans are accustomed. Half-holidays, or afternoons off, might be given on Thursdays and Saturdays. Sundays were free of classes but at least partially filled with church services.

At the age of twelve or thirteen, grammar-school days were done and the erstwhile pupil might go on to a variety of fates. Some had no more formal schooling. A member of the gentry who was tired of books might simply occupy himself with hunting, or with helping his father oversee the estate. Most families favored a few years at a university, perhaps followed by a few more years at the Inns of Court in London, but there was nothing compulsory about this sequence. A boy from the mercantile classes might become an apprentice, perhaps in the family business. A fairly large proportion, however, went on to spend some time at a university.

No one seemed to think the schoolboy's five years of studying Latin rhetoric and literature a waste of time—that is, no major segment of society held this opinion; the boys may have had their doubts, especially during the duller stretches. Latin was not considered a dead language; the queen could speak it extemporaneously with foreign ambassadors, as could many of her ministers, and while the average grammar-school boy was not likely to find himself in such high conversational circles, a glamour attached nevertheless. If he traveled abroad in educated circles, he was more likely to encounter foreigners who spoke classical Latin instead of English, the latter still being considered a provincial and not very important language.

Closer to home, Latin was intrinsic to the Church and the law, and it had a prestige, an association with authority and sophistication, that was more than skin deep. The rhetorical techniques the boys learned in Latin carried over into English and enhanced their daily doings, for the Elizabethans loved language and admired those who could express themselves accurately, forcefully, and with embellishment befitting the occasion. Finally, the content of the readings was considered highly valuable in itself. Classical studies had, after all, been at the heart of the humanist movement in the early sixteenth century. To become familiar with great minds and great civilizations was perceived as a liberating enterprise, not a restrictive one.

The Universities

Universities were open to men only, a limitation that was to persist until the late nineteenth century. In the sixteenth century, entering students were not only male but were considerably younger than the age we associate with college, often matriculating at thirteen or fourteen, although some colleges tried to persuade parents not to send their sons until they were fifteen.

The two universities, Oxford and Cambridge, were roughly fifty miles from London in their respective directions, and while individuals and families might have strong loyalties to one or the other, there has never been a general consensus that either is superior. William Harrison, having attended both, declares himself unable to praise one over the other. In speaking of either, "I cannot but describe the other; and in commendation of the first, I cannot but extol the latter; and so much the rather for that they are both so dear unto me that I cannot readily tell unto whether of them I owe the most good will."[5]

Each university consisted, as is still the case, of a number of separate and quite individual colleges. Harrison lists fifteen for Cambridge and eighteen for Oxford, with the addition in the latter case of nine "hostels, or halls," several of which later evolved into full-blown colleges. The founding of new colleges had been a favorite form of charity through the sixteenth century, with patrons including at various times Cardinal Wolsey, Henry VIII, and Queen Elizabeth, along with a number of prosperous merchants and other well-wishers to the cause of education.

Today's American visitor often finds the colleges of Oxford and Cambridge something of a dizzying maze, a sequence of gothic courtyards unfolding out of one another like puzzle boxes, and labeled with what seem to be interchangeable names. Both Oxford and Cambridge have a Corpus Christi College; Cambridge has a Christ's College and Oxford a Christ's Church College; both have a Jesus College; Oxford has a Magdalen College and Cambridge a Magdalene College, with an *e*; each has a Saint John's College and a Trinity College, and Cambridge adds a Trinity Hall. Oxford has a Queen's College, honoring Edward III's Queen Philippa, and Cambridge a Queens' College—the plural form— honoring Henry VI's Queen Margaret and Edward IV's Queen Elizabeth, sequentially patrons of the college and an odd combination in view of the political background. To the students, of course, past and present, each college is so much an individual entity that confusion is unlikely and the possibility, if suggested, rather startling.

Then, as now, a student had more sense of belonging to his individual college than to the university as a whole. The university, a rather vague entity, administered examinations and awarded degrees, but the college had a solid spatial presence and was populated by tangible friends and mentors.

What we would call classical studies, Latin and Greek, comprised the heart of most students' reading lists. Room could be made for individual pursuits, and the libraries got better and better. Sir Thomas Bodley, for example, restored Oxford's library in the late 1590s and did such a good job, giving generously himself and persuading his friends to follow suit, that the library now bears his name, the Bodleian.

Unlike today's American student, who takes a certain number of separate courses and earns a grade in each, accumulating course credits until he can turn them in, like chips in a casino, for the appropriate degree, the English student spent his college years preparing for the examinations which would determine at one fell swoop whether he got a degree or not. It must be added that many students did not aspire toward a degree and left without one, under no dire disgrace as far as public opinion was concerned, and presumably in possession of more knowledge than they had entered with.

University Jargon

Like all specialized environments, Oxford and Cambridge developed their own vocabulary, and since specimens of it often appear without explanation the American reader may find the following list helpful. Some of these terms are not in present-day use, but as they turn up quite often in literature they are explained in the present tense.

Bachelor. As in America, the holder of the first or lowest degree granted by a university. Most frequently, then as now, this was the bachelor of arts.

Chancellor. The titular head of a university, sometimes an honorary post. Among those holding the office in Queen Elizabeth's time were Robert Dudley, earl of Leicester, chancellor of Oxford; and Lord Burleigh, chancellor of Cambridge. Both took a strong interest in the well-being of their universities and made their influence felt.

Commoner. A student who pays for his commons, or food and other expenses. Students whose expenses were met from other sources included those in need of aid as well as the outstandingly bright; commoners were those who fell into neither of these categories and paid up. At Cambridge a commoner might be called a pensioner. In this context the word *commoner* has nothing to do with whether or not the student holds a hereditary title.

Dean. At Cambridge and Oxford, a resident fellow with responsibility for the behavior of a group of undergraduates. This was not a particularly high post. At European and Scottish universities, a dean was the president of a faculty, or of a department of study in a university; this is the usage which has become current in America.

Don. A head, fellow, or tutor of a college. In literary references, we need only imagine a don as a person ranking higher than an undergraduate, having some authority over him.

Fellow. Many meanings; can refer to all incorporated members of a collegiate foundation, and often to a student who has stayed on after getting his bachelor's degree and holds a stipendiary position with the college. The fellows outrank the undergraduates and usually form a group apart from them.

Fellow-commoner. An undergraduate who dines at the fellows' table, where the food is better. Since this privilege costs extra, the fellow-commoner may be assumed to be relatively wealthy.

Gentleman-commoner. The same as a fellow-commoner.

Master. Two meanings, in the academic context: 1) the holder of a master's degree, a step up from the bachelor's; 2) the presiding officer of a college, a quite responsible position.

Pensioner. Another word for commoner, used at Cambridge; an undergraduate who pays his own dining-hall bill.

Proctor. A disciplinary officer, often described as patroling the streets seeking offenders—undergraduates out after hours, perhaps.

Scholar. A student receiving money from college funds for defraying the cost of his education, usually a reward for merit. Scholars often wore distinctive academic regalia and had special seats in the dining hall and at chapel. The word in a similar restricted sense is often used in American institutions today.

Servitor. The Oxford word for an undergraduate whose expenses are paid, all or in part, and who acted as a servant to one or more of the fellows. The work seems to have been fairly light, that of a page or attendant, rather than all-day drudgery. A servitor might be sent by his master to bring a lighted candle when evening fell, but he probably would not be responsible for carrying loads of wood to the fireplace.

Sizar. The Cambridge word for what at Oxford was called a servitor.

Life after Graduation

Then as now, the holder of a college degree might take a number of paths on leaving the groves of academe, some of them quite traditional and others less so. He might, of course, choose to stay where he was—taking root, so to speak, and staying on for a master's degree and perhaps a fellowship at his college. Or he might enter the Church, a very usual course, or become a teacher in a grammar school. He might go on to the Inns of Court and a law career. Or, especially if he expected to inherit his family estate, he might simply return to it and take up life as an educated gentleman.

Literary history includes a number of writers who followed these courses, and also some who chose another option, that of going to London, cultivating acquaintances among the powerful, and seeing what might turn up. This was not quite so Mr. Micawberish a plan as it might sound. Many interesting projects were under way, and appointments were made on the basis of personal knowledge. A likely young man, well educated, might well encounter some open doors.

Spenser, for example, who had entered Pembroke Hall (now Pembroke College) as a sizar and earned a bachelor's and then a master's degree, became secretary to John Young, bishop of Rochester, whom Spenser had known when Young was master of Pembroke College. Two years later another personal connection, this time resulting from Spen-

ser's acquaintance with Sir Philip Sidney and his literary circle, brought
a quite adventurous appointment, that of secretary to Arthur Lord Grey,
lord deputy to Ireland. Spenser went with Lord Grey to Ireland in 1580
and stayed there the rest of his life, filling a variety of official posts after
he left Lord Grey's service. He eventually became owner of an estate
north of Cork, where he wrote much of his poetry. Spenser made occasional visits to London to see his works through the press; in these
poems appeared in allegorical guise, along with many other public figures and personal friends, Sidney, Bishop Young, and Lord Grey.

Friendship with the Sidney circle was also useful to Samuel Daniel,
whose sonnet sequence *Delia* is today the best known of his works.
Daniel entered Magdalen Hall (later Magdalen College), Oxford, as a
commoner, and left three years later without a degree. He became tutor
to William Herbert, Shakespeare's patron early in the latter's career.
Herbert's mother, the countess of Pembroke, was the sister of Sir Philip
Sidney and was widely respected for her learning and literary taste.
Daniel's poetry was published with her encouragement.

Christopher Marlowe's career would seem to have been decidedly
nontraditional, at least in some aspects. While still at Corpus Christi
College, Cambridge, Marlowe appears to have formed some connection
with the Elizabethan secret service; university authorities hesitating to
grant his degree because of his absences from Cambridge were reassured
by a letter from the Privy Council explaining that Marlowe had been
about matters of benefit to the country. On taking his degree Marlowe
went to London, where his plays were an immediate success, but he
seems to have kept up some rather dubious connections through the rest
of his short life.

Marlowe was one of a group of writers whom literary historians have
since labeled the "university wits," having in common not only a certain
amount of higher education but the ability to earn a living with their
pens—or a living of sorts, rather, for penury often prevailed. Thomas
Lodge, of Trinity College, Oxford, is usually included in this group; his
fictional works included *Rosalynde*, the source of Shakespeare's *As You
Like It*. Lodge, however, sought greener financial pastures than the new
profession of free-lance writing could promise, eventually taking an Oxford degree in medicine and settling down as a respected physician.

Two university wits who found a relatively refined audience were
John Lyly, a graduate of Magdalen College, Oxford, whose *Euphues*

stories were filled with rhetorical devices and classical allusions; and George Peele, of Christ Church, Oxford, whose plays were well received at court. Peele was a versatile writer, as he also produced scripts for the popular stage, the Lord Mayor's show, and other City spectacles.

Among the less financially successful of the university wits were two graduates of St. John's College, Cambridge, Robert Greene and Thomas Nashe. Both developed quick reflexes as they supplied the reading public of the 1590s with whatever literary commodity they thought would sell. Greene wrote pastoral romances (among them *Pandosto,* a source for Shakespeare's *The Winter's Tale*) and then moved on to realistic sketches such as the "cony catching" pamphlets, warning newcomers to London of the traps set for the unwary. Greene's last works took a confessional turn, describing and perhaps exaggerating the dissipations of his and his friends' lives. Thomas Nashe, an associate of Greene's in various ink-slinging feuds, is remembered for his picaresque novel, *The Unfortunate Traveler, or the Life of Jack Wilton.* Like Greene, Nashe spent some of his time grumbling at the impertinence of upstart writers who had the impudence to come to London and write successful poems and plays, all on a mere grammar-school education and without a touch of college.

10

Literary Stereotypes: Religious, Occupational, and Regional

Stereotypes function as a kind of shorthand, conveying a complex of associated ideas in a few brief strokes. For the present-day reader, recognizing an Elizabethan stereotype usually depends on making a connection with the context in which the stereotype occurs, a connection this book attempts to further. The stereotype of the London gallant, for example, appears in the chapter dealing with his natural habitat.

The figures in the present chapter are sufficiently complex to benefit from individual attention, although naturally they have associations elsewhere. Religious stereotypes are grounded particularly in chapter 4, with its idea of a cosmic harmony echoed in man's social world. The stereotype of the lawyer may be connected with these ideas and also with education, as treated in the previous chapter; medical men are generally encountered, in literature, in the places where they practice— surgeons are called for on battlefields, for example. References to foreigners often occur in their native climes, some of which are discussed in chapter 12, below. In short, Elizabethan literature reflects an interconnected world.

Puritans in Literature

To Americans who have spent their elementary-school years drawing pictures of the Puritans welcoming the Indians to harvest festivals at

Plymouth, it is a simple matter to conjure up a literary character who has been presented under this label. A tall black hat, large shoe buckles, and an aura of rustic self-sufficiency does the job, against a background of pumpkins and wild turkeys.

The Elizabethan stereotype of the Puritan might have included the sober dress and earnest air, but the reader also catches a tone of mockery foreign to the American version. Puritans were seen in literature as figures of fun, not as founding fathers. As pointed out in chapter 4, above, the Puritans occupied the austere end of the Protestant spectrum, resisting elaboration in worship services or in daily life and inveighing against the theater as well as against many types of literature—popular journalism, for example—that they saw as either frivolous or downright harmful. Since popular stereotypes were generated by the very writers the Puritans held in low esteem, a certain lack of sympathy resulted.

Puritans were seldom depicted as downright villains, however. The typical Puritan appears as a harmless caricature, amusing because of his solemnity and self-importance. Shakespeare's Malvolio, in *Twelfth Night,* is described by Maria as "a kind of Puritan" (2.3.139), but she adds that his main flaw is his self-centeredness, as Olivia has also observed (1.5.90).

Ben Jonson does up a more detailed Puritan in *Bartholomew Fair.* Zeal-of-the-Land Busy demonstrates by his name the Puritan habit of putting doctrinal meaning into everything; as godfather to another of the characters, Busy has named her Win-the-Fight, though she is called Win and acquaintances assume she is a Winifred. Busy declaims in biblically fulsome language against the evils of the fair, and particularly against the roast pig sold there, but manages to eat quite a lot of it himself. He then overturns a gingerbread stall, decrying the decorated gingerbread-man cakes as an "idolatrous grove of images" (3.6.93), and is put in the stocks.

Another of Jonson's Puritans, Tribulation Wholesome, appears in *The Alchemist* among the victims of the rapscallion con men Face and Subtle. Puritan traits which the audience would have recognized as part of the caricature include the fact that Wholesome and his subordinate, Ananias, have taken up residence in Amsterdam, seen as a hotbed of Puritanism. "The brethren," for whose benefit Wholesome hopes to make an advantageous alchemical deal, is presumably one of the numerous small sects. Puritans tended to form quite small groups, perhaps because of their dislike of large organizations and elaborate hierarchies but also, possibly, because of their tendency to disagree on minute matters of doctrine, so that congregations were more likely to split among themselves than to unite with another body.

The name Ananias, incidentally, represents another variety of stereotyped Puritan name, the biblical but unusual. (The Bible mentions three Ananiases, minor figures, all of them in the Book of Acts.) Again, even in using a fairly familiar biblical name, Puritans were likely to choose a less familiar form of it, preferring Hannah to Anne, for example. Another method of Puritan child-naming was said to be that of opening the Bible at random and using the first name that met the eye. One "Machabyas Chylde," who married one "Edmounde Spenser," possibly the poet, in 1579, may have received her name by this means; Maccabees is a portion of the Apocrypha, and the Geneva Bible, favored by Puritans, contains it.

Spenser's Duessa and the Catholic Menace

While mainstream Elizabethans saw the Puritans as generally harmless, they took a quite different view of Roman Catholicism. Here we have, quite simply, the enemy. England was surrounded by large and often hostile Catholic countries, poised, or so it was easy to think, to unite and overthrow the English government. Then there were the English Catholics, many of them unreconciled to the new faith; Queen Mary, Elizabeth's Catholic sister, had done her best to restore England to Rome and, had she managed to give birth to an heir, might have succeeded. Since in Elizabeth's time no one knew how active this fifth column might be, a typical nightmare scenario involved a joint effort of foreign invaders and their secret supporters among the seemingly loyal English.

A focus for Catholic plots real or imagined could, for eighteen years, be found in the person of another Mary, this one the queen of Scotland, whose talent for getting into trouble had brought her to England in 1568. Escaping from the captivity into which her own nobles had put her (among other irregularities, she was suspected of having plotted with her third husband to bring about the murder of her second), Mary fled across the border to beg for refuge and found herself imprisoned instead. Here she attracted conspirators eager to push Elizabeth off the English throne and put Mary on, for as a descendant of Henry VII she could claim English as well as Scottish royal blood. In 1586, after catching Mary red-handed in a plot which had been set up to entrap her, Elizabeth's ministers brought her to trial, and she was beheaded in February of 1587.

In Spenser's *Faerie Queene,* the figure Duessa represents the concept of falsehood and also some more specific falsities. At different times she takes the role of each of these Catholic queens named Mary, as well as that of the Roman Church itself; many of the images that surround Duessa—wealth, power, jewels, and the color red—are frequently associated in Elizabethan stereotype with the Roman church.

Duessa first appears to Redcrosse, the Knight of Holiness, as a beautiful woman, and since he is in the early stages of his quest he fails to recognize her true character and is quite taken with her (1.2.13). His infatuation, however, does not survive Duessa's union with the giant Orgoglio. If Duessa here represents Mary Tudor, Orgoglio can be seen as this queen's husband, Philip II of Spain (1.7.16). Duessa then appears in the guise of the Whore of Babylon from the Book of Revelations (chapter 17), mounted on the seven-headed beast that figures therein. English Protestants frequently associated this pair with the Catholic Church. The Geneva Bible, in fact, includes a marginal note identifying the woman on the beast with "the newe Rome which is the Papistrie." Redcrosse is then thrown into prison, but eventually, with the help of the genuinely beautiful Una (representing Truth, and specifically the Church of England), he is able to see Duessa for what she is, a monstrous witch (1.9.46), and he resists her wiles thereafter.

But Duessa reappears from time to time, harassing the other characters, and in Book 5 the Knight of Justice, Artegall, is present at her final scene. Queen Elizabeth, as the allegorical figure Mercilla, presides over Spenser's version of the trial of Mary Queen of Scots, where some of the ominous practical and theoretical aspects of condemning a sovereign to death are presented. "High alliance unto forren powre" [sic] (5.9.45.6), mentioned by the figure Daunger, echoes England's fear of French or Spanish retaliation. An allegorical advocate for Duessa is the figure "Nobilitie of Birth," a reminder that the shedding of royal blood is not to be taken lightly. But Mercilla, like Elizabeth, feels the "strong constraint" of circumstances (5.10.4.6). Elizabeth and her ministers had recognized that Mary, a focus of plots domestic and foreign even when imprisoned, could not be allowed to live. Her death (and Duessa's) was inevitable.

King James and Guy Fawkes

While Guy Fawkes is not exactly a literary stereotype, he does evoke a specific complex of ideas and has, in a sense, entered the realm of folklore. He started out as a quite real person, the central figure in a 1605 Catholic plot to blow up King James and his Parliament by packing with gunpowder a cellar beneath the House of Lords. The plot was discovered just in time and the conspirators were hung. Guy Fawkes Day, November 5, still celebrates this narrow escape with fireworks, masked children begging for pennies, and bonfires in which effigies of Guy Fawkes are burned. English children grow up with several rhymes about the event, including this one:

> Remember, remember, the Fifth of November,
> Gunpowder, treason, and plot;
> I see no reason why gunpowder treason
> Should ever be forgot.

The effigy, or guy, incidentally, is usually a quite ragged and disreputable-looking object, and the term *guy* came to mean, in England, a badly dressed and grotesque person. To call an Englishman a "regular guy" can thus be the reverse of complimentary.

Jews as Seen by the English

In theory, at least, the Elizabethans did not know any Jews, for Jews had been banned from England since the late thirteenth century. There was, nevertheless, a small Jewish community in London, temporary residents in that the authorities could throw them out at any time. They were not part of the general environment, and the typical Englishman had neither a personal acquaintance with individual Jews nor any detailed knowledge of Jewish culture. Headline cases, so to speak, such as the trial and execution of Roderigo Lopez, a physician to Queen Elizabeth who was accused of plotting to poison her, simply confirmed the stereotype.

The stereotype was lurid indeed. Jews, to begin with, were already barred from spiritual salvation by their ancestors' having preferred Barabbas to Christ when Pilate offered to free one or the other (Matthew 27:21); there was thus no hope for them and they could be considered in a sense nonhuman. In the popular imagination, Jews spent most of their time kidnapping Christian children for sacrifice in secret rites. During leisure moments, they arranged loans at high interest and extorted payments from helpless victims. Each possessed piles of ill-gotten wealth which it behooved honest Christians to take away from them. And each usually possessed, as well, a beautiful daughter who wanted nothing more than to be rescued from her cultural fate by some handsome Christian.

Variations on these patterns can be found in Shakespeare's *The Merchant of Venice* and Marlowe's *The Jew of Malta*. Most present-day readers find Shylock a sympathetic character, one who rebels against the nonhuman label that society has put on him: "Hath not a Jew eyes? Hath not a Jew hands, organs, dimensions, senses, affections, passions? . . . If you prick us, do we not bleed?" (3.1.59ff.). We lack sufficient evidence to postulate Shakespeare's personal opinions on what today would be called anti-Semitism, but certainly he has sensed a rich venue for dramatic conflict. Marlowe's reminiscently named Barabas [sic] seems closer to the stereotype of pure villainy. In both plays, it is taken for granted that the state has the right to confiscate Jewish property more or less at the state's convenience. Similarly, the torture contrived for the Jewish villain Zadoch, in Thomas Nashe's *The Unfortunate Traveler*, is noteworthy not only for its ferocity—Zadoch is impaled on a spit and roasted alive—but for the narrator's tone of brisk accomplishment, seeming to take for granted that his readers are cheering the torturers on.[1]

Under Oliver Cromwell, the Puritan leader who headed the government between 1649 and 1660, Jews were allowed to settle in England with a much greater degree of safety. England's mercantile position promptly improved. What the Elizabethans had seen as the demonic and unnatural piling up of wealth, usury in all its horror, had been in fact part of an increasingly effective system of international finance.

Professional Stereotypes: Lawyers

In moments of annoyance, our cultural ancestors tended to see lawyers as a pompous, unnecessary, and even tyrannical group, dominating ordinary people with an arcane mumbo-jumbo that might well contain less than met the eye. Thus a follower of Shakespeare's Jack Cade suggests, "The first thing we do, let's kill all the lawyers" (*2 Henry VI*, 4.2.76), a proposal to which Cade assents at once. (This quotation presumably strikes some chord among Americans today, as it has been seen emblazoned on a canvas tote bag for sale at the Folger Shakespeare Library.)

The law in Elizabethan times was a major avenue for the advancement of bright young men. Money as well as prestige were available; J. H. Baker points out that "at the top of the profession, a leading advocate or a senior court official in 1600 could earn as much as £1,000 a year, enough to build a great house such as Montacute or Blickling, enough indeed to join the ranks of the nobility and found a dynasty."[2]

Lawyers in literature are sometimes pictured as stirring up or encouraging controversy. "Lawyers seek out still / Litigious men, which quarrels move, / Though she and I do love," John Donne remarks in "The Canonization." (Donne, incidentally, had had a legal education.) Shakespeare's Rosalind implies that lawyers are one-track creatures, doing either their work or nothing; time, she says, stands still "with lawyers in the vacation; for they sleep between term and term" (*As You Like It*, 3.2.331–32). Portia, however, in *The Merchant of Venice*, represents law in the best of lights, as the means of correcting injustice and restoring truth.

Students at the Inns of Court

In order to become a barrister and enter the upper echelons of the legal profession, training at the Inns of Court in London was essential. These institutions—the Inner Temple, the Middle Temple, Lincoln's Inn, and Grey's Inn, housed in venerable gothic buildings beside the Thames—provided libraries, lectures, and such exercises as "moot courts," in which students argued set cases for practice. Students also had access to the actual cases being heard in the law courts of Westminster Palace.

There were no entrance requirements specifying a degree from or attendance at any other university, though it was generally agreed that seventeen years was a minimum age for entrance. Students had often spent two or three years at Oxford or Cambridge before enrolling; as we have seen, higher education began quite early by our standards. Latin would have been a necessity at most stages of schooling and certainly at the Inns of Court, since legal proceedings and records were carried on in the traditional tongue.

John Stow, in his *Survey of London* (1603), says that the barristers-to-be spent "seven years or thereabouts" at their learned exercises, "whereby growing ripe in the knowledge of the laws"[3] they were called to the bar, as our own idiom still puts it, and allowed to plead cases in the courts.

Law students, even if hard-working, had their recreative moments and particularly liked plays. Records indicate that the *Comedy of Errors* was performed at Grey's Inn in 1594 and *Twelfth Night* at the Middle Temple in 1602. Somewhat less respectable amusements figure in the memory of Justice Shallow in the second part of *Henry IV*; his and Falstaff's sojourn at Clement's Inn seems to have focused on brawling with the neighborhood apprentices and frequenting houses of ill repute (3.2).

Clement's Inn, incidentally, was not one of the four main Inns of Court devoted to training barristers but a sort of preparatory school with a special connection with Lincoln's Inn, its "big brother" school, in a sense. Attending one of these subordinate "inns of chancery," as they were called, did not obligate one to go on to a higher level, and many students came simply to spend a few years in London and pick up some useful information.

The Justices of the Peace

Since American associations with justices of the peace usually have to do either with getting married or paying traffic fines, perhaps it should be noted at once that the Elizabethan version does not entirely fit this picture. Weddings took place only in churches, and traffic in the modern sense of torrents of automobiles had not been invented.

The typical justice of the peace in Elizabethan England was so familiar a figure that the literary stereotype was immediately recognized. In the "seven ages of man" speech in *As You Like It*, Shakespeare describes, tongue in cheek and with an eye to the essential comedy of role-playing, "the justice,"

> *In fair round belly with good capon lin'd,*
> *With eyes severe and beard of formal cut,*
> *Full of wise saws and modern instances.*

(2.7.153–56)

Justice Shallow, a more complete sketch, is probably a bit more fuddy-duddy than the average real-life counterpart, but his failings are human and familiar, and his heart is in the right place. When duty requires him to provide soldiers for the king, he sincerely wants to get the best available and does not understand Falstaff's profit-making shenanigans (3.2.-). But unlike the Lord Chief Justice in the same play, who is considerably closer to the ideal of justice, Shallow is not above a bit of partiality. His servant, Davy, hopes that Shallow will deal leniently with one William Visor, Davy's friend, whose offense is not specified but whose name puts him in a suspicious light; a "visor" can be a vizard or mask. Visor, Davy admits, is an arrant knave, but he is the more in need of mercy, for "an honest man, sir, is able to speak for himself, when a knave is not" (5.1.46).

The justice of the peace filled a variety of functions—officiating at petty sessions as well as quarter sessions, sitting on the boards that licensed alehouses, and performing other chores so numerous that a handbook of their duties became a best seller.[4] Except for a small wage for attending quarter sessions, the justice served without pay, a demonstration of the Elizabethan commitment to an orderly society—or, perhaps, in view of the stereotype's tinge of pomposity, a demonstration of the human fondness for dressing oneself in a little brief authority.

Despite the justice's function as part of the law of the land, no specific legal training was required. Many incumbents, like Justice Shallow, happened to have spent some time at one of the Inns of Court, but this experience was more or less a coincidence.

Medical Practitioners

The literary stereotypes of the medical profession fall into three categories, as did the practitioners themselves. These were the physicians, who at one point in their history were forbidden to shed blood; the surgeons, who might shed any quantity of it; and the apothecaries, chiefly concerned with medicines.

Physicians were at the top of the status ladder, and in literature they sometimes appeared as genuinely wise and effective; Helena's father, for example, in *Measure for Measure* has left his daughter a valuable "receipt" (2.1.104–9) with which she is able to cure the king. (The fact that this cure has been kept secret and has not been announced to the world sometimes disturbs present-day readers, but secrecy was quite within the ethical norm of the typical Renaissance physician.)

On the other hand, physicians were sometimes seen as overly concerned with money, not an unfamiliar charge today. The doctor in *Macbeth*, after witnessing not only Lady Macbeth's sleepwalking episode but the decline in Macbeth's kingly prospects, regrets his own presence at the castle:

Were I from Dunsinane away and clear,
Profit again should hardly draw me here.

(5.3.61–62)

Physicians held a degree in medicine from either Oxford or Cambridge, during the pursuit of which they immersed themselves in the works of Hippocrates and Galen, Greek authorities of the fifty century B.C. and first century A.D., respectively, and they became learned in astrology, a subject then taken quite seriously. The works they studied were either written in Latin or translated into it from the original tongue. This requirement in itself was not a sign of stagnation within the discipline, for Latin was the language that reached the widest audience of learned readers; the most up-to-date medical treatises were written in it. Nevertheless, particularly in England, the prestige of ancient tradition held sway, and physicians were not encouraged to experiment. Students who wanted more advanced training often went abroad. William Harvey, for example, who in the early seventeenth century discovered the true nature of the circulation of the blood, had studied anatomy at the University of Padua.

On taking his degree, the Elizabethan physician was examined by the Royal College of Physicians, a regulating body which served the function of a guild although it projected a more elitist aura, and, if he passed, licensed to practice.

It had been during their medieval association with the Church that physicians had been forbidden to shed blood, and the traditional proscription continued. Physicians thus limited their endeavors to diagnosing disease (often after consulting the patient's horoscope) and prescribing remedies. Both diagnosis and cure were often based on the doctrine of the traditional "four humors," in which the human body is said to be compounded of phlegm, black bile, yellow bile, and blood; disease results when these ingredients get out of balance, and remedies must be devised to restore the right proportions. Literary references to physicians and to diseases often include allusions to the humors as well as to the assumption that sickness and health are determined by the stars. (Another familiar literary stereotype, the astrologer, was often presented in a more questionable light than was the physician, as possessing greater potential for fraud. Astrologers might gain individual followings, as many of them did, but they did not possess a recognized society or guild, they did not regulate themselves or require any specific training, and they could not draw on any collective dignity as a body.)

Beneath the physician in status was the surgeon, whose trade had evolved in conjunction with that of barbering; both callings make use of sharp-edged tools and handy basins. In the early sixteenth century, barbers and surgeons formed a corporation, "The Masters or Governors of the Mystery or Communality of Barbers and Surgeons of London"; a painting by Holbein commemorates Henry VIII's granting of a charter to this group.

The surgeon's job, which he learned by serving an apprenticeship rather than by attending college lectures or reading books, included splinting broken bones, bandaging wounds, and digging out arrowheads and bullets; surgeons and barbers seem to have shared between them the chore of pulling teeth. Operations which involved opening the body cavities were seldom attempted because the age knew neither anesthetics nor antiseptics, and success was unlikely. Amputations of arms or legs were performed on fully conscious patients. Because surgeons often had to work under makeshift emergency conditions, they sometimes made accidental but useful discoveries. A French surgeon, for example, Ambroise Paré, ran out of boiling oil while dressing battle wounds and discovered that turpentine (at room temperature) worked much better.

The literary stereotype of the surgeon was not a particularly detailed or vivid one, perhaps a surprising fact in view of the possibilities for melodramatic gore. Surgeons are mentioned rather offhandedly in scenes of physical violence. Cassio calls for one when Iago stirs up a street brawl in Cyprus (*Othello*, 5.1.30), as does Sir Andrew when Sir Toby is attacked by the person thought to be Caesario (*Twelfth Night*, 5.1.172).

John Earle, in his *Micro-Cosmographie*, sees the surgeon as a mercenary figure with no sympathy for the regulation of violence, as he "sighs for the flashing age of sword and buckler, and thinks the law against duels was made merely to wound his vocation . . . his envy is never stirred so much as when gentlemen go over to fight upon Calais sands, whom he wishes drowned ere they come there, rather than the French shall get his custom."[5]

Apothecaries were socially the lowest of the three categories, although the unfortunate specimen appearing in *Romeo and Juliet* (5.1) would seem to be well below the usual standard. (This character was not supposed to be English in any case.) Under Henry VIII, apothecaries were recognized in 1543 as practicing a specific trade, and in the early seventeenth century they shared a guild for some time with the grocers before becoming a separate corporation in 1617. Like the surgeons, they were trained through apprenticeships rather than through some more academic method. Despite their low social status, apothecaries could do quite well, especially if they dealt in tobacco as well as medicines.

Regional and Foreign Stereotypes

Literary characters created for an English-speaking audience must themselves speak English, if the story is to make any progress, so that an author can make only limited use of dialect and foreign languages. The pronunciation used by Shakespeare's Welshmen is indicated in the texts by a substitution of unvoiced for voiced consonants; Fluellen claims that Pistol uttered "as prave words at the pridge as you shall see in a summer's day" (*Henry V,* 3.6.63). Jamy, the Scot, in the same play, and Macmorris, the Irishman, similarly advertise their origins by an occasional dialectical twist. "It sall be vary gud, gud feith, gud captens bath," says Jamy (3.2.102), while Macmorris, annoyed with the world, complains "the town is beseech'd, and the trumpet call us to the breach, and we talk, and be Chrish, do nothing. 'Tis shame for us all" (3.2.107–9). Presumably the actors simply used these hints to produce the regional accent required, taking care to make their lines intelligible to the London audience. It is noteworthy that this particular group—Fluellen, Jamy, and Macmorris—represents the use of regional stereotypes to demonstrate an ultimate solidarity within what the present-day reader sees as an English army, rather than merely to make fun of speech and customs different from the supposed norm.

Doctor Caius, in *The Merry Wives of Windsor,* partakes energetically of the standard stereotyped English view of the Frenchman—excitable, ungrammatical, and, of course, not as irresistible to women as he thinks he is. Like many French characters in Elizabethan literature, he sometimes lapses into his native tongue, suggesting that some proportion of the audience understood the language. This was no doubt the case; however, Caius's French lines become intelligible in context, and he sometimes translates them himself. On eloping with quite the wrong person, he exclaims that he has married "oon garsoon, a boy" (5.5.205). We do not see Caius in a professional role, no one happening to need a physician, but relative to the other characters he is of sufficiently high social status for Mistress Page to consider him an eligible suitor for her daughter, Anne.

Another stereotype, that of the Moor, was a more ominous figure. Moors, unlike Frenchmen, were not part of the familiar Elizabethan scene, and their precise identity is open to question. Ancient writers of history spoke of the natives of Mauritania, in northern Africa, as Moors, and the name was given to the Islamic North African people, partly Arab, who conquered Spain in the eighth century and were driven out, after long and complicated struggles, in the fifteenth. In Elizabethan times a Moor was assumed to have a dark skin, but some variation obtained in further details. Hair and facial features are sometimes described as Arabic, sometimes as Negroid. Shakespeare's Othello would seem to belong to the latter group, as his skin is described not just as black but as "sooty" (1.2.70), and his lips as "thick" (1.1.66). Othello appears to the audience in a positive light—or more positive, at least, than many of his fellow Moors; Aaron, for example, in *Titus Andronicus,* is a zestfully remorseless villain, though he does show loyalty to his own flesh and blood. Jaques and Zanche, Moors in Webster's *The White Devil,* are servants, abettors of dubious doings, and the duke of Florence eventually disguises himself as an Othello-like Moor of military experience. Throughout Elizabethan literature, the stereotype of the Moor appears as an unknown entity, the dark side of the globe in a sense, a power which even if temporarily subordinated within some more familiar social order nevertheless belongs to a world of its own—less immediately alarming than the world of Catholicism because farther away, but a disquieting and challenging presence just the same.

11

Outsiders: Witches, Criminals, and Vagabonds

That a society so aware of beauty, so eager to debate the principles of religion and justice, and so confident in pursuing a vision of harmonious social order should at the same time have been so indifferent to the sufferings of a sizable proportion of the individuals within that society astonishes not only present-day Americans but present-day Englishmen as well. Empathy, like religious toleration, has come a long way.

Some justification, even if slight, may perhaps be found for the harshness with which the Elizabethans treated those who, through choice or through circumstances, found themselves outside the approved patterns of behavior. Civilization was still thin on the ground, after all. Many criminals went uncaught, a factor influencing the harshness with which the caught ones were punished. Again, with regard to the more innocent victims of poverty and a changing economy, we cannot help noticing that our own society has not succeeded in determining, to the satisfaction of all concerned, precisely what is to be done about vagrants or the mentally ill, for example, and precisely who is to do it. Nor have we risen entirely over the temptation to find and persecute a convenient scapegoat when things go wrong—to conduct a witch-hunt, in short.

Witches in the Courts of Law

The majority of accused witches in England, as elsewhere, were old women, poor and helpless, likely to beg a piece of bread or borrow small

156

sums of money. Recent studies, among them Alan Macfarlane's *Witch-craft in Tudor and Stuart England,* suggest that accusations of witchcraft rose during hard times, when relationships between neighbors became strained;[1] a villager who turned down an old woman's request for help might suspect her of having vengefully caused the next misfortune that happened to occur.

Compared to their counterparts in Scotland and on the Continent, English witches seem to have lived rather unexciting lives. The testimony produced against them did not ordinarily include membership in a coven, sexual encounters with the Devil, flying through the air, or attending witches' sabbats; this agenda belongs to the more melodramatic European pattern. English witches, according to the accusations, contented themselves with killing their neighbors' cows, deforming children's toes, or causing trees to fall on barns.

If she were brought before a Church court rather than a court of common law, the witch would meet a gentler punishment and would have some chance of escaping even that. The Church courts dealt with only the less serious cases of witchcraft in which no death or serious injury were involved. If the alleged witch denied the accusation, she would usually be ordered to "purge" herself, to bring in three or four neighbors to swear to the truth of her denial. Should these neighbors turn out to be on her side, the accused witch would be let off at once. If the witnesses substantiated the accusation, however, she would be condemned to some form of public penance. Typically, she would have to appear in church wearing a white sheet, to declare her repentance and ask the forgiveness of God and her fellow parishioners.

A sterner fate awaited women brought before the courts of common law. Here witchcraft was categorized as a felony, and almost all felonies carried the death penalty. Records indicate, however, that a sizable proportion of defendants were found not guilty, or, if found guilty, were pardoned. Also, the courts often made a distinction between a first and second conviction. A first conviction might carry a penalty of a year's imprisonment, with periodic six-hour ordeals of standing in the pillory; a second conviction usually brought the death penalty.

Unless the crime of witchcraft were combined with some other charge, such as petty treason, which carried with it the punishment of death at the stake, condemned English witches in the sixteenth and seventeenth centuries were hanged, not burned. Oddly, however, even

at this time Englishmen persisted in assuming that their witches went
up in smoke. Macfarlane quotes several contemporary illustrations of
this popular belief and suggests a lingering memory of medieval times,
when witches were categorized as heretics rather than felons and were
sent to the stake.[2] This situation still obtained in many parts of Europe,
and Englishmen who followed news from abroad may have assumed that
their own country had not changed. Literature may have been another
cause of error in this regard. Joan of Arc, burned in France in 1431
under legal circumstances quite different from those in force in sixteenth-
century England, figured in, among other works known to the Elizabethan public, the second part of Shakespeare's *Henry VI*.

Specialists in Witch Lore: Scott, King James, and Hopkins

Three men with an interest in the subject—in chronological order, a
sixteenth-century country squire and member of Parliament, a sovereign
of Scotland and England, and a seventeenth-century entrepreneur—left
writings which give the present-day reader an idea of what a witch-
believing atmosphere is like.

Reginald Scott (or Scot), whose *Discoverie of Witchcraft* was published in 1584, wrote in defense of reason and justice, and in sympathy
with the many victims who, he felt, were falsely accused. To make his
point, he turned his book into a compendium of murky superstitions,
bizarre logic, and stomach-turning examination methods. To make sure,
for example, that the Devil was not protecting the allgeged witch from
pain, sharp instruments might be thrust beneath her fingernails. While
this inspection was being carried out, Scott adds, the examiners might
make "semblance of great a doo," bringing in manacles and instruments
of torture, and producing someone to make "lamentable shrieks" in the
next room.[3]

As Scott points out, such techniques could hardly produce a reliable
result. "How can she, in the middest of such horrible tortures and torments, promise unto herself constancy or forbear to confess anything?
Or what availeth it her, to persevere in the denial of such matters, as
are laid to her charge unjustly; when on the one side there is never any

end to her torments; on the other side, if she continue in her assertion, they say she hath charms for taciturnity and silence?"[4]

Scott did not entirely repudiate the idea of witches or devils, particularly since these beings were mentioned in the Bible. He felt, however, that the Scriptures are not very precise about them and that we should not take upon ourselves to invent details.

Meanwhile, far to the north, an authoritative figure with a firm belief in witches and in his duty to protect his subjects from them was going about his business. King James, who on ascending the English throne in 1603 ordered Scott's book burned, in 1597 wrote a book of his own, *Daemonology,* in which he argued that devilish arts do exist and that they merit severe punishment. In the form of a dialogue between "Philomathes" and "Epistemon," the book describes witches making contracts with the Devil, flying to distant places, and attending unholy gatherings. Scotland, as the reader will realize, was plugged into the more dramatic European tradition of witchcraft.

Epistemon, King James's voice of authority, claims that "who denieth the power of the Devil, would likewise deny the power of God," and explains to his more naive friends that women are more likely than men to succumb to occult temptation; "that sex is frailer than man is, so is it easier to be entrapped in these gross snares of the Devil, as was over all proved to be true, by the Serpent's deceiving of Eva."[5] Asked what form of punishment is suitable, Epistemon replies that "they ought to be put to death according to the Law of God, the civil and imperial law, and municipal law of all Christian nations"—a weighty assemblage. Fire is appropriate, Epistemon adds, but the method does not matter as long as the job gets done.

King James did more than theorize. Several years earlier, he sat in on some of the examinations of one "Dr. Fian" (or Fiennes), a schoolmaster accused of evil practices, and his accessory witches, a case described in the anonymous *Newes from Scotland,* published in 1591. The witches seem to have done most of the work. They sailed the sea in a sieve, kissed the Devil's buttocks, christened a cat (the name they chose is not recorded), and above all cast spells against the king himself—"the greatest enemy he hath in the world," as the Devil is supposed to have specified.[6] The king must have found all this quite riveting. "The said christened cat," bound to portions of a human body and then deposited in the sea outside Edinburgh, caused several marine misfortunes, including the wreck of a boat arriving with "sundry jewels and rich gifts" for the new queen of Scotland, Anne of Denmark. The cat, or its spirit presumably, also caused a contrary wind to buffet a ship on which the king himself was traveling, but to no avail; as one of the accused witches explained, the king's faith was strong enough to prevail over his attackers' best efforts.

Dr. Fian, the alleged ringleader in these doings, refused to confess and was tortured, a standard process under Scottish law at the time. When needles thrust under his fingernails had no effect, the nails were torn off, and finally his feet were put into the infamous "boot" and crushed, "that the blood and marrow spouted forth in great abundance." *Newes from Scotland* specifies that Fian was strangled and then burned; his followers are last heard of in prison "till further trial, and knowledge of his majesty's pleasure."

Not surprisingly in view of King James's post-1603 influence, England in the seventeenth century became increasingly conscious of the witch menace. The religious upheaval of the civil wars gave further scope for extremist views. England's only professional witch-hunter, Mathew Hopkins, followed his trade in the troubled 1640s; thus he did not directly influence the literature with which we are chiefly concerned in this book. Hopkins's directions for identifying witches often relied on folklore, however, which would have been known to earlier authors and their readers.

Hopkins's handbook, *The Discovery of Witches,* is in the tradition of similar treatises which had appeared in Europe considerably earlier. The *Malleus maleficarum* ("Witches' Hammer"), written by two Dominican friars, Heinrich Kraemer and Johann Sprenger, was published in the late fifteenth century. Here the relationship between witches and the Devil, complete with sex, was codified and detailed. A section of questions and answers was included for the convenience of inquisitors who, while the victims were under torture, might read out the questions and await the expected answers.

Hopkins's book is based on his experiences as he traveled from town to town, charging the municipal authorities twenty shillings to purify the premises, rather like an exterminator in search of termites. Hopkins's methods followed a standard pattern. Suspects who refused to confess were kept awake for days and nights at a time; they were walked (or run) about by their examiners; finally, in a triumph of unreason, their thumbs and toes were bound and they were thrown into the nearest pond. Suspects who floated were thought to have been aided by the Devil, and their guilt was assumed. Suspects who did not float were fished out and attempts were made, not always successfully, to revive them.

Hopkins's victims confessed to a considerable range of demonic familiars, mostly taking the form of domestic animals, with colorful names—"Sack and Sugar," and "Griezzell Greedigutt." Names like these, said Hopkins, are proof of dealings with demons, for no mortal mind could have invented them.

Hopkins's victims are variously estimated at between forty and seventy in number, mostly women but a few men. One of the latter was a vicar nearly eighty years of age who was allowed to read his own burial office before being hanged. It was another vicar, one John Gaule, who brought about Hopkins's end. Although, he said, he himself believed in witchcraft, Hopkins went too far. "Every old woman," proclaimed Gaule in a published sermon, "with a wrinkled face . . . a squint eye, a squeaking voice, or a scolding tongue, having . . . a spindle in her hand, and a dog or cat by her side, is not only suspected but pronounced for a witch."[7] According to one story, a movement was set afoot to test Hopkins by his own criteria; he failed, floating ignominiously about the pond, and was subsequently hanged.

Witches in Literature

The matter of trafficking with demons was taken seriously in literature as well as in life, as Marlowe's *Dr. Faustus* illustrates. Many in the original audience would have seen Faustus's act of bargaining away his soul and his eventual departure for hell as a stark piece of spiritual reality despite the play's comic scenes.

Female witches in Elizabethan literature overlap occasionally with other stereotypes of romance, such as the beautiful but wicked enchantress. Spenser's Duessa and Acrasia fall respectively into this category. Duessa has numerous overlapping identities with the allegory; she represents falsehood, particularly religious falsehood, and is able to change both her own appearance and that of others, at one point turning two characters into trees (1.2.42). Acrasia, a figure of intemperance, is something of a Circe type, inhabiting a magical island and transforming her lovers into animals when she tires of them (2.12.85).

A more everyday Spenserian witch is the old hag in Book 3 with whom Florimel takes refuge from her constant pursuers. This witch, with her son, lives in a little cottage, built of sticks and sod, apart from her neighbors; the narrator explains that her isolation is of her own choosing, as she does not wish her neighbors to know of her "divelish deedes / And hellish arts" (3.6.7–8). Unlike Duessa and Acrasia in their elegant attire, the old woman is dressed in rags, thus demonstrating the paradox inherent in the so-called witches of real English villages; if she's so powerful, one wants to ask, why isn't she rich? Ragged or not, once her devilish arts are in gear, Spenser's witch contributes to both the allegory and the romance plot, sending a baleful beast after the fleeting Florimel and, once it is plain Florimel has escaped, contriving a substitute out of snow, mercury, and other curious ingredients (3.8.6).

Another group of recognizable witches is the crew in *Macbeth*, who, like much else in the play, seem calculated to interest King James. These witches' prophecies are closely connected with events in the plot, but their side activities also give them a special authenticity. Their familiar spirits—Graymalkin, Paddock, Harpier—are mentioned without explanation, and the witches pass their time doing everyday witchy things. "Killing swine," says one, asked where she has been (3.1.2). In line with Maclane's hypothesis about the kind of events which precipitated accusations of witchcraft, we could assume the swine belong to a person who has refused some request. Similarly, a sailor's wife who munched roasted chestnuts but drove away the witch who cried "Give me" has brought upon her husband the gloomy fate of being drained "dry as hay" (1.3.18). To carry out this errand, the witch plans to use that means of supernatural transport of which King James is already aware, a sieve.

The Witch of Edmonton, by Rowley, Dekker, and Ford, was produced in 1621, shortly after the execution of Elizabeth Sawyer, the witch of the title; her real name is used in the play. Elizabeth Sawyer seems to have been a quite typical case. She was old, poor, and isolated, and it is her neighbor's assumption that she must be a witch that teaches her how to act the part. Once she has got the idea, she quite enjoys it. Revenge after years of humiliation clearly has its sweet side. Her familiar spirit, "Black Dog," played by a human actor, first appears after she curses a landowner who has beaten her for trespassing and gathering sticks for fuel. Since for the most part he is invisible to others, Black Dog might be interpreted as a hallucination, were it not for the awkward fact that one of the comic characters accidentally calls him up. Elizabeth Sawyer's crimes include striking horses lame, preventing butter from coming in the churn, and through her evil arts inciting a man to murder his wife—or, rather, one of his wives, for the plot is a complicated one. Dekker, who is usually credited with having written the witch portions, has done so with sharp psychological insight and a good deal of sympathy.

Criminals: Traitors, Felons, and Others

Although present-day readers find it hard to include these alleged witches, a group which by our standards is automatically innocent of the charges made against them, in a category with criminals who may have actually done their deeds, to the Elizabethans and Jacobeans a malefactor was a malefactor. Crimes were classified as treason, felonies (including many witchcraft cases), and misdemeanors, the large-scale division still current in America today.

The crime of treason included a much wider range of misdoings than Americans would tend to recognize. Our Constitution finds treason in "levying war against them [the United States], or in adhering to their enemies, giving them aid and comfort"—a fairly straightforward prohibition, though "aid and comfort" can have flexible interpretations. By contrast, English tradition stressed loyalty to the monarch in person, rather than to the abstract idea of a nation, though the latter concept was not entirely absent. "High treason," the offense we will examine here, thus had a large scope. It was treasonous to rape the queen; treasonous to counterfeit coin. Since the sovereign was defender of the faith, adherence to the wrong religion or to atheistic doctrines might also be considered treasonous. And, since the official view of what was right and wrong in religion was subject to change, so were the details of what was or was not treasonous. Subjects had to keep up to date.

The term *petty treason,* incidentally, labels a different category of crime and does not have to do directly with the sovereign, although there is a connection by way of hierarchical patterns. Petty (or petit) treason consists of harming a person to whom one owes obedience, as a wife to her husband, or a servant to his employer. For a wife to kill her husband was considered particularly heinous, and the punishment often assigned (though usually commuted to hanging) was burning at the stake. The term *treason* when used alone usually refers to high treason, as we shall use it here.

A felony might be loosely defined as a crime carrying the death penalty, ranging from murder down to some rather minor forms of theft. The category of misdemeanors, not usually punishable by death, included among many possibilities using false measures in selling wheat, disturbing the peace, and a variety of acts or conditions which in themselves did no harm to society but which the authorities felt would lead to worse things. Vagabonds, for example, were viewed as thieves in embryo if not in fact.

Treason and Torture

Since treason was at least theoretically the worst crime one could commit, persons condemned for it or even only suspected of it were treated more harshly than other prisoners. There are two kinds of exceptions here. Members of the nobility sometimes lived relatively comfortable lives, their prison cells furnished with fireplaces and books, until the day they mounted the scaffold. And a few traitors were pardoned by the crown—young and naive counterfeiters, for example, or people who had only followed in a revolt led by somebody else.

In examining a treason suspect, especially a suspect thought to be part of a conspiracy against the sovereign's person, torture might be used to extract information such as the names of coconspirators or details of the alleged plot. It was the king's authority, in person or as exercised through the Privy Council, which permitted this departure from the standard way of doing things. Torture was not ordinarily a part of English common law; even with regard to treason, it was used only to force out information and not assigned as a punishment once the criminal was convicted. (From the perspective of the accused, of course, this difference might seem academic.)

The Tower of London specialized in political prisoners and it was here that torture was more or less taken for granted. The rack seems to have been the favorite instrument. This contrivance was a horizontal frame within which the prisoner was placed, with ropes attached to his wrists and ankles. The ropes were wound around cylindrical rollers at each end of the frame. When the rollers were turned, the prisoner might eventually be pulled apart at his joints, though he usually chose to cooperate with his examiners before this happened. The rack's advantage was that the pain could be applied gradually, allowing the victim to sense what was coming and to decide that he might as well talk now as later. The tension of the ropes might be held at any point by means of ratchets; thus the technician operating the machinery could be sent out of the room while the examiners, privileged to deal in state secrets, took down the prisoner's words.

The playwright Thomas Kyd was racked in 1593 after supposedly atheistic papers denying the deity of Christ were found in his possession. Kyd claimed the papers had been left with him by Christopher Marlowe, his roommate at an earlier point. In this case the racking process does not seem to have been severe enough to cause permanent disability, although Kyd did die the following year. Marlowe's mysterious death occurred only a few weeks after Kyd's arrest; the connection, if any, is unknown.

In literary references, the rack usually implies a slow and excruciating pain in which the victim feels helpless. Othello's cry to Iago, as the latter describes Desdemona's supposed betrayal, is, "Avaunt! be gone! thou has set me on the rack" (3.3.335). And as other characters try to revive the dying King Lear, Kent says,

> Vex not his ghost. O, let him pass, he hates him
> That would upon the rack of this tough world
> Stretch him out longer.

(5.3.314–16)

Treason and the Death Penalty

High-ranking traitors might sometimes be granted a privileged execution, so to speak—to be beheaded rather than hanged, and to undergo this process in relative privacy. For ordinary traitors, whose fate was intended to edify the onlookers and dissuade them from similar careers, a higher quotient of both gore and publicity was in order. Executions for treason, however, seem to have been less often treated as large-scale public events than executions for felony, though this effect of moderation may result simply from the fact that there were not so many of them.

The usual sentence called for the condemned traitor to be "hanged, drawn, and quartered." Women were exempt from the drawing and quartering part, presumably on grounds of feminine delicacy, and the official alternative was for them to be burnt instead. (Burning was associated with heresy, an offense akin to treason if church and state were considered one.) Usually, however, women condemned for treason were simply hanged, without elaboration.

Part one of the three-part masculine program, hanging, might or might not actually extinguish the prisoner's life. The design of the gallows did not allow a long, fast drop that would instantly break the prisoner's neck, and death came instead through strangulation. If the authorities overseeing the process wished to be merciful, they might let the prisoner hang long enough to get pretty thoroughly dead, or even order the executioner or a member of the crowd to pull on the prisoner's legs and hurry things along. To be in accord with the spirit of the sentence, however, the prisoner was cut down only partially strangled and still conscious.

After taking him down from the gallows, the executioner cut off the prisoner's genitals, an act intended to symbolize, according to John Bellamy, that the traitor's issue "was disinherited with corruption of blood."[8] Drawing, the next step, involved slitting the abdomen, removing the intestines, and finally cutting out the heart. An occasional prisoner remained conscious, talking or praying, until his heart was removed, still beating. Several of the Catholic priests executed under Queen Elizabeth astonished the crowds with their endurance to this point, and one wonders if the effect of their deaths may have been the opposite of that intended. The head was cut off, finally, and shown to the crowd.

The prisoner being now completely dead, his heart and entrails were burned, symbolically purging his disloyal thoughts and deeds. Finally, the body was cut into quarters to be exhibited in various public places. The head was also an important showpiece, and most municipalities had a special place for displaying them. Claes Janszoon de Visscher's famous engraving of London in the early seventeenth century shows the southern gateway to London Bridge bristling with traitor's heads impaled on poles.

Appalling as a condemned traitor's death might be, there were other aspects of his end which might serve as a further deterrent to friends, family, or undetected coconspirators. Chief among these was the fact that a condemned traitor's property, or large portions of it, became forfeit to the Crown. This provision impaired any revenge the traitors' families might have gone in for, as they were now impoverished, and of course it strengthened the sovereign's position. If a condemned traitor's property were hard to get at, Parliament might pass a special act of attainder clearing the way. There were even cases in which property was seized by act of attainder as soon as the suspect was indicted for treason; should he be acquitted after all, there was no requirement that the Crown return what it had taken.

Finally, not all forms of treason were considered equally dire. If one had harmed one's sovereign not by plotting against his or her life but merely by spreading scandal, say, the wheels of justice might turn more gently, and one might only have a bit of one's tongue nipped off. Persons who had not originated traitorous acts but had merely followed along might also get away with their lives while their leaders suffered the fuller penalty. The 400 or so followers of Sir Thomas Wyatt (son of the poet) in his rebellion against Queen Mary begged for pardon by kneeling before the queen, each with a noose tied around his neck. The queen was sufficiently touched by this spectacle to pardon the followers, though Wyatt, needless to say, was executed.

Felonies, Public Hangings, and the Pillory

Murder, piracy, theft of horses or cattle, and highway robbery are among the many offenses categorized in the sixteenth and seventeenth centuries as felonies. William Harrison in his *Description of England* adds some others. "Carrying horses or mares into Scotland," for example, reflects the military situation; Scottish horses were generally smaller than English ones, and the English authorities wanted to keep their advantage. "Hunting by night with painted faces and visors," "rape, or stealing of women and maidens," and "embezzling of goods

committed by the master to the servant above the value of forty shillings"
also come under this varied heading.[9]

Most felonies were punishable by death, although, as we will see,
there were some loopholes. Harsh penalties were thought necessary on
the ground that a small proportion of criminals were actually caught,
and the risk of loss of life would presumably discourage criminals before
they started. Both these principles seem questionable. A person who
steals out of desperation is unlikely to spend a great deal of energy
calculating the risks, and there are no reliable statistics on how many
criminals were not caught. Nevertheless, Elizabethans and Jacobeans
perceived themselves as living in the midst of great lawlessness, about
which something had to be done.

In line with the educational aim of punishment, the hanging of felons
usually took place before a large crowd. London especially was famous
for hangings. Throngs lined the streets, including tradesmen and their
apprentices who had taken the day off, and others came for the sake not
only of the spectacle but of the crowd itself. Fruit- and gingerbread-
sellers could count on a good day, as could pickpockets; if it had been
theft which brought the accused to the gallows, the deterrence theory
might be said to be disproved on the spot. Other vendors offered ballads
describing the crime in rough-and-ready verse, with woodcut illustrations. These ballads sometimes included the condemned man's last words
on the scaffold—needless to say, a creative act on the part of the ballad's
author. The author may in fact have recited his work directly to the
compositors setting up type in the print shop the night before; the hanging usually followed the trial very speedily, leaving little time for entre-
preneurial preparation.

In London, most hangings took place at Tyburn, outside the city
walls, at what is now the northeast corner of Hyde Park, near Marble
Arch and the Speaker's Corner. Here, for the more than merely routine
hangings, bleachers were put up and seats sold for prices varying according to the notoriety of the star attraction. The gallows itself was a
large horizontal beam, stoutly supported, somewhat resembling a goal-
post in American football except that the vertical supports did not extend
into the air. The cart in which the one or more prisoners had taken their
last ride was brought underneath the beam so that the ropes might easily
be adjusted about the prisoners' necks.

Prisoners often made speeches from the cart. The authorities encouraged this sort of thing provided the theme was repentance, as it often was, though sometimes the prisoner expressed an undue amount of defiance. The crowd approved an air of nonchalant courage and would cheer if the prisoner struck the right note. Then the priest who had accompanied him in the cart heard his final prayer, the noose was adjusted, and the cart moved forward, leaving its main passenger swinging in the air behind it.

The prisoner continued to perform a cautionary function after death, for his body was exhibited as an example of the consequences of crime. Since felons were not usually cut into pieces, a humiliation reserved for traitors, the bodies were not only left in one piece but an effort was made to keep them that way. The body, when cut down from the gallows, was put into an iron framework, a sort of harness called a gibbet, and suspended beside a street or in some other public place. Here, slowly decomposing, the body might remain for years.

Benefit of Clergy

In pre-Reformation days, clergymen were exempt from many strictures of the common law and might escape hanging for a felony conviction. To earn this privilege, one showed that one could read; this association between reading and holy orders went back to medieval times when the Church had a monopoly on literacy. After the Reformation, it was still possible to plead "benefit of clergy" on a first conviction, regardless of whether or not one were actually in orders, and upon a successful demonstration the sentence would be changed to imprisonment or branding. Among those who successfully pleaded benefit of clergy was Ben Jonson, who killed a fellow actor in a quarrel.

The test was often performed on the first verse of the fifty-first Psalm: "Have mercy unto me, O God, according to thy loving kindness; according to the multitude of thy tender mercies, blot out my transgressions"—an appropriate choice for the circumstances. It would not have been impossible for a felon simply to memorize the passage, generally known as the "neck verse." However, as the Latin text was used, the task would be difficult for a beginner, and if the authorities suspected the performance to have been rehearsed, they could, of course, choose another verse.

As the years passed, and as reading became a more frequently encountered accomplishment, the list of felonies for which benefit of clergy could not be invoked came to include murder, burglary, piracy, and horse stealing, among other things. In the nineteenth century, the loophole was closed altogether.

Lesser Offenses and Their Punishments

For misdemeanors such as small-scale thefts, frequent punishments included amputation of all or part of an appendage, branding, the stocks, or the pillory. Imprisonment for a fixed term was assigned as a punishment to some extent, but not with the frequency that is usual today. Part of the reason was economic; keeping prisoners cost money, even though conditions were strictly no-frills. And rehabilitation was not seen in terms of long-term education or training but in terms of repentance, which the criminal might just as well do on his own time.

Amputating some much-needed portion of the criminal's anatomy, such as a hand, was so severe a punishment that it was relatively scarce. One of the judges in the celebrated case of John Stubbs (also spelled Stubs or Stubbe), condemned to lose his right hand after writing a pamphlet the authorities considered seditious, objected to the barbarity of the sentence and was removed from the bench.[10] Stubbs's behavior when the sentence was carried out impressed the crowd; as his right hand was struck off, he removed his hat with his left and cried, "God save the queen."

A more frequently imposed sentence deprived the offender of some relatively expendable item, such as an ear, or part of an ear. This type of punishment was useful as identification; should the accused find himself in trouble again, he could not claim to be a first-time offender. And, in the meantime, persons having dealings with him might be warned after a casual check of the state of his ears to remain on their guard.

The branding iron was also useful for identification and could be more specific than the knife in indicating the crime for which the offender had suffered. "T" meant "thief," for example; during military cam-

paigns, a deserter might be branded with a "D." The place chosen for
the brand varied in conspicuousness from the forehead or cheeks, where
it would be the first thing a stranger might notice, to the more easily
concealed base of the thumb. As the last choice was a frequent one, a
judge preparing to give a sentence often asked to see the offender's hands
in order to check his record, so to speak.

The pillory and the stocks provided punishment in the form of dis-
comfort and humiliation, with some more permanent or dangerous options. Offenders were sometimes nailed to the pillory by the ear; at the
end of the stipulated time (several hours, say), an official might pull the
nail out with pincers, but he might take the easier course simply of
slitting the ear. Pillories were also designed to hold their prisoners without impalement; the head would protrude through a hole to face the
jeers and sometimes the projectiles of the crowd. Since he could not use
his hands to protect his face, offenders of whom the crowd disapproved
were sometimes killed or blinded. Stocks, by contrast, in which the
prisoner sat on a bench or rail and was held by the feet, seem almost
benign. In *King Lear,* Cornwall's ordering Kent into the stocks is seen
as a presumptuous thing for Cornwall to do to the king's messenger, but
Kent apparently is not outrageously uncomfortable (2.2.155). If the rail
on which the offender had to sit were narrow or sharp, however, the
session might become excruciating indeed.

Whipping might be combined with the above punishments, especially
the pillory and the stocks, or it might make up the entire sentence. Theft,
prostitution, various forms of cheating and conniving, and, as we will
see, vagrancy and related offenses were punishable by whipping. The
prisoner might be immobilized, perhaps tied to a whipping post; but if
he had been sentenced to be "whipped out of town" he might shorten
the ordeal by moving briskly. The whips used for this purpose had fairly
short lashes and were not designed to cut to the bone but to lacerate the
skin. The sentence might prescribe a certain number of lashes—twenty
or thirty, say, for a case of theft tried before a quarter sessions; the
military sometimes stipulated a much higher number. Alternatively, the
sentence might simply require that the offender be whipped until his or
her shoulders were bloody. Sometimes the authority presiding over the
ceremony was empowered to decide when the offender had had enough.

Women were sentenced to whipping quite regularly; like men, they
were required to strip to the waist for the ordeal. A few punishments,

such as the ducking stool and the scold's bridle, were particularly associated with women.

The mechanism of the ducking stool varied but often involved a post-and-beam arrangement, with pulleys, set up beside the village pond. Women convicted of prostitution, lewd behavior, scolding, and other disturbances of the peace were tied into the chair and sent under. Occasional accidents happened—the constable kept the chair under too long, something went wrong with the machinery, or the offender panicked and choked; few people could swim or were accustomed to finding themselves out of their native element.

The scold's bridle, or "brank," also existed in many variations, but its essential form was that of an iron cage for the head. The tonguepiece, a flat metal plate, extended into the wearer's mouth, and once the cage was closed and locked she could not speak. Often the bridle included a ring with an attached chain, by which the scold might be led to the marketplace and tied to the pillory or some convenient fixture. This sentence was usually exacted by the judges of quarter sessions or by a local magistrate; the plaintiff might be the woman's neighbors but might also be her husband. The meaning of the word *scold*, incidentally, has become milder with the passing centuries until it now means nagging or chiding; in the sixteenth century, scolding was a loud and obstreperous affair, much embellished with profanity.

Vagrants, Lunatics, and Other Wanderers

In the ideal world the Elizabethans would have liked to live in, a rather wistful construction in a landscape of changing social conditions, every individual belonged to one single and identifiable locale—one parish, in fact—and was not supposed to go anywhere else. People did move, of course; the growth of London is evidence. Changing one's residence was not illegal, for the feudal system and its power to bind serfs to the land had withered away. And as long as a newcomer remained solvent and did not become a drag on his new neighbors, mobility was excusable. But his neighbors declined responsibility for him under less happy conditions. An impoverished vagrant reduced to begging might be found to have committed the offense of coming to wher-

Exploration and conquest. Theodore de Bry, a Flemish engraver who spent some years in London, here illustrates the landing of Columbus in *America* (1595). The costumes and ships are Elizabethan, however, and the scene may well accord with Europeans' imaginings of the New World. Some of the natives have taken flight; others do what their visitors would consider the proper thing by presenting remarkably elaborate gifts. (*Courtesy of the Folger Shakespeare Library.*)

Life before fax. The post boy, laden with urgent messages, was required to blow his horn to warn other traffic to get out of the way. Title pages of Nicholas Breton's *Post with a Mad Packet of Letters* (1602). Breton's lively bits of imaginary correspondence were popular enough to go through many editions. (*Courtesy of the Folger Shakespeare Library.*)

A pleasant ride on a sunny day; getting around without benefit of the internal combustion engine. From a collection of early seventeenth-century English watercolors. (*Courtesy of the Folger Shakespeare Library.*)

A player upon the virginals, a smaller form of the harpsichord, is joined by a viol player and another companion acting as a human music stand. The London music publisher Henry Playford chose this illustration for the title page of his *Banquet of Music* (1688), subtitled "A Collection of the newest and best Songs sung at Court, and at Publick Theatres." (*Courtesy of the Folger Shakespeare Library.*)

Tennis was an indoor and elite pastime. In the second part of *Henry IV,* Prince Hal teases Poins for having played no tennis lately because he has no spare shirt to change into after a sweaty match. From a French work, *Le centre de l'amour,* around 1650. (*Courtesy of the Folger Shakespeare Library.*)

Football in an early form. Rules were rudimentary and violence was frequent. In *King Lear,* the Earl of Kent insults Oswald by calling him a "base football player." The picture is from *Minerva Britannia* (1612), an emblem book by the many-talented Henry Peacham. (*Courtesy of the Folger Shakespeare Library.*)

Sausage making, using the standard kitchen appliances. Country households in Europe as well as England were self-sufficient to an extent hardly imaginable today. This illustration appears in a 1657 edition of the works of the Dutch poet Jacob Cats. (*Courtesy of the Folger Shakespeare Library.*)

A game of cards and a bite to eat. The increasing comfort of everyday English life encouraged many forms of recreation. From a collection of early seventeenth-century watercolors. (*Courtesy of the Folger Shakespeare Library.*)

Midwives at work. Presumably the baby is to be washed in the shallow tub in the foreground. Meanwhile, discreetly turning away from the human side of the event, astrologers await the exact moment of birth in order to compute the baby's horoscope. Jacob Ruff, a Zurich surgeon and writer, includes this illustration in his *De conceptu et generatione hominis* (1580). (*Courtesy of the Folger Shakespeare Library.*)

An efficient execution. Four men are being hanged simultaneously; once the nooses are adjusted, all that need be done is to drive the horse forward. From Holinshed's *Chronicles of England, Scotland and Ireland* (1577). (*Courtesy of the Folger Shakespeare Library.*)

Before the development of anesthesia, amputations were performed only if the patient would otherwise die of gangrene, or whatever the problem might be. This patient is apparently being distracted by having his arm pinched as the main order of business begins. From the title page of *The French chirurgerye* (1598), by Jacques Guillemeau. Guillemeau had been a student of Ambroise Paré, one of the century's most innovative medical practitioners. (*Courtesy of the Folger Shakespeare Library.*)

ever he had been apprehended, and he could be assumed, moreover, to be a thief, even if he had not yet got around to his thievery.

Such a policy naturally jumbled together actual criminals, potential criminals, and law-abiding wanderers who had taken to the roads because they had lost their jobs and hoped to find work someplace else. Thus the poor classes merged with the criminal classes in a sociological and ethical gray area that is still with us today, greatly as some conditions have changed.

A series of "poor laws," constructing a system of taxation for the relief of the deserving poor, were enacted during the sixteenth century in an attempt to fill the gap left by the monasteries' charitable institutions. These projects lagged behind the need, but they demonstrate the government's increasing sense of responsibility toward the helpless members of the state. Those who did not appear to be all that helpless were another matter, however. "Sturdy beggars," men strong enough to work but averse to holding a job, seemed to local authorities an obvious threat to good order and were sent away with a whipping. Other beggars—feeble beggars, one might say—were seen as proper objects of charity and were given licenses to beg.

Among the most pitiable of the vagabonds, to present-day sensibilities, were the insane, who wandered and begged in the company of their delusions. Care of the insane had not reached an advanced state. London's Bethlehem Hospital, pronounced "Bedlam"—a word that has entered the language to indicate noisy confusion—specialized in the insane, who were kept in shackles and sometimes, by way of treatment, whipped. Some Bedlam inmates were given the privilege of an official license to beg and allowed to wander over the countryside. Thus the word *Bedlam* for the Elizabethans came to denote any itinerant beggar who seemed not all there, as we would say, whether or not he had actually come from the hospital.

The "Bedlam beggar"–disguise persona invented by Shakespeare's Edgar in *King Lear* describes himself as "Poor Tom, that eats the swimming frog, the toad, the tadpole, the wall-newt . . . swallows the old rat and the ditch dog; drinks the green mantle of the standing pool; who is whipt from tithing to tithing, and stock-punish'd and imprison'd" (3.4.129–35). A "tithing" was a territorial division; a beggar's being whipped out of one and into another demonstrates the local authorities' usual policy of moving the problem on to another jurisdiction.

"Poor Tom," wandering in his rags over the cold moor and raving at his hallucinatory devils, achieves a strangely convincing reality and becomes a more vivid character than his putative creator, Edgar. In a sense, of course, Tom is quite as valid an entity as Edgar, equally bodied forth from the poet's imagination, and representative of Shakespeare's compassion as well as his powers of observation.

Rogues and Vagabonds in Literature

If Poor Tom can be classified among the deserving vagabonds, the literature of the period also paid a good deal of attention to the undeserving ones, the rogues or potential rogues, with their scams and disguises and sneaky tricks. A certain amount of escapist fantasy might underlie the popularity of this genre. To flout the law, live by one's wits, belong to a secret world with its own hierarchies and language, has an undeniable if usually unacknowledged appeal to the respectable classes; and this luxury might be enjoyed from a properly righteous stance if one were reading about—and, of course, condemning—other people.

Thus we have the long chain of "rogue literature" through which the Upright Man leads his harem of doxies, his Abraham Men, swigmen, and rufflers (pretending respectively to be madmen, peddlers, and returned soldiers), and the rest of the crew of hypocritical beggars and agile thieves. The Elizabethans read about this assortment with such delight that pamphleteers served them up again and again, often transcribing their fellow authors in large chunks without acknowledgment. As far as thievery goes, today's reader begins to feel, some people certainly picked the right subject. Copyright laws had not developed, however, and the pamphleteers often led lean and desperate lives, so perhaps they should not be harshly judged.

Among these exposés, John Awdelay's *The Fraternitye of Vacabondes* [sic], published in 1565, supplied the idea of an organized society of wandering rogues, along with some of the special vocabulary. A year or so later Thomas Harman, in his *Caveat or Warening for Common Cursetors Vulgarely called Vagabones* [sic], made the rather uncommon gesture of mentioning Awdelay's book while borrowing material from it, and went on to add a great many details on his own. Many of these he claimed to have collected himself, questioning the beggars who came to his door in the Kentish countryside and exploring criminal haunts in London. Harman's vocabulary of the vagabonds' "pelting speech," or "cant terms," was widely borrowed by later writers.

Among the many writers who lifted Awdelay's and Harman's material without acknowledgment was Robert Greene, whose "cony catching" pamphlets in the early 1590s describe the rogues' victimization of the naive "cony" (rabbit). Thomas Dekker in turn made free with Greene's work for *The Seven Deadly Sins of London, The Bellman of London,* and *Lanthorne and Candlelight,* all published in the first decade of the seventeenth century.[11] In one or the other of these incarnations, Greene's or Dekker's but more often Greene's, the Upright Man and his carefree companions enter today's literary anthologies and proceed to divert the reader as much as they did in their own day. The author's assumption, after all, is that his reader knows nothing of these unscrupulous schemers; his business is to warn the reader in detail, and the passages are consequently self-explanatory.

12

Travel and Exploration

Today's Americans, as well as today's Englishmen, are so accustomed to a landscape filled with roads—highways, motorways, cloverleafs, underpasses, flyovers, all paved and shouldered and brightly lighted—that to imagine a world without such amenities requires an effort. Hikers may be among the best prepared for this bit of time travel. Many sixteenth-century roads bore a similarity to the Appalachian Trail, although a close comparison might find the trail better maintained and easier to follow.

As for longer journeys—London to Venice, say—perhaps the outstanding difference is in the factor of the unknown, taken for granted by these earlier travelers. There were no package tours, no picture postcards, no travel agents' pamphlets; one ad-libbed one's way, so to speak. The overland traveler could not consult a road map, as no maps of such detail and accuracy existed, but hired a guide or asked his way one segment at a time. For seafarers, navigational charts did exist but were sometimes conjectural. If the destination were unknown, if the object were to find a new trade route or beat the Spaniards to a rumored group of islands, then the journey became a stalwart advance into the unknown.

This sense of wonder to be found in adventuring to unimagined places, in comparing different ways of life and also—for these were practical explorers—in reconnoitering the profit possibilities of these new surroundings, are reflected in the literature. Spenser, for example, uses metaphors of voyages as he conducts his reader through the allegorical geography of *The Faerie Queene*; his fairyland becomes the reader's willingness to try new things, to flex his thoughts and allow for unsuspected possibilities. For, Spenser reminds his reader, we learn

> *dayly how through hardy enterprize*
> *Many great Regions are discovered,*
> *Which to late age were never mentioned.*
> *Who ever heard of th' Indian Peru?*
> *Or who in venturous vessel measured*
> *The Amazons huge river, now found true?*
> *Or fruitfullest Virginia who did ever vew?*
>
> (2.Prol.2)

This journeying of the imagination was not new to the Elizabethans but seems an intrinsic part of the human makeup. The ancient Greeks were fascinated by the faraway, as the detailed itineraries in Homer can witness. Similarly, readers today turn to science fiction for its promise of new dimensions in space and thought. As Spenser points out, we sometimes find that reality is catching up very quickly.

Road Traffic in England

Because of England's rainy climate and the mud that resulted, roads were not well adapted for carts and wagons. Only the nine or so main roads fanning out from London, several of which followed routes laid out by the Romans a thousand-odd years previously, were wide enough for wheeled vehicles. Even on these, one needed dry weather and plenty of luck to get to where one was going.

Despite this lack of what we would consider passable roads, people were more mobile than we might assume, accustomed as we are to thinking of overland transport in terms of wheels exclusively. Walking was a quite reasonable way to get someplace; the chief hazard of present-day pedestrians, being run over, was after all nonexistent. Inns were accustomed to guests who walked through the door with knapsack and staff, having spent the day striding along the paths between the hedge-bounded fields.

Anyone who could afford to ride a horse generally did so, however. Horses with comfortable gaits, particularly the "amble," were especially esteemed. An ambler, in America sometimes called a pacer, is able to move the legs on each side simultaneously, in a gait resembling a trot but much smoother. (In the trot, the legs move in diagonal pairs.) Women as well as men traveled on horseback, women riding sidesaddle. A woman might also ride on a pillion, a cushion fastened behind a regular saddle, and steady her balance with a hand on the waist of whoever was in the saddle. Often the harness included a little board for her feet.

The humbler packhorse, sometimes called load horse or loader, was chosen not for his trot or amble, since he would not be going that fast, but for surefootedness and endurance. Farmers' packhorses took grain to the mill or produce to the market, picking their way along tracks too narrow or too muddy for wagons. For longer distances, strings of pack-horses, tied nose to tail in single file and loaded with goods put into the custody of the "carrier" in charge of the expedition, made their way through forests and over hills, splashing through fords, following trails that sometimes vanished and were often unmarked, even at crossroads. If the destination were London, the pack train would progress eventually to main-traveled roads where signs of civilization were more frequent and the footing better, and where other travelers might appear.

The carriers were the truck drivers of Elizabethan England. Shake-speare gives us a glimpse of their lives in *1 Henry IV.* Here, at an inn where they have found less than perfect accommodation, the carriers prepare their horses for the final day of their journey to London, making sure the saddles don't rub their backs and also keeping an eye on the health of the cargo; one pannier contains live poultry. Other items include "a gammon of bacon and two razes [roots] of ginger, to be deliver'd as far as Charing Cross" (2.1.24–25).

The Post System

The English post system was developed in the sixteenth century as a royal enterprise, a means of carrying official dispatches. Henry VIII replaced the older and less efficient arrangements with a sequence of stages at which postmasters were required to keep horses for the use of royal messengers. The postmasters might also hire their horses out to ordinary travelers, provided, of course, the king's messengers were given priority. These private customers made the system profitable enough to work fairly smoothly.

As the post system developed, the Crown authorities found that it was not always necessary to send dispatches in the care of a single messenger who, after all, might get tired even though he was provided with fresh horses. The postboys employed by the postmasters might be entrusted with royal dispatches, to be taken in a special pouch from one stage to the next, where they would be passed on to the next postboy. If, however, there were space left in the pouch after the dispatches had been tucked in, ordinary letters from private persons, called bye letters, might be carried. This expansion of the post business also added to the profit margin.

Thus reference to the "post" in the sixteenth and seventeenth centuries might have several meanings. The letter-carrying one, still with us today, is used by Nicholas Breton in the title of his early seventeenth-century collection of prose sketches, *A Post with a Mad Paquet of Letters*; here the "post" is the postboy. Again, "to travel by post" or simply "to post" can refer to traveling by a series of hired horses, the quickest way to cover long distances. Hamlet has this meaning in mind as he ponders his mother's hasty marriage to her brother-in-law.

> *O, most wicked speed, to post*
> *With such dexterity to incestuous sheets.*
>
> (1.2.156–57)

Foreign Travel

Travel abroad required a "license to travel," obtainable from the sovereign or the Privy Council. Usually these were not hard to get.

In addition to the ambassadors and other official dignitaries who represented England in the royal courts of Europe, the sixteenth century saw two other kinds of travelers increasingly make their way abroad. Merchants expanded England's trade; and young men of good family

embarked upon what later came to be called the "grand tour," putting
a polish on their education by encountering strange sights and curious
customs.

This last group provoked a somewhat ambivalent response from their
countrymen at home. Voices were raised against the whole idea. It was
claimed that impressionable youths might return home in worse shape
than they set out, wearing absurd foreign fashions or, worse, damaged
in their religious beliefs, having fallen prey to Jesuits or other wily pros-
elytizers. Others disagreed, among them Francis Bacon, who in his late
teens had spent several years in Paris as a member of the household of
the English ambassador to France.

Bacon's advice to young travelers serves to remind us of the newness
of this kind of undertaking. The taken-for-granted ease with which students today hop from country to country was still far in the future. One
should always, Bacon says, take along a tutor who knows the country
and the language—although the young traveler himself should, of
course, have at least begun to learn the language before setting out. The
tutor was to direct his pupil's sightseeing; Bacon gives a list of the kinds
of things one should see, including churches, courts of justice, and libraries. The young man should immerse himself in the country he is
visiting, avoiding his own compatriots as much as possible and frequenting places "where there is good company of the nation where he traveleth."[1] He should keep a diary of his travels and, on returning home,
maintain a correspondence with the most worthy of those he has met.

Usually these young travelers, their tutors, and their servant or servants traveled on horseback, as they would have done in England. They
could hire post-horses, but it was cheaper and just as convenient, since
they did not have to go at top speed, to buy horses at the beginning of
the journey and sell them at the end of it. Europe also offered an amenity
not yet widely available in England, the public coach, drawn by relays
of horses changed at coaching inns. The English tended to look askance
at coach travel—they thought it sissified—but in foreign countries it did
provide a chance to practice the languages.

Most Englishmen traveling for curiosity and education spent only a
year or so abroad before returning to their home pursuits, but some
found themselves hooked, so to speak. Two who kept going were Fynes
Moryson, who in the 1590s spent six years wandering about Europe and
parts of Asia Minor, and Thomas Coryate, who a few years later covered

almost two thousand miles on foot, traversing various countries of Europe. Coryate later set out again and made his way from Constantinople to northern India, learning several oriental languages as he went and encountering English merchants at Agra; he died, rather suddenly in his early forties, in Surat, near Bombay. Both Moryson and Coryate wrote about their travels.[2] Such information as the mileage between one city and another, or the relative values of foreign coins, was not readily available elsewhere and made their work much appreciated. The present-day reader will also find details that illuminate the almost taken-for-granted dangers of this kind of enterprise. Moryson, for example, warns the traveler who can swim against letting his fellow passengers know this fact. "My self have known many excellent swimmers, whereof some in the sight of the wished Land, have perished . . . by the weight of their fearful companions, knowing their skill, and so taking hold of them."[3]

The dangers of foreign travel were, in fact, such that any traveler setting out faced a good chance of not coming back again, and the bizarre custom developed of betting on oneself to do so, a kind of life insurance in reverse. The odds usually given were five to one. The prospective traveler left a sum with a goldsmith, moneylender, or private speculator and, on turning up again, could claim five times his investment. If he did not return, the moneylender naturally kept it. Puntarvolo, in Ben Jonson's *Every Man Out of His Humour* has a scheme to turn this procedure to profit. "I am determined to put forth some five thousand pounds, to be paid me, five for one, upon the return of myself, my wife, and my dog from the Turk's court in Constantinople. If all, or either of us miscarry in the journey, 'tis gone; if we be successful, why, there will be five and twenty thousand pound to entertain time withall" (2.3.245ff.). Puntarvolo's listeners solemnly advise him against taking the dog. The distance would be long for a dog unaccustomed to travel, and the holders of the money might try to arrange "divers attempts . . . against the life of the poor animal." The scheme does in fact come to grief before Puntarvolo can gather his party together.

Unknown Paths to Unknown Places: The Trading Companies

English exploration, like that of other countries, was strongly pushed by the profit motive. It was the trading companies that followed in the track of the explorers, developing routes and setting up trading stations. Often, in fact, the trading companies *were* the explorers.

In Europe and the Mediterranean, companies such as the Merchant Adventurers, which held the English monopoly on trade with the Low Countries and Germany, and the Levant Company, which specialized in Turkey and its environs, grew in power through the sixteenth century. (The term *adventurers,* incidentally, with its overtones of derring-do, referred to the company's willingness to venture money, to take a risk— a dashing enough concept, after all.) Other English traders developing markets in the eastern hemisphere included the Muscovy Company, a relatively short-lived concern concentrated on the White Sea, and the East India Company. This last, after starting life as an offshoot of the Levant Company, went on in the seventeenth century to establish what was to become one of the pillars of the British Empire.

In both the Old and New Worlds, English explorers and traders had to cope with the fact that they had been dealt out of the game, so to speak, a century earlier. Pope Alexander VI, shortly after the return of Christopher Columbus, had presided over the division between Spain and Portugal of the unclaimed and/or undiscovered portions of the globe. As eventually adjusted, all lands east of an imaginary line at approximately fifty degrees west longitude were assigned to Portugal; lands west of it, to Spain.

This portioning-out was complicated by the fact that ascertaining longitude was a difficult and controversial undertaking, and remained so for some time. A century later, Philip II of Spain offered a reward for the discovery of a reliable method of ascertaining one's longitude at sea, but to no avail. (Latitude was easier; as sixteenth-century navigators knew, one made measurements from the polestar.) Finally, in the late seventeenth century, England set up the Greenwich Observatory to determine the angles formed by heavenly bodies, and the longitude problem was on its way to a solution; but in the meantime, mapmakers and sailors had to muddle through.

By the late sixteenth century, Portugal had been concentrating for some time on Africa and India, with some attention to Brazil, which stuck out of South America into the Portuguese sphere, while Spain took over South America and Mexico, along with parts of what would become the United States. This high-handed dealing did not suit the convenience of other European countries with exploring or colonizing ambitions. The basic English attitude was that both Spain and Portugal had asked for it; if English ships seized Spanish treasure or Portuguese slaves, the seizure should be seen as a justified response to the latter's act of aggression in 1493.

Drake and the Golden Hind

Francis Drake, on his voyage in the late 1570s that was eventually to circumnavigate the globe, subscribed to this anti-Iberian feeling, as did the financial backers of his expedition—investors who hoped for a large return on their money. When Drake sailed around the tip of South America and found himself on the Pacific coast—backstage, so to speak—the pickings were rich. The Spaniards expected no trouble from that direction and were going about their business of harvesting treasure. Gold and silver, newly mined or taken from the Indians, had been collected in storehouses; cargo ships, only lightly armed, shuttled along the coast picking up the stored treasure and taking it to a collection point on the Pacific side of what is now Panama. Here the treasure would be loaded on pack animals—the canal, of course, would not be dug for another 300 years—and carried to the Atlantic side, where well-guarded convoys would begin the final stage of the journey home. But the Spanish warships were on the wrong side of the continent to deal with Drake, and after a few raids his ship, the *Golden Hind,* was loaded with as many ingots as she could carry.

Coming home the long way round, Drake and his men sailed across the Pacific for sixty-eight days without sight of land, arriving eventually at what is now called Indonesia. The *Golden Hind* picked her way among the islands, trading for spices. Then she crossed the Indian Ocean, rounded the tip of Africa, and sailed north into waters familiar to English sailors, so that captain and crew were fully aware of what they had done. It is true that the globe had been circumnavigated fifty years before by an expedition under Ferdinand Magellan, a Portuguese in the service of Spain, but Magellan had been killed on the voyage and did not get to enjoy the rewards of his achievement. Drake enjoyed his quite fully. The appearance of the *Golden Hind* in the autumn of 1580, almost three years after she had sailed away, delighted the English, especially those who had bought shares in the voyage, and the queen knighted Drake as he knelt on the deck.

The Slave Trade

Another type of maritime enterprise which pleased English investors, few of whom brooded about the ethics involved, was the slave trade, developed by John Hawkins in the 1560s. Hawkins worked out a triangular route on the first leg of which he acquired slaves on the west coast of Africa, in Guinea or Sierra Leone. Accounts vary on the means of this acquisition. In some cases Hawkins made his purchases from native chiefs who had captured them as prisoners of war; some historians suggest that Hawkins was not above assisting the winning side in these wars. Another method favored by English traders was simply to raid the Portuguese, who kept slaves in coastal fortresses awaiting shipment to plantations in the West Indies and elsewhere; all the English had to do, if they could avoid the Portuguese warships and duck the fortresses' cannon, was swoop down.

After loading his human cargo, Hawkins headed for Haiti, Venezuela, and other places where field labor was in demand. His Spanish and Portuguese customers were not supposed to buy from any but their own suppliers, but convenience is a great persuader with a harvest to bring in, and the English had no trouble getting a share of the market. The cane sugar for which they traded was of much greater relative value than is the case today—not because sixteenth-century sugar was better than ours, cane and beet sugar being the same product as far as the consumer is concerned, but because the supply was smaller. Hawkins's eastbound cargoes were welcomed in England almost as if they had been spices.

English Colonies in the New World

In 1604, England's state of reflex-action enmity with Spain and Portugal, the latter temporarily under Spanish rule, ended as King James and his ministers negotiated a peace. Two years later the Virginia Company was chartered for the purpose of trade and settlement in a part of North America not already occupied by the Spanish. Stockholders became members of the company either by purchasing shares, entitling them to a part of the company's profits, or by moving to the colonies as planters; many people did both. The venture was better capitalized and managed than Sir Walter Raleigh's ill-fated Roanoke Island colony had been, and it survived despite Indian massacres and other setbacks. King James presumably had no trouble identifying with it; the first settlement was named Jamestown, on the James River. The chief cash crop, tobacco, did not reflect the English monarch's taste, but it increased the colony's profits. The Virginia Company, acting as proprietor of the province it had founded, appointed resident governors and other functionaries, much as a present-day corporation staffs its executive offices.

Meanwhile, in what came to be called New England, a variety of settlements grew up. The colonists at Plymouth in 1620 had originally aimed for a more southerly territory controlled by the Virginia Company, which had given them a patent to settle there, but having been blown off course they simply drew up their own constitution before disembarking from the *Mayflower*. Shortly thereafter Boston was settled by the Massachusetts Bay Company, chartered by King James after a reorganization of earlier enterprises.

In New England, colonists were often less centered on making money and more centered on establishing a form of government in accordance with their religious preferences; this, rather than financial profit, had been the object for which they crossed the seas. Like the Virginians, they often found their goal harder to obtain than they had at first supposed. Disagreements developed; sifting and shifting had to be done. Some of the early settlers in Connecticut, for example, moved there because of their discontent with the autocratically theocentric government of Massachusetts.

Literature and Far Horizons

The men and women who actually settled the English colonies seem to have been too busy to do much reading, though they got around to it as the decades passed, and they also became strong advocates of education. Back at home, however, Elizabethan and Jacobean readers consumed travel tales in quantity. Some of these had a strong fantasy element; others were, or purported to be, factual eyewitness accounts. For the present-day reader it is sometimes hard to sense the difference.

The outstanding collector and editor of the real-life accounts, Richard Hakluyt, had been fascinated by geography since boyhood. A graduate of Christ Church College, Oxford, and ordained in the Church of England, Hakluyt lectured on discoveries and voyages, and urged overseas expansion among his influential friends; he was at one time chaplain to the English ambassador to France, and had been helped in his church career by Lord Howard of Effingham, commander-in-chief of the English navy. Hakluyt supported Raleigh's colonizing efforts, helped petition the Crown for patents to settle Virginia in 1606, and, looking in the other direction, supplied geographical information to the organizers of the East India Company.

But Hakluyt's most lasting monument is his collections of travel narratives. The largest of these, the *Principal Navigations, Voyages, and Discoveries of the English Nation,* enlarged to three folio volumes for its edition of 1600, contains among much else an eyewitness account by one (or perhaps several) of Drake's companions on the "famous voyage" around "the whole globe of the earth"; a description of the last voyage of Sir Humphrey Gilbert, explorer of Newfoundland, during which Gilbert went down with his ship in a storm at sea; and a "brief and true report" by Thomas Heriot, a member of Raleigh's colony in the 1580s, of the "new-found land of Virginia." Raleigh's "Last Fight of the *Revenge,*" describing the English commander Sir Richard Grenville's fight to the death against the overwhelming number of Spanish warships attacking him, is of the same genre as much of Hakluyt's collection, though it was published separately.

Writers who stayed home nevertheless incorporated the idea of a wide, rich, and exciting global domain into their imagery and patterns of thinking, whatever the subject of their work might be. To John Donne, for example, this new mental world was a natural habitat. In "Elegy XIX: To His Mistress Going to Bed," the lady is a rich continent—"O my America! my new found land"—for the exploration of which the poet's hands beg to be duly licensed.

Michael Drayton's "Ode to the Virginian Voyage," first published in

1606, takes some of its details from passages in Hakluyt's *Principal Navigations,* the reading of which, Drayton says, "shall enflame / Men to seek fame." The poem illustrates several misconceptions later to be disproved by the colonists' experience, among them the easy availability of "pearl and gold" and the harvests ready at hand without need for toil, but it reads as an invigorating call to adventure.

Finally, to choose a last example of the pervasive awareness of faraway places in literature, Shakespeare's magic island in *The Tempest,* though in a literal sense set in the Mediterranean so that characters en route from North Africa to Naples can be deflected there, nevertheless evokes the New World in its wonders and its hard-to-categorize inhabitants. Gonzalo is inspired to describe the ideal commonwealth, where "All things in common Nature should produce / Without sweat or endeavor" (2.1.160–61); Trinculo longs to turn Caliban into a sideshow exhibition, the fate of some unfortunate New World captives (2.2.31–33). And much of the audience would have had in mind, as Shakespeare very likely did, an adventure that had just befallen one of the Virginia Company's expeditions. All the ships except one arrived safely at Jamestown; the other, blown off course, had wrecked off Bermuda, then uninhabited and certainly a candidate for a paradisiacal island. Officers and crew made their way ashore, where they found fresh water, food (some of it in the form of wild pigs), and cedar trees. With the last they built two small ships and sailed on to Jamestown, arriving ten months after they had been given up for lost. Several accounts of the voyage were published in England between 1610 and 1625; presumably they would have been known to Shakespeare's audience and to Shakespeare himself.

13

The Military: Arrows, Cannon, and Sails

The Elizabethans had no regular standing army. The navy was in a slightly different situation, as warships had to be built and maintained whether needed that week or not, but a naval emergency still required the help of ships—armed merchant vessels, for example—which spent most of their time doing something else.

Another difference noticeable to present-day readers is the gap between officers and enlisted men, as we would use the terms. No mechanism existed for promotion from the ranks. Enlisted men might have entered the service as volunteers, thus revealing their lack of better prospects, or might have been "pressed" (impressed) into it. Either way, their lot was seldom a happy one. Of the officers, some were aristocrats to whom military glory was a family tradition; others, army captains especially, regarded their commissions as business monopolies and made the most of what came their way.

The reigns of Elizabeth and James, respectively, were peaceful by comparison to other eras. Such military action as did occur took place far from public view. Ireland continued to resist English attempts at conquest or pacification, despite the fact that the English had been making these attempts for four centuries, and absorbed one campaign after another without permanent effect, a sort of green hole in space. In Europe, England was allied by religious sympathy with the Protestant parts of the Netherlands but tended to avoid entanglement as much as possible. Although English troops did go to the Low Countries in the 1580s, in one of which engagements Sir Philip Sidney was killed, these conflicts did not loom large in public awareness. Sea battles seem to have evoked more general interest, possibly because of Hakluyt's publicizing zeal and also, perhaps, because the defeat of the "Invincible Armada" in 1588 had taken place close to home.

Musters and Recruiting

Even without a paid standing army, the expense of which would have been unthinkable in the sixteenth century, national defense required that the population at large have some rudimentary military training. It was also useful to have some idea of how many potential soldiers the country had. These goals were addressed by the shire (or county) muster, held usually every four years, with occasional extras in times of crisis. An out-of-synch muster was held in 1587, for example, under the threat of Spanish invasion. Every able-bodied male from sixteen to sixty was required to turn up, be counted, and receive instruction in military drill.

In quest of a higher level of preparation, a few, more elite groups, "trained bands," or "train-bands," convened at more frequent intervals. London's trained bands drilled on a common at Mile End, east of the city. Shakespeare's Parolles, in *All's Well that Ends Well*, claims that Captain Dumaine once served as a drill instructor at Mile End, implying that this is the limit of Dumaine's military experience (4.3.269). Fortunately for the latter's reputation, no one believes Parolles on any point.

Members of trained bands had their weapons provided at the expense of the shire, but they were not professional soldiers in that they had to continue their regular trade, whatever it might be, in order to earn a living. If called up for active service, they would be paid. (The queen, economical in this as in other matters, called up her trained bands as seldom as possible and dismissed them as quickly as possible.) Service in these bodies offered several advantages: one could learn the management of pike or musket, exercise one's patriotic energies, enjoy a break in routine, and protect oneself from being recruited for foreign service— the trained bands were considered vital to the defense of the realm and were not ordinarily sent abroad.

When the sovereign did decide to undertake a foreign military campaign, soldiers were provided in several ways. Shire musters, which theoretically ensured that the men who ended up in the ranks would not be entirely green, were not used for actual recruiting; this method presumably would have been too cumbersome. Instead, recruiters sometimes tried marching about with a drummer, collecting volunteers. Or the recruiter, having been granted the power of "impressment," might order the local justices of the peace to provide him with the requisite number of men. In a pinch, these "press gangs," as they were called, were known to snatch men off the streets and bear them away. Dekker's Ralph Damport, in *The Shoemakers' Holiday,* undergoes this fate.

These recruits could only metaphorically be described as "in uniform," since army clothing of the sixteenth century presented a varied pattern. Some soldiers were not issued clothing but had to manage as best they could in what they had started out with. At other times some high authority, perhaps a member of the Privy Council, would decide that men bound for such-and-such a campaign would wear garments of a certain color. These choices might have been made for symbolic reasons or personal taste, or they might represent bargain offers by the merchants supplying the army. It would be almost two centuries before the English army looked as we are accustomed to imagining it, in red coats with ornamental facings and perhaps a pouch-belt over the shoulder.

An exception is found in the Yeomen of the Guard, the sovereign's personal bodyguard established by Henry VII, which wore a royal-red tunic with purple facings. The Yeomen of the Guard were also an exception in that they might be said to constitute a permanent military body, but as their numbers were quite small, 200 or so in the time of Queen Elizabeth, the objection seems a technical one. The Yeoman of the Guard is still in existence today, performing ceremonial functions; they should be distinguished from the yeomen warders of the Tower of London, who also wear red Tudor uniforms.

Army Organization

The basic unit in Elizabethan armies was the company, a group of 100 to 200 men serving under a captain who, in a sense, owned it. Often he had been responsible for its recruitment. All dealings with the individual soldiers went through the captain; their pay was sent to him, for example, to be distributed. He was responsible for clothing and feeding them—making deductions from their pay to cover expenses—and for finding replacements to fill up vacancies.

Obviously, the opportunities for lining one's own pockets were many, and a captaincy could become quite a lucrative post. A soldier who died or deserted would still be paid—or, rather, his pay would be sent to the captain until the captain got around to reporting the loss—and it was easy to neglect these reports. If his men persisted in surviving, a captain unencumbered with scruples could hurry things along by sending them off on dangerous missions. The resulting information gap was, of course, unfortunate for the army as a whole, as the higher-up commanders often had no idea how many men they really had. Surprise inspections did not always work. The authorities had no way of ascertaining that the names on the captain's muster book corresponded with the soldiers the captain had produced; captains sometimes temporarily filled the gaps by borrowing from another company.

It should be pointed out that some captains resisted these temptations and functioned with the sense of feudal obligation characteristic, at least theoretically, of the earlier period in which the system had evolved. This was especially the case when the captain knew his men—if he had raised the company himself from among his family's tenantry, for example, a traditional procedure but an increasingly scarce one. Opportunism seems to have been more the coming thing.

The company's size (or its supposed size, given the discrepancy between muster lists and actuality) varied according to its job. A cavalry company generally numbered about a hundred, while an infantry company might be up to twice as large. The captain was supported by one lieutenant—his understudy, in a sense—as well as by other company officers. Among these were the ensign bearer, who carried the flag—an important office when battlefield communications were primitive; two sergeants, who drilled the men; two drummers, useful for morale; a surgeon, for rough-and-ready repairs; and several corporals, who oversaw the men's equipment.

Major military decisions, including numerous directives intended to keep the captains in line, were made by the sovereign and the Privy Council. Directly beneath this body was the general, appointed by the sovereign for the campaign at hand. Aristocratic rank was an understood prerequisite for such an appointment.

The regiment, more or less an amalgamation of several companies headed by a colonel, took its first evolutionary steps during Elizabeth's reign, so that by the turn of the century the army had considerably more coherence than had been the case some decades earlier. The kind of regimental identity and loyalty typical of the army in later centuries had not yet developed, however, and the basic unit remained the company, for better or for worse.

Falstaff as Army Captain: The Wrong Stuff

Tracing Falstaff's failings as officer material requires a reversal of the sequence of events in the two parts of *Henry IV.* A close-up view of Falstaff's recruiting methods appears in part two, while a battle, Shrewsbury, takes place in part one.

In part two, Justice Shallow, doing his duty as "one of the king's justices of the peace," has rounded up some potential recruits among whom Falstaff is to choose. The group—Mouldy, Shadow, Wart, Feeble, and Bullcalf—has a decidedly motley air. In a private conference with Bardolph, Falstaff's lieutenant, Mouldy and Bullcalf arrange to buy their way out, and Falstaff quietly accepts the bribe. Justice Shallow is unaware of this transaction and protests Falstaff's passing these two over: "Sir John, do not yourself wrong. They are your likeliest men, and I would have you serv'd with the best" (3.2.254–56).

In part one, Falstaff has received from Prince Hal "a charge of foot" (3.3.186), or commission as captain of an infantry company; has been given "money and order for their furniture" (equipment); and now marches through Warwickshire, recruiting as he goes. The recruitment process is not acted out for us but Falstaff cheerfully describes it: "I have misus'd the King's press damnably" (4.2.12). Falstaff's method has two main phases. In the first phase, he recruits (or threatens to recruit) men who have strong motives not to go—family men and prospective bridegrooms, "contracted bachelors, such as had been ask'd twice on the banns." These prospects, as Falstaff knows, are sufficiently well off to buy their way out, and they have done so, netting him "in exchange of a hundred and fifty soldiers, three hundred and odd pounds." Phase two, of course, consists of actually scraping together some men to fill the company, and for this purpose Falstaff has accumulated 150 beggars, vagrants, and others down on their luck, a highly unimpressive assemblage. A passerby, Falstaff says, "told me I had unloaded all the gibbets and pressed the dead bodies." Falstaff might, of course, provide his ragged men with clothing from the money he has been given, but he has no intention of doing so; "they'll find linen enough on every hedge," spread out to dry by unsuspecting householders.

It is at this point that Prince Hal happens by, perplexed by the "pitiful rascals" he has seen on the road, and Falstaff for all his shrewdness now shows his own blind side. He is unable to see the situation from the prince's perspective; the coming battle is, after all, in defense of what will ultimately become the prince's right to the throne of England. But Falstaff clings to his blithely cynical view of reality and tells the prince it doesn't matter if his men are less than adequate fighters: "Tut, tut, good enough to toss, food for powder, food for powder; they'll fill a pit as well as better" (4.2.65–67).

Falstaff's behavior during the battle is consistent with his principles, or lack of them, and we find that he has got rid of his men: "I have led my ragamuffins where they are pepper'd; there's not three of my hundred and fifty left alive, and they are for the town's end, to beg during life" (5.3.35–38). These events take place offstage, and may be overbalanced, as far as the audience is concerned, by Falstaff's ebullient charm. Prince Hal, however, irrevocably turning into a grownup, sees a larger picture. Falstaff's attitude here contrasts with Hal's on the night before Agincourt, two plays farther along, when as king he tries to raise his army's morale and ponders his own spiritual responsibility in sending men into battle.

Army Weapons: The Longbow versus the Musket

During the two previous centuries, the longbow had served as something of a secret weapon. That is, other countries (France, for example) knew England had the longbow, but they did not use it themselves and tended to forget about it, remembering too late at Crécy or Agincourt. National myth thus swayed the authorities when it came to choosing weapons for the army. Economy played a part as well; the longbow, once mastered, was a much cheaper weapon than the gun.

Because shooting the longbow took years of practice as well as considerable strength, the English authorities did their best to make it part of every young man's growing up. Parliament passed acts requiring bowyers to stock low-priced bows in small sizes, and municipalities were expected to hold archery contests.

Times changed, however, and advocates of firearms for military use increasingly made their voices heard. Cannon and other heavy artillery, most of it not very mobile and used mainly for besieging fortresses, had been familiar since the early fifteenth century. The concept of a miniature cannon, so to speak, which an individual soldier might carry about with him, could be seen as a natural development, but there were technical problems.

Much of this awkwardness had to to with the problem of mobility. An archer's equipment was lightweight, simple, and familiar; he needed his bow, a bowstring or two, and a supply of arrows. The user of a firing piece first had to carry the weapon itself, ranging from heavy to very heavy depending on its type. Then there was gunpowder, which had a tendency to separate into its original components (sulphur, charcoal, and saltpeter) when shaken by travel, and which would not explode properly unless the proportions were exactly right. ("Corned" gunpowder, mixed into a paste with alcohol and then dried, eventually solved this problem.) The lead balls had to be the right size to fit the barrel—a concept of exactitude to which the sixteenth century was unaccustomed. The older-style cannons had fired whatever was put into them, including stones. The soldier also needed a ramrod, often attached to the gun, and paper for wadding. Juggling all these components, he had to assemble them under the pressure of battle, ignite the charge, and hope the gun would not explode at the wrong end. Metal alloys improved slowly, and sometimes the powder charge, even if correctly measured out, proved over-excitable.

With these disadvantages, it is a wonder firearms made any headway at all, or that readers of literature were expected to recognize references to them. Three types of firearms, nevertheless, became fairly well known to the public. These were, in descending order of size, the musket, the caliver, and the pistol.

Earlier models of the musket had been managed by two-man teams, but by the late sixteenth century this weapon could usually be carried by one man. It had to be braced on a special stick for firing. Another century would pass before muskets were made sufficiently light to be fired from the shoulder, and even then the kick was considerable. The musket was not very accurate, but then neither were other firearms; perhaps it was felt that in a battle all one had to do was aim at the enemy in general. "Rifling," or putting spiral grooves on the inside of the barrel to give a twirl to the bullet and increase accuracy, did not come into use until the eighteenth century.

The caliver was shorter than the musket, three feet or so in length, and was designed to be fired from the shoulder. Shakespeare mentions it as the usual weapon for new recruits. "Put me a caliver into Wart's hand, Bardolph," Falsfaff says, and compliments Wart on the drill exercises the latter then performs—to the distress of Justice Shallow, who claims that "he doth not do it right" (3.2.278).

Elizabethan pistols were larger than the pocket-sized weapons that figure in American murder trials, but they were still small enough to wear at the waist and to fire from horseback. Standards of marksmanship under these circumstances were not very high. Prince Hal implies that Hotspur, despite his fearsome reputation, could not really "ride at high speed and with a pistol kill a sparrow flying" (2.4.345). Sixteenth-century pistols were not only inaccurate but dangerous to the user, being more likely than the larger weapons to explode backwards. Both these qualities are evoked in Shakespeare's unpredictably fiery character Pistol.

It should be added that most references to firearms in Shakespeare's history plays are anachronistic. The real Hotspur could not have owned a pistol, and nobody could have carried a caliver into battle in 1405. The problem does not seem a major one. Shakespeare was portraying certain kinds of personalities in certain kinds of situations, and his audience got the effect.

Swords, Armor, and Horses

Some components of the military picture were not in the least newfangled, and sixteenth-century readers had little trouble imagining them. With regard to traditional items such as swords, armor, and horses, the same situation obtains for today's reader, and most references are self-explanatory.

The sword had an elite connotation as the weapon of the upper classes. Lower-class foot soldiers might be issued pikes, spears up to twenty feet long, the efficient use of which required some training but not a great deal, or bills, a spiky kind of ax with a shaft about six feet long. The use of the bill seems to have been left largely to instinct. Swordplay, by contrast, whether practiced on foot or on horseback, required the lengthy instruction and practice available only to the more leisured. Gentlemen were expected to own their own swords, though armories—that in the Tower of London, for example—usually kept swords, along with pikes and bills, ready for emergencies. Of the swords which a gentleman might wear with pride, the most prestigious was the Toledo blade from Spain, subject of an exercise in one-upmanship in Jonson's *Every Man In His Humour* (3.1.-). Some styles of swordplay called for the participants to use a dagger as well, a weapon in each hand, and many swords were made with a matching dagger.

Armor had gone through various evolutionary phases by the late sixteenth century, trying to strike a balance between protection and mobility; the heavier the protection, the less the mobility, and a knight could be quite helpless if he fell off his horse. Armor was complicated as well as heavy, and putting it on before a battle required expert help.

In literature, armor often serves as a convenient vehicle for symbolism, but as explanations are usually provided in the context for the various colors, emblematic designs, and so forth, the present-day reader is not at a disadvantage. Real-life battle armor was usually more functional than ornamental, the designer being more concerned with deflecting arrows than with making a visual statement. However, many noblemen had armor especially made for tournaments and other ceremonial occasions, and this could exhibit great chivalric splendor. Another convenient feature of armor is that of concealing the wearer's identity, an advantage used in real life only on rare occasions but quite frequent in literature. Spenser's Britomart, for example, comes to Faeryland on purpose to seek Artegall, whom she has seen in a magic mirror wearing the legendary armor of Achilles (3.2.24–25). But Artegall is wandering about in a quite different armor, dark and mysterious, with his visor down, and a whole series of adventures occur before Britomart finds out who he is (4.6.25–26).

War-horses in literature differed from their real-life counterparts in the former's remarkable endurance and ease of maintenance. Actual war-horses were of course vulnerable to the problems of equine flesh and blood, and required looking after even when quite sound. They were very strong, as they had to carry not only an armored rider but a quite heavy saddle and other accoutrements, but they were specialists in battles and tournaments and would hardly have been able to travel on day after day in search of adventure. They also had to be very carefully trained. A battlefield is an assemblage of things a horse does not like—loud noises, unfamiliar sights and smells, miscellaneous things underfoot, and, sometimes, the need to travel on a line that takes him away from the other horses. He is not to panic and run, and, furthermore, he must do exactly as his rider signals him; a few inches one way or another can make all the difference as his rider attempts to use his own weapons and avoid his opponents'.

This choreography required training and practice not only for the horse but, of course, for the rider as well, and peacetime exercises in the management of the "great horse" were popular among those members of the upper classes for whom riding a horse into battle was a feasible ambition. Sidney describes such an occasion in Sonnet 41 of *Astrophil and Stella*:

> *Having this day my horse, my hand, my launce*
> *Guided so well, that I obtain'd the prize,*
> *Both by the judgement of the English eyes*
> *And of some sent from that sweet enemy France.*

The reason for his victory, the poet explains, is that Stella was watching. Later, in Sonnet 49, he works out an analogy between the control he has of his mount and the control Love has of the poet himself, putting him through his paces; "and while I spur / My horse, he spurres with sharp desire my heart."

Henry V *and the Battle of Agincourt*

Shakespeare's battle scenes are reasonably clear to the present-day reader, provided the reader has kept the characters straight and followed the political patterns that govern the clashing swords. Battles involving English factions, waged between contenders for the English crown, are especially tricky in this regard as the participants are prone to switch sides. The major foreign battle, that of Agincourt in *Henry V*, offers no difficulty in sorting out English and French opponents but does portray an event which had become so much a part of the national myth that present-day Americans are at something of a disadvantage.[1] Many members of the original audience knew not only the basic outline of the story but the more detailed versions in Holinshed and elsewhere, and were well equipped to follow the Chorus's suggestion that they use their imaginations to supply the horses, space, and sweep missing from the stage version.

In August of 1415, as Shakespeare depicts in the third act of the play, King Henry crossed the channel from the port of Southampton, with a fleet of 1,500 ships carrying 10,000 men. On disembarking, the army "sat down before Harfleur," as military writers say, meaning that the people of this small port at the mouth of the Seine shut themselves inside their walls, and the English besieged them.

The siege lasted for over a month, during which time the English soldiers were kept supplied by their own ships crisscrossing the channel. The weather was hot, a point Shakespeare mentions (3.2.106), and dysentery thinned out the English troops. Sanitation was not understood, and a crowded camp was a natural site for disease. The people of Harfleur hoped for rescue from the direction of Rouen, where Charles VI presided over a somewhat disorganized court, but none came, while the English bombarded them with cannon and dug tunnels in an attempt to collapse the walls.

Unlike the smaller firearms which anachronistically find their way into Shakespeare's early fifteenth-century plays, these cannon were really there, representing a fairly new wrinkle in siegecraft. The tunnels or "mines" (specifically, passages dug beneath a wall) were more familiar to tradition, and Shakespeare's Fluellen enjoys displaying his knowledge of the Roman ones (3.1.57–64). Harfleur surrendered on September 22, thus avoiding damage to its walls or other facilities.

The English then faced the question of what to do next. The prudent thing would have been to go home, leaving an occupational force in Harfleur, and come back the next summer. But they were trying to prove a point, that the English king was entitled to the French throne, and rather than withdraw they decided to march across a section of the land they were claiming. Their destination was Calais, on the French coast northeast of Harfleur and almost directly across the channel from Dover, thus providing a convenient exit. Calais would not need to be besieged, since at that time it was under English control anyhow.

But the English had not taken into account the autumn rains or the swollen rivers which prevented their making a simple march along the coast. When Shakespeare's French lords, still trying to decide what to do about the invasion, ponder the news that "he [King Henry] hath pass'd the river Somme" (3.5.1), they refer to a quite desperate crossing which the English army, now in a cold and hungry state, had finally achieved after going a long way upstream in search of an unguarded bridge or ford. Their march in this unplanned direction, a sharp right turn, so to speak, had taken them away from their own coastal supply line and had also brought them, in a weakened condition, far into enemy territory. The French decided to act, as Shakespeare portrays them doing. They set out after the English, who were making their way toward Calais, and caught up with them on October 24.

The battle that took place the next day pitted some 25,000 Frenchmen against 5,000 to 6,000 Englishmen, according to modern historians' estimates. Shakespeare gives a larger figure, 60,000 French to 12,000 English (4.3.3–5), but the ratio remains in the neighborhood of five to one. In accounting for the victory, we should give full measure to English courage, as Shakespeare does, but there are two other aspects of the case which he does not mention. The original audience would have been aware of them anyhow. These are the devastating effect of the English archers, and the nature of the place.

The battle was fought on an expanse of ploughed land, just sown with winter wheat and soggy from the rain. Woods on either side narrowed the field slightly at the English end and prevented the French forces, when they charged, from spreading out. As the French knights reached the English line, the archers who had been shooting at them stepped back, revealing pointed stakes set in the ground at an efficient angle for impaling horses; and as the knights pulled up, tried to turn, collided with one another, fell off their mounts, and lay helpless in the mud, the English archers continued their fast and accurate onslaught. When the French commanders realized things were not going well, they sent in another wave of knights and armored foot soldiers, reinforcing defeat in the worst way as these too became hopelessly mired and tangled. Eventually the lightly clad English found themselves leaping about on piles of living and dead, dispatching the enemy with whatever weapon they happened to have—knives, mallets—and no doubt realizing with dawning joy that they had not only escaped what had seemed certain death but were winning an amazing victory.

One wonders why Shakespeare did not mention the archers. In other plays he seems properly sentimental about the English longbow. It would, of course, be quite frustrating to try to put archers on the stage, as one could show either the beginning or the ending of an arrow's journey but not the whole thing. Or perhaps the stage tradition of hand-to-hand combat was overriding.

Except for this omission, *Henry V* would probably have won the approval of members of the audience who knew their Holinshed. King Henry's order that the Englishmen kill their prisoners (4.6.37) appears in the sources; the king was worried that, with numerical odds on their side, the French might manage to regroup, releasing and rearming the prisoners.[2] A group of Frenchmen who lived in the neighborhood did attack the English baggage wagons and kill the boys guarding them (4.7.1–8). Finally, the small number of English fatalities agrees with historical evidence. Shakespeare lists only four "of name," ranking as gentlemen or higher, and "of all other men / But five and twenty" (4.8.105–6). The French, by contrast, lost so many men that they had to dig great pits to bury them, and the number of bodies, according to modern historians, was some 6,000.

Ships and Tactics

England's land forces during the sixteenth century did not make any major technological advances except for the gradual advance of firearms over bow and arrow. But in ship design, England was ahead of her opponents, especially the Spanish, despite the fact that the English vessels looked far less prepossessing. Spanish warships were not only large in size but stood so high in the water that those on the decks could literally look down on the English—or, more to the point, shoot down on them with muskets. Spanish warships carried large numbers of soldiers as well as a crew of sailors, and a favorite tactic was to seize an enemy ship with grappling hooks and then send the soldiers swarming aboard, swords swinging and pistols blazing.

The English preferred to rely on their skill in maneuvering the ship itself, bringing into play the cannon installed on and below the decks. The position of these guns was fixed, a necessary limitation in the days of sailing vessels. One could hardly fire from a movable turret without hitting one's own rigging. In order to aim the guns, consequently, one had to aim the whole ship, and the preferred technique was a sort of sideways swipe at high speed, a "broadside" raking the target with all the guns on one side of the ship. The attacker then curved away from its opponent, reloading while it came around for another pass.

The Spanish, of course, also had cannon and knew how to use them, and, in fact, from a present-day perspective there are probably more similarities than differences in the two nations' respective ships and skill in seamanship. All the ships were quite tiny when compared even to vessels we think of as small. Many of the ferries into which we drive our automobiles, for example, could swallow up an Elizabethan warship or two without crowding the other cargo, except, of course, for the masts and sails. One wonders if the energy the seamen displayed in scampering about the rigging might have owed something to the relief of escaping from the cramped spaces below. The sails were made of linen, cotton being not yet available in large quantities, and the ropes were of hemp; the industries that supplied these materials were more developed than either is today. And the ships were built of wood; the notion that metal might be made to float was several centuries in the future.

But the major difference between seagoing vessels in Elizabethan times and our own was, of course, that there were no engine rooms— no furnaces burning wood or coal, no paddle wheels, no screw propellers. Windpower was it. Oared vessels had not disappeared, especially in the Mediterranean; in the Battle of Lepanto, in 1571, when Spanish and Italian forces defeated a Turkish fleet, galleys were used on both sides. Philip II even sent some galleys along with the Armada in 1588, but they did not take a major part in the action.

In controlling their speed and direction, sixteenth-century sailors were amazingly skilled. Only a complete calm left them helpless, and these were rare on the oceans. A wind blowing in an inconvenient direction could be a disadvantage if it were sending them toward shore, or into rocks or sandbanks without enough room to maneuver. But under ordinary circumstances the seamen knew how to make almost any wind take them where they wanted to go and could perform all sorts of tricky changes of direction and variations in speed.

The Invincible Armada

In 1588, Philip II of Spain was sixty-one years old, and a great deal had happened in the world since his marriage to Queen Mary of England in 1554 and her death four years later. (On the dynastic front, Philip had in fact been married twice since and had had three children, as well as a son by a wife who had preceded Mary.) It now seemed obvious to Philip that the well-being not only of Spain but of the entire Catholic world required that he conquer England, and he worked out a plan for doing so. His great fleet, the Invincible Armada, was to link up with his land forces stationed in those parts of the southern Netherlands then under Spanish rule; soldiers were to be brought across the channel in barges from Dunkirk (not included in French territory at that time) while the Armada dealt with the English navy, and England was to be overrun.

In accordance with this program, the Armada appeared off the southwestern coast of England on the twentieth of July,[3] a hundred or so warships and thirty supply ships carrying a total of some 30,000 men, and proceeded slowly toward the rendezvous point almost 300 miles east. The Armada could travel only at the speed of its slowest members, for none could be left behind to fall prey to the English. Defense also dictated the Armada's traveling formation, the famous crescent moon. The trailing tips of the crescent, about six miles apart in the vast panorama of masts and sails, were made up of powerful warships ready to close in on any English vessel which tried to cut out a ship from behind.

The English, of course, tried to do just that, and harried the Armada for eight days as it moved slowly along the English Channel. They had no major success but did lure the Spanish into wasting ammunition by firing at them while they stayed just out of range. The English admiral, Thomas Howard of Effingham, earl of Nottingham, and his vice-admiral, Sir Francis Drake, commanded almost 200 ships, many of them quite small; others, though larger in size, were really merchant vessels armed with a few cannon. The number of men aboard is usually estimated at between 16,000 and 17,000.

Since the Armada's objective was unknown to the English, they assumed that it might attack Southampton or any of the channel ports and prepared their defenses as the fleet moved along. But on July 28, having passed most of the English coastline, the Armada anchored off Calais, opposite Dover and less than thirty miles west of Dunkirk. Calais was at this time no longer in English hands, having fallen to the French in the 1550s, and was a neutral in the present conflict.

Shortly after reaching Calais, the Spanish encountered two pieces of bad luck. One was the discovery that their troops in the Netherlands would not be joining them. Weak links had developed in the chain; among other things, the barges meant to take the soldiers across the channel had not been finished. Another misfortune was that the wind was now blowing toward the French coast, giving the English a maneuvering advantage in addition to the fact that their ships were more agile anyhow.

Another misfortune followed. It was on this night that the English, on the advice of Drake, sent out their fire ships—eight sacrifices, one might say, coated with pitch and manned by crews who lined them up abreast, pointed them at full speed toward the Armada, set them alight, and sprang at the last minute into the boats which took them back to safety. Fire ships were not a new weapon, and the Spanish commanders had already instructed their captains not to break formation and to return to their original positions if they had to move temporarily out of the way. But the psychological effect of the blazing ships, bearing down on the fleet like giant torches driven by the wind, was too much. There was physical danger as well, not only from the fire itself but from the cannon the ships carried, primed to go off as soon as the flames reached them. The Spanish ships cut their cables and fled into any open water they could find. Some ran aground, others collided, and when dawn came the English found that the Spanish formation had finally broken. Ships were scattered for miles and could not protect one another.

Squadron after English squadron selected a victim, queued up, and raced past the target, one ship behind the next, delivering almost continuous broadsides. Slowly, the Spanish cannon fell silent as ammunition ran out. Their crews, certainly as determined and courageous as their enemy, fought on with muskets. When the English had reduced a ship to relative helplessness they did not take the time to sink it but went on to another, leaving the crippled Armada blowing helplessly toward the coast. This was another danger, for the coast was no longer that of neutral France or the Spanish part of the Netherlands but the Protestant part of the Netherlands, where beached Spanish vessels would have been immediately attacked.

The next day, as the English prepared to continue the fight, the Armada was saved from total defeat by a change of wind. Instead of being blown toward shore, the ships were able to shake out their sails, gather into formation once again, and head into the North Sea. The English had by this time used up their own ammunition and had no choice but to return to port.

This victory was unlike that of Agincourt because it was not immediately evident. The English did not know how badly the Armada had been hurt. The ships had sailed away, after all, and they might sail back again or have other tricks up their sleeves. The queen's great address to her troops in camp at Tilbury, urging vigor in the defense of the country, took place in August after the danger had actually passed. Then the reports that had been coming in gained coherence and validity, and it was known that the Armada had been struggling around the coasts of Scotland and Ireland, swept by storms and losing ship after ship as the surviving crewmen fought to keep from sinking or running aground. Some eighty vessels finally returned to Spain, many of them crippled past repair. Two thirds of the men had perished. King Philip, though he lived another decade, lost heart, and Spain was never again to be a serious threat to England's security or her sea power.

English appreciation of this retrospectively triumphant turning point, when it did come, was enthusiastic. Spenser transfers the conflict from sea to land in his battle between Prince Arthur and "the Souldan" (*The Faerie Queene*, 5.8.28–42), but the reference is not hard to see. The Souldan rides in a very high chariot, "with yron wheels and hooks arm'd dreadfully," which the prince cannot approach without danger, but "still he [Arthur] him did follow every where" (5.8.33.7). The prince then draws the cover off his magic shield, and the blinding light of it causes the Souldan's horses to panic:

> *So did the sight thereof their sense dismay,*
> *That backe againe upon themselves they turned,*
> *And with their ryder ranne perforce away.*

> (5.8.38.2–4)

The incident is usually taken to refer to Drake's fire ships. As the horses continue to run, the storms off the west coast of Ireland come into allegorical play, and eventually the chariot is thrown

> *Quite topside-turvey, and the pagan hound*
> *Amongst the yron hookes and graples keene*
> *Torne all to rags, and rent with many a wound,*
> *That no whole peece of him was to be seene.*

> (5.8.42.5–8)

It is tempting to point out that King Philip, here a "pagan hound," due to Spenser's view of the Catholic Church as a false idol, had saved all of Christendom from some actual pagans, the Turks, seventeen years earlier at the Battle of Lepanto. But war is partisan by definition.

14

Life's Extras

Unprecedented luxury seems to have been the impression registered by William Harrison, our faithful eyewitness reporter of sixteenth-century England, as he surveyed the changes in living conditions within his own memory. Ordinary villagers now slept on mattresses, and some even had pillows; the better off were putting glass panes in their windows; dining tables now displayed not the old wooden bowls and spoons but pewter ones, and households on their way up the social ladder even had dishes of silverplate.[1]

It must be admitted at once that sixteenth-century prosperity was not evenly spread over the social landscape. Some fortunes fell as others rose, and hard times occasionally afflicted almost everyone. Furthermore, any view of the period taken from a literary perspective is forced into a sociological bias, for its focus must rest most sharply upon the classes with the closest connections to literature—the several classes, that is, from the nobility through the various middle strata, that produced the writers and also the readers. We thus find ourselves in a snobbish stance, fixing our attention on the brighter peaks of the social landscape and seeming to imply that the lower slopes did not exist, that there were no crowded laborers' cottages, no children fed on crusts and parings. And yet, without denying the crippling effects of poverty, there is reason to assume that life for many people whom we would consider quite poor nevertheless held much satisfaction. Family stability was high; most people enjoyed the psychological security of living among neighbors whom they had known all their lives; leisure, even though they had comparatively little of it, was the more cherished. And, by and large, leisure was increasing, while life for a growing segment of the population became more than a matter of scraping together the barest necessities.

Houses and Furnishings

The Tudor age had seen the end of internal warfare in England. The Civil War in the seventeenth century was to bring a brief return of battles and sieges, but these were temporary, not a way of life, and the English were eager to return to the domestic peace to which they had become accustomed. During Queen Elizabeth's time, a nobleman on his country estate need no longer assume that at any moment his neighbor might ride over the hill at the head of an armed troop. It was consequently no longer necessary to live within thick walls or peer out through arrow slots. To celebrate this new freedom, noblemen built houses with ornate glass windows, designed gardens instead of moats, sent for a troupe of players to give a performance in the great hall, and invited the neighbors in to watch. Often the invitation list went much higher. Several of Queen Elizabeth's courtiers built great houses on purpose to entertain their sovereign, a form of competition which the frugal queen naturally encouraged.

The plans of these aristocratic dwellings varied, but usually the two- or three-storied building enclosed or partly enclosed a courtyard or a series of them. Indoors, the "great hall" represented a holdover from the medieval castle, but the grand staircase, with its carved posts and generous proportions, was a Tudor innovation. Earlier staircases had been circular and cramped, often built into a tower, with arrow slots at intervals. The upper stories now often contained a "long gallery," where ladies might walk on rainy days or do fancy needlework, and a library displaying not only the family's growing collection of books but curiosities brought home from the sons' foreign travel.

The bedrooms in stately Tudor houses sometimes give present-day visitors a feeling that something is wrong, a vague trepidation traceable to the fact that architects had not yet invented the corridor. Consequently, one room opened into the next in a way that gave the occupants no way to shut the door and achieve some privacy without disrupting traffic. Occasionally a room built off the mainstream might be closed off, and these were called "closets"; Ophelia, sewing in hers, may well have enjoyed a many-windowed private study and should not be visualized in a tiny cubicle among the coat hangers (*Hamlet,* 2.1.74).

Interior furnishings, even in great houses, combined the functional and rather bare look of earlier centuries with the Elizabethan love of ornament. Chairs were of wood, for example, not very comfortable by our standards, but they were often richly carved. Chairs were, in fact, a luxury; backless stools were much more common. Chests were a favorite item of furnishing, since they provided storage space as well as extra seating and displayed carving to advantage. Tapestries and embroidered hangings added elegance and were practical in shutting out drafts. Imported Turkish carpets were more likely to be used to cover tables than floors; the floors themselves were often left bare, especially in upstairs rooms, while the flagstones on the ground floor might be covered with straw or rushes.

Less affluent households often achieved similar effects though on a smaller scale. Diamond-paned windows, wooden paneling, and ceilings of ornamental plaster gave an air of comfort to small manor houses as well as to aristocratic mansions. Heating depended on open fireplaces; the room-size stove had not come into use, let alone furnaces and radiators.

Gardens and Flowers

Outside the house, the "orchard" contained not only fruit trees but flower beds and, often, kitchen herbs; the Elizabethans loved rosemary and lavender, mint and thyme. Gardeners laid out beds in intricate geometrical patterns, controlling nature in a quite straightforward fashion. The revolution in landscaping that began in the late eighteenth century, when designers strove for romantic wildness and gardens were planned to look unplanned, was still in the future. Instead, Elizabethan gardens with their well-defined walkways, their balanced and often symmetrical plantings, might be seen as reflecting the age's preference for visible authority. Gardens in literature often symbolize harmonious human society; the gardeners in *Richard II* (3.4.40–47) draw a detailed analogy.

The rose was and remains the queen of flowers, but the sixteenth-century version was looser and fluffier than today's hybrid teas. The old-fashioned cabbage roses to be seen in Dutch paintings are closer to the Elizabethan model. Second most popular was the lily, of which several varieties were grown. The white madonna lily was similar to the plant Americans call the Easter lily. The fleur-de-lys, although Perdita calls it a lily (*The Winter's Tale*, 4.4.127), is actually an iris.

Carnations, or gillyflowers, were among the Elizabethan's favorite garden flowers and looked much as they do today. The pansies which Opelia gives Laertes, or thinks she gives him, "for thoughts" (*Hamlet*, 4.5.176) were not today's round, happy-faced blossoms, a recent horticultural development, but a smaller relative something like a violet. Heartsease and love-in-idleness were other names for the same plant.

Of the wild flowers that begemmed the English countryside, the violet and the daffodil, respectively, have not changed form or nomenclature over time or space, and our mind's eye can supply the picture the English poet expects. The woodbine of Titania's bower (*A Midsummer Night's Dream*, 2.2.251) is another name for honeysuckle. The type that grows in England is similar to but less aggressive than the Japanese honeysuckle with which American gardeners have a love-hate relationship.

Wildflowers mentioned in English literature but not native or naturalized in America include the oxlip and the cowslip; the resemblance of the yellow blossoms to a bovine mouth is slight, but flower names are, after all, expressions of the imagination. The oxlip is slightly larger. Both are related to the primrose, which also grows wild in England. (Primroses are, of course, not related to real roses.) Some confusion has been set up by the early settlers in America, who tended to call vaguely familiar-looking flowers by the names they knew. Thus, for instance, we have the Virginia cowslip, an attractive blue flower but not precisely the one Ariel planned to lie in the bell of (*The Tempest*, 5.1.89).

Hunting of the Deer and Other Beasts

Hunting was a privileged pastime in the hierarchical Elizabethan world. Members of certain social strata might pursue certain beasts or fowl, while others, lacking the requisite territorial rights, could take no part in such sports at all—at any rate, not legally.

The sovereign was chief hunter, so to speak, in this very feudal order of things, holding sway over the "royal forests," or game preserves, and occupying a central position in the etiquette of the chase.[2] A forest in this sense did not necessarily have to have trees in it. Nor did it have to be enclosed; people simply knew where the boundaries were. Here the sovereign and his or her courtly guests pursued the "beasts of the forest," traditionally defined as the hart, the hind, the hare, the boar, and the wolf. Of these, wolves had almost disappeared by Elizabethan times, but the quite dangerous boar was a favorite quarry, pursued by dogs and killed with a spear. Usually the professional huntsmen in charge of the practical proceedings did the actual killing of the boar.

The hart and the hind, to continue the list of "beasts of the forest," were the male and female, respectively, of the red deer, the largest deer native to England. The hart might also be called a stag. These, too, were hunted with dogs, the pursuers usually on horseback, and the weapon was the bow and arrow.

The smallest of the "beasts of the forest," the hare, was also hunted, or coursed, with dogs, sometimes with greyhounds, who work by sight rather than smell.

Not surprisingly, references to hunting practices and terminology make frequent appearances in Elizabethan literature. Horned creatures lent themselves to cuckoldry jokes, as mentioned in chapter 8, above. Again, the lover as hunter becomes a natural metaphor, as in Sir Thomas Wyatt's sonnet:

> *Whoso list to hunt, I know where is an hind,*
>
> . . . .
>
> *Who list her hunt, I put him out of doubt,*
> *As well as I may spend his time in vain;*
> *And, graven with diamonds, in letters plain*
> *There is written her fair neck round about:*
> Noli me tangere, *for Caesar's I am,*
> *And wild for to hold, though I seem tame.*

(Tradition has it that the elusive prey in this instance was Anne Boleyn, in whom King Henry VIII had become interested at the time the poem was written.)

Orsino, in *Twelfth Night,* varies the metaphor and alludes to the legend of Actaeon, who spied on the goddess Diana and was changed into a stag, to be run down by his own hounds. When he first saw Olivia, Orsino claims,

> *That instant was I turn'd into a hart,*
> *And my desires, like fell and cruel hounds,*
> *E'er since pursue me.*

(1.1.19–22)

The royal forests were administered under forest law, a quite ancient body of tradition existing apart from common law, though it seems to have had a common-law justification in that the king in the thirteenth century was held to have the right to establish a forest where he pleased.[3] Often the result was that the king owned the hunting rights while the land itself was owned, or rather held, by someone at a lower level of the feudal pyramid. Restraint in the establishment of royal forests was one of the reforms forced upon the Crown by the rebellious barons of King John. The sanctity of the "king's deer" gives drama to the Robin Hood stories; their locale, Sherwood Forest in Nottinghamshire, occupied an area twenty miles long and from five to nine miles broad. Forest law disappeared with the forests—that is, with forests in the sense of royal game preserves—during the English Civil War.

The crown also permitted—or franchised, in a sense—hunting rights for the nobility through royal grants allowing the establishment of a chase or park. (The grant did not bestow the land, merely the right to hunt on land the nobleman already owned.) The chase, by definition, was not enclosed, while the park was. Many of England's stately homes still retain their deer parks, although these have often been greatly reduced from their original size.

In either a chase or a park, the privileged nobleman and his guests might hunt the five "beasts of the chase": the buck, the doe, the fox, the marten, and the roe. Once again hierarchical distinctions required a specific use of terminology which might become a bit looser in other Elizabethan contexts. Bucks and does, for example, were deer, as we might assume, but of a different and smaller variety than the higher-ranking red deer; these were fallow deer. Roe were also deer, the small-est variety native to England. The marten, related to the sable, was hunted for its pelt, while the fox was thought of as vermin and was hunted, when at all, in order to get rid of it, or just to give the dogs a run. It would be another two hundred years before fox hunting became popular and developed what we now think of as its traditional form.

Another type of game enclosure, ranking below the chase or park but still carrying considerable prestige to the holder of the right to hunt there, was the warren, a word that has since come to mean a piece of ground where wild rabbits live in burrows. In Elizabethan terminology this was a place where one might hunt the hare (double listed, in a sense, as it was also a "beast of the forest"), the cony, or rabbit, the pheasant, and the partridge. As with the higher-ranking types of game preserves, the right to establish a warren came originally from the Crown. By the sixteenth century many hereditary country squires hunted the same grounds, modest by comparison to the neighboring earl's deer park but satisfying nevertheless, that their forefathers had.

Falconry: The Fascination of What's Difficult

The hunting of birds presented a special problem, assuming one had in mind a sporting occasion and did not plan merely to trap them. The shotgun as we know it had not been invented; firearms, in fact, came into use slowly for hunting because they were not very accurate for small, elusive targets. So the Elizabethans, like their predecessors for centu-ries, hunted birds by a means which had become a sport in itself, that of falconry.

A good hunting falcon represented a compromise between two quite contrary principles. The falcon had to be tame enough to fly back to her master after she had been released to hunt. But she also had to be able to hunt, and this skill was best learned in the wild. A young bird taken from the nest and raised by hand would be tame but less likely to catch the prey she went after, if indeed she quite got the point of going after prey at all. A wild bird caught and trained would have less trouble bringing down prey but might decide to revert to her earlier way of life and not be seen again. By and large, the preference was for the second choice, the skilled huntress taught to ride on the falconer's glove and return to his lure.

The term *falcon* refers to the various types of hawks that were trained for this sport, and usually the word is further restricted to the female. Female hawks are larger and somewhat more tractable than males, or tiercels. They hunted such prey as pheasant, partridge, or quail, and water birds as well; large falcons were flown at wild duck, for example.

With one exception, the names of the hawks used for falconry offer no difficulty to present-day American readers, either because the word still has the same meaning for us or because we have no prior associations to confuse with it. The peregrine falcon, for example, considered by many Elizabethan falconers the ideal bird because of its balance of tractability and hunting skill, has had some publicity in the United States as an endangered species. The merlin, smaller than the peregrine, was a favorite with lady falconers; in America it is often called the pigeon hawk. The sparrowhawk is the subject of some transatlantic confusion, as the English use the term for one of the true hawks (accipiters) and Americans use it for the slightly smaller kestrel. The general effect is the same, as far as the reader's imagination is concerned.

The word *buzzard,* however, sends Americans right off the track. The word properly belongs to hawks of the genus *Buteo,* which includes the bird we now call the red-shouldered hawk. To the early settlers in America, however, a large bird was a large bird, and they gave the name *buzzard* to the enormous turkey vulture, a carrion eater and an entirely different sort of creature. The buzzard, properly so called, was seldom used for falconry because it is slow-flying and tends to prefer small mammals to birds, but it should be recognized as a bird of prey.

Literary associations with falconry often focus on the difficulty of training what is, after all, a wild animal. Othello refers to Desdemona as a "haggard," that is, a bird which has lived in the wild before being caught and which might fly away again. Should that happen, Othello says, he will make no effort to reclaim her, "though that her jesses [straps attached to the falcon's feet] were my dear heart-strings" (3.3.261).

Petruchio uses many metaphors from hawking in *The Taming of the Shrew*; the audience would have taken the implied point that Katherina's wildness and self-sufficiency will make her, once tamed, a more valuable bird than a meek, hand-raised one—Bianca, perhaps. Bianca displays a will of her own at the end, but she is not dependable, and Katherina defeats her in a contest that is overtly aligned to a sporting wager.

The Pleasures of the Table

Food for the Elizabethans was, for the most part, a very local matter. With no refrigeration, perishable items could not be sent very far, even if the roads allowed for more than packhorse traffic. Villages were self-sufficient in many ways, and towns depended on meat and produce brought in from a comparatively short radius.

Not surprisingly, social gradations were very evident from the perspective of kitchen and table. The aristocracy favored meat dishes, serving up the game brought back from the hunt. Merchants and others of the middle class lived thriftily much of the time, keeping an eye on expenses, but splurged on feasts for special occasions; a favorite project of the trade guilds was giving themselves ceremonial dinners. The country gentry and the better-off farmer used their resources with versatility; and the poor made the best of what they could get, often (though not always consistently) helped by the charity of their neighbors.

The cooks in high-ranking households went in for quite elaborate doings, chopping food into bits and reassembling it in unrecognizable forms, with much use of spices and secret ingredients. The spices may have been a practical necessity in case the meat had gone a bit off. Sugar was a favorite additive to almost everything.

Present-day readers are usually familiar with traditional English festive foods—or with the idea, if not the actuality, as in the case of the boar's head associated with Christmas. The peacock, roasted and with a few of its own feathers added for effect, was also a Christmas dish, though for some reason it seems to have dropped out of the legend.

Menus for festive occasions, or even fairly ordinary occasions, were often immense. Gervase Markham in one of his encyclopedic works suggests fifteen courses for a family meal with a few friends, as follows: 1) brawn (pork) with mustard; 2) boiled capon (chicken, specifically a castrated cock); 3) boiled beef; 4) roasted beef; 5) roasted neat's (cow's) tongue; 6) roasted pork; 7) baked chewets (various chopped meats, mixed with spices and fruit); 8 roasted goose; 9) roasted swan; 10) roasted turkey; 11) roasted venison; 12) venison pasty (pie, in a pastry crust); 13) "a kid with a pudding in its belly"; 14) olive pie; and 15) a custard or dowsets (sweet dishes).[4]

It is a relief to know that diners were not expected to eat their way through all these courses. Instead, one simply chose what one would like. Uneaten food did not go to waste but was given to the servants. It is also a relief, in view of the relentless protein content of the above menu, to note that Markham recommends side dishes of fresh vegetables. His suggested list of "sallats" would not look amiss on a present-day salad bar, including scallions, radishes, young lettuce and cabbage, boiled onions, asparagus, cucumbers, "the fine thin leaf of the red Coleflower," bean-cods, samphire (a plant growing on seaside rocks, often pickled), and "skirrets" (a type of water parsnip).

Bread would have accompanied the meal, probably the more expensive and fine-textured kind. Bread made with a higher proportion of bran or with an admixture of rye flour would be eaten on more ordinary occasions.

Drink might have included wine, a status symbol in England as it had to be imported. Beer was just coming into use with the innovation of growing hops to flavor it. England's traditional drink was ale, usually made locally. As it could be had in various strength and quality, it too denoted the status of the repast.

Markham's menu does not include fish, being intended presumably for a non-Lent or non-fasting day. Fish was eaten in great quantities, however. The government saw the fishing industry as important not just in itself but as a training school for seamen and thus a factor in national defense. The Church of England, far from giving up fast days when it parted from Rome, added some more; a statute during the reign of Queen Elizabeth provided that flesh (red meat) was to be forbidden not only during the forty days of Lent but during any of the Wednesdays, Fridays, and Saturdays of the year. The ban was to be lifted for Christmas, should it fall on a fast day.

Alehouses, Taverns, and Ordinaries

Elizabethan England lacked both fast-food franchises and five-star restaurants, as we know these phenomena, but their counterparts existed to some extent. An Elizabethan who lived in lodgings, or who had his own household but sometimes found himself at a distance from it, would not starve.

Alehouses varied in status but inclined to the low end of the social spectrum. As their name implies, they emphasized the drink rather than the food. Patrons might order something to eat, perhaps a meat pie, or fresh or dried fruit, but they would not expect much choice. The ale itself was locally brewed, often on the premises. Its quality (or lack of it) was a major factor in the alehouse's reputation.

Greater variety obtained at a tavern, where wines (including "sack," or Spanish sherry) might be on hand as well as local ale and beer. Beer, flavored with the pistillate cones of the hop vine, was a new wrinkle in sixteenth-century beverages. With regard to food, taverns could usually provide whole meals, not just snacks. Falstaff's bill at the Boar's Head (*1 Henry IV,* 2.4.535–39), cited in chapter 5, above, probably exaggerates the proportion of drink to food, but the items themselves (wine, bread, chicken, and anchovies) would have seemed plausible to the original audience. Eggs, butter, and cheese were usually kept on hand as well, along with dried, smoked, or pickled foodstuffs with a long shelf life, as we might put it. For special occasions one consulted with the host beforehand, so that the meal could be bought and cooked to order.

An "ordinary" was, in England, an eating-house providing meals to the public at a fixed price. (Americans may have encountered this word as it was used in eighteenth-century Virginia, referring more broadly to any sort of tavern or inn.) At an ordinary, the fare might be fresher than that available at a tavern, as meals were the main business and the proprietor could assume that everything he bought at market would be eaten. Patrons did not order from a menu; they simply sat down. Thomas Nashe writes of a "pease porridge ordinary,"[5] a class of fare which would have been low in price and reasonably nourishing. "Porridge" (or "pottage"), incidentally, meant a stew of vegetables, sometimes with bits of meat added; the word's association with oatmeal and other cereals did not become fixed until the later seventeenth century.

Generally, one can assume that the ordinaries based their offerings on what was available in shops and markets. In London, for example, whole streets of bakers had their loaves of wheat or rye bread ready to sell by early morning. The proprietor of an ordinary, as a steady customer, would have arranged to have his daily order delivered. Other items on the shopping list would have required personal selection. Smithfield

Market, just outside the city walls to the northwest, sold just-butchered beef, mutton, and pork under conditions which we would find remarkably unsanitary. Within the city, adjacent to a wharf near the tower, stood Billingsgate Market, specializing in fish and other seafood as well as any vegetables or fruit which had arrived by water. Since the word *billingsgate* has entered the language as a synonym for verbal abuse, one assumes the transactions were lively. The proprietor of our hypothetical ordinary would, of course, be quite used to it, as he would have been to the piles of animal entrails in Smithfield. By midday, the ordinary's customers—neighborhood tradesmen, city gallants, countrymen in London on business—would be sitting down to their meal of, say, boiled mutton, plenty of bread and cheese, boiled vegetables, reasonably good ale, and perhaps a favorite Elizabethan dish, eel pie.

The Tobacco Controversy

Tobacco smoking was introduced in the 1580s, and the debate at once began as to whether or not it was a good thing.

On the positive side was Sir Walter Raleigh, who popularized tobacco as a product of the New World. The story, possibly apocryphal, is told that one of Raleigh's servants, seeing his master breathing smoke, assumed he had caught fire and poured water on him.

Health claims were many. Spenser's Timias, from time to time an allegorical representation of Raleigh, is cured of a battle wound by a magical herb which may have been, the narrator says, "divine tobacco" (*The Faerie Queene,* 3.5.32.6), although he declines to commit himself and mentions other possibilities. More specifically, tobacco is described by William Barclay, physician and author of *Nepenthes, or the Virtues of Tobacco* (1614), as a "happy and holy herb," curing, among other things, melancholy and epilepsy.[6]

Fashionable London gallants hastened to learn the art of smoking, or "drinking tobacco," and heated up the economy as they did so. Tobacco and the long clay pipes for smoking it could be bought from apothecaries, but a smoker did not have to carry his equipment around with him. Up-to-date taverns offered "a pipe of tobacco," to be ordered as easily as a glass of ale.

On the negative side could be heard the voice of King James, who published *A Counterblaste to Tobacco* in 1604, shortly after ascending the English throne. The king finds fault with the origins of tobacco; why imitate "the wild, godless, and slavish Indians, especially in so stinking a custom?" He also expresses sympathy with nonsmoking wives: "Moreover, which is a great iniquity, and against all humanity, the husband shall not be ashamed, to reduce thereby his delicate, wholesome, and clean complexioned wife, to that extremity, that either she must also corrupt her sweet breath therewith, or else resolve to live in perpetual stinking torment."[7]

Ben Jonson's characters frequently take up this question, with points scored on both sides. Abel Drugger, in *The Alchemist,* is naturally pro-tobacco, as he intends to sell it. Justice Clement, in *Every Man in His Humour,* faced with Cobb the water carrier's complaint that Captain Bobadill has beaten him for speaking against tobacco, vigorously joins the attack; Cobb is in the wrong "to deprave, and abuse the virtue of an herb, so generally received in the courts of princes" (3.3.112–13); and Cobb, who has come seeking redress, finds himself threatened with prison. But Justice Overdo, in *Bartholomew Fair,* surely as authoritative a figure as Justice Clement, has a novel argument against "that tawny weed," displaying a certain ecological awareness as well as a vivid picture of life in the New World: "And who can tell," he says, "if, before the gathering and making up thereof, the Alligarta hath not pissed thereon?" (2.6.26–27).

Fashions in Dress

Wealth, status, and class distinctions supply the scaffolding for the ebullience of Elizabethan costume. The queen, at center stage, played her part in glittering brocades, starched ruffs, jewels, and ermine; foreign ambassadors were impressed by the power such luxury implied, as they were meant to be, and the English people were pleased to see their sovereign transmitting so unambiguous a message. The queen's court glittered as well, but as the contemporary eye traveled down the social ladder it began to find scope for criticism.

Sartorial extravagance became a standard subject of complaint by the writers of the time. Courtiers and would-be courtiers were wearing their fortunes on their backs; good Englishmen were being led astray by foreign fashions; merchants, and especially their wives, were dressing above their rank; and one could no longer tell at a glance who was what. Most commentators seem to have spoken from the implied premise that their own style of dress, whatever it might have been, was appropriate to the dignity of their station in life, while all those other people were projecting images they had no right to.

In the interest of hierarchical clarification, the Privy Council and Parliament passed a series of "sumptuary laws" spelling out exactly what people could and could not wear. In the 1550s, for example, only dukes, marquesses, and earls might wear cloth-of-gold fabrics or sable furs. Blue velvet was forbidden to everyone ranking lower than an earl, a baron, or a Knight of the Garter. The cut-off point for embroidered garments was placed at a baron's son, a knight (any kind), or a gentleman with an income of 200 pounds a year. Ruffs of lace or finely woven linen, some of which went to luxuriant extremes and made the wearer's head seem to rest on a platter, provided instantly measurable status displays, and the government attempted to regulate the diameters appropriate to varying social ranks. Not surprisingly, none of this legislation worked, and early in the seventeenth century Parliament repealed it.

Like any new consumer enthusiasm, the flowering of fashion encouraged the development of new industries, in some cases literally cottage industries. Knitting made its first commercial appearance in the 1550s, an astonishing fact in view of how easy it is; surely someone would have thought of it. Cloth weaving, after all, a much more complicated enterprise, had been done for centuries, if not millennia. The answer seems to be that nobody really saw the potential. Knitting had been developed in Scotland and spread slowly to England, knitters at first turning out woolen caps before moving on to hosiery and finding an eager market. Earlier stockings had been cut from woven cloth and seamed up, with an inevitable bag at the knees, while knitted articles were more comfortable and more flattering. Housewives who combined knitting with their other duties could clothe their families or bring in some income, as they chose. Mechanized production arrived with the development of the stocking frame in the late sixteenth and early seventeenth centuries.

Another minor industry springing up with the new fashions was the art of starching the controversial ruffs and other trimmings of lace, holland, and cambric. These artisans not only did the washing and starching but made their own starch as well. Joan Thirsk describes the lengthy process of steeping wheat bran in water, drying, and grinding it. This undertaking could easily be combined with pig fattening by giving the pigs the bran that was strained off as the starch was refined.[8]

For the present-day reader, understanding references to specific garments often becomes a matter of decoding the names of things. This terminology tends to shift over time, as fashion likes to think of itself as constantly changing and will often give a new name to an old garment. Also, Elizabethan and Jacobean clothing could be remarkably fragmented, breaking itself up into separate items such as sleeves and stomachers, and the items can be hard to visualize.

The following list should be helpful in making a start. For men's costume:

Bombast. Stuffing, as for puffed sleeves; usually cotton batting, of low quality. Cotton was not widely used as a woven fabric until machinery was developed for spinning a strong thread, centuries later.

Codpiece. An appendage at the front of the trunk-hose (see below) for the wearer's private parts, often ornamented and, from a present-day viewpoint, scandalously conspicuous.

Doublet. A close-fitting jacket. This might end at the waist, or might have short skirts.

Hose. The word meant whatever was worn on the legs and was not limited to stockings. (Stockings, however, were confusingly called "hosiery.") "Trunk-hose" refers to the upper part, covering the thigh, sometimes padded with bombast.

Jerkin. A jacket worn over the doublet, with slightly longer skirts.

Points. Laces or ties for attaching separate pieces of garments, such as the hose to the doublet.

Sleeves. As we would expect, but often detachable, to be mixed and matched with other garments.

Women's sleeves were also detachable. Other articles of women's clothing:

Bodice. Close-fitting upper part of the dress, often separate from the skirt.

Farthingale. A hoop petticoat varying in shape from round to oval.

Girdle. Not an undergarment but a sash worn around the waist.

Kirtle. A skirt.

Smock. A woman's undergarment, worn next to the skin.

Stomacher. Did not have to do with the stomach, though it was worn on the front of the torso, under the bodice and showing through the laces, or filling in the low neckline. Often ornamented with jewels.

Music

Present-day music historians become impatient with Tudor England because of its isolation from the European trends leading ultimately toward opera, the full symphony orchestra, modern harmonic theory, tempered scales, and much else. Sixteenth-century English music still relied on polyphony, or interwoven melodic lines, rather than the chord-based harmony being developed elsewhere.

England's nonprogressive condition had been caused in part by the Reformation and its disapproval of musical ornamentation that might distract from the verbal content of religious services. If, for example, a composer set a psalm to music, he must be sure the words came through clearly; the melody must match the text, one note per syllable, with no crowding and no extraneous elaboration. In Catholic countries, by contrast, composers such as Palestrina found in the Church a patron of musical innovation.

Meanwhile, most Englishmen had no suspicion that they were languishing under a cloud and went on enjoying their music—an enjoyment shared, needless to say, by many present-day musicians and listeners. Brisk progress from one chapter to the next in a textbook of music history is, after all, not the only criterion.

Elizabethan music was, for a large part of the population, a participatory delight and not merely an auditory one. People had no way of reproducing a musical performance, or of calling up music to order by pushing a button; one had to have the real thing. People thus learned music not only for their own pleasure but for that of their friends. Among these amateur musicians had been, in the earlier part of the century, King Henry VIII, who sang, played several instruments, and composed pieces for voices and viols which are still performed. The king is also said to have composed several masses, now lost.

The lute, emblematic of poetry as well as music, is perhaps the archetypal sixteenth-century instrument. The virginals, a keyboard instrument something like a spinet, almost always called by the plural form even if one is speaking of only one of them, was a favorite of Queen Elizabeth and many others. Other popular instruments included various sizes and pitches of recorders, the wooden flutes which regained popularity in the twentieth century, and several members of the violin family.

Many Elizabethans had learned to sing at sight and could, as the saying went, "bear a part" among a group of friends gathered to try out the latest book of "ayres" (relatively simple part songs) or madrigals (more elaborate contrapuntal compositions). Other sixteenth-century composers were William Byrd (not related to the eighteenth-century Virginia writer), who wrote many pieces for the virginals; Orlando Gibbons, considered the last great figure of the English polyphonic school; John Dowland, famous for his lute songs; and Thomas Morley, who specialized in madrigals. Morley held the monopoly for printing ruled music paper and songbooks, a lucrative privilege, and brought out many of his own works. Among these was a textbook, *A Plaine and Easie Introduction to Practicall Music,* destined to remain popular for nearly 200 years.

In learning to sight-read, Elizabethan singers often began with the "gamut," a group of six consecutive notes in which the only semitone, or half-step, occurred between the third and fourth note.[9] The syllables sung were "Ut-re-mi-fa-sol-la," which will sound familiar to present-day readers, though in a truncated manner as we are used to adding "ti" and then going up one more semitone to finish the scale. The gamut goes back to the eleventh century, however, long before the day of scales, when church plainsong was sung in modes; and as a learning device it simply taught the singers where to put the semitone. The gamut was a relative system, not an absolute one, and when the instructor wanted to teach his pupils to read more notes he simply moved the gamut up or down the written clef, overlapping it with the one previously learned if necessary to get the semitone properly placed between "mi" and "fa," and off they went again, looking at the written notes and singing the mnemonic syllables. Learning the gamut was a beginners' exercise, and one suspects that pupils learned to sight-read as quickly as possible in order to escape from it.

Shakespeare's Hortensio, in *The Taming of the Shrew,* uses the gamut as the framework of his love letter to Bianca (3.1.73–78). Before she realizes what the note contains, Bianca objects to reading it because, as a fairly advanced music student, "I am past my gamut long ago." After reading it, she says she prefers the traditional one.

Dance

Dancing was an art that, like so much else in the ordered Elizabethan world, needed to be learned; one did not just go out on the floor and do something. Nor did the couple function as a self-contained unit, spinning about on its own with no concern for the other dancers except to avoid bumping into them. Instead, one learned to dance as one would learn any complex pattern, and then everyone danced together. This idea, and often the experience as well, is familiar to many American readers because of the continuing popularity of the country dances brought over by our immigrant ancestors.

Compared to the country dances, those done at court were usually more elaborate. Here, under a strong French influence, courtiers could display their mastery of the latest steps, some of them quite acrobatic. In *Twelfth Night,* Sir Andrew's wondrously deluded view of himself as an accomplished gallant is encouraged by Sir Toby, who praises the former's aptitude for the galliard, a lively dance with three beats to the measure—speeded-up waltz time, so to speak; the coranto or "running dance," also in triple time; and the cinquepace, a figure in the galliard (1.3.125–33).

But dancing meant more to the English than an opportunity to show off. Queen Elizabeth danced all her life, not only at courtly entertainments but sometimes just for fun, with her ladies-in-waiting on the spur of the moment. Poets used the dance quite consciously as an emblem of harmony and order. The whole cosmos was seen as performing an elaborate dance; the stars revolved in their stately courses, and all smaller microcosms reflected the heavenly example. E. M. W. Tillyard, in *The Elizabethan World Picture*, quotes lines from Sir John Davies's unfinished poem, *Orchestra*, describing the relationship of the sea to the moon:

> *And lo the sea, that fleets about the land*
> *And like a girdle clips her solid waist,*
> *Music and measure both doth understand;*
> *For his great crystal eye is always cast*
> *Up to the moon and on her fixed fast.*
> *And as she danceth in her palid sphere*
> *So danceth he about his center here.*[10]

Shakespeare's plays include many dances; his comedies often end with them, reaffirming the link between social and heavenly harmony in a way that is typical of the genre.[11] In *The Merry Wives of Windsor*, Falstaff is made a victim in the final dance; as the figure in the center, not so much honored as entrapped, and complete with a set of horns, he is mocked by the other dancers and pinched by the elves. But in the closing lines Mistress Page invites him along with the rest of the company to return to the shelter of an orderly and happy society:

> *Heaven give you many, many merry days!*
> *Good husband, let us every one go home,*
> *And laugh this sport o'er by a country fire—*
> *Sir John and all.*

> (5.5.240–43)

In *Much Ado About Nothing*, Benedick expresses his sudden enthusiasm for the married state as well as his forgiveness of Claudio with a general invitation to the dance: "Come, come, we are friends. Let's have a dance ere we are married, that we may lighten our own hearts and our wives' heels. . . . Strike up, pipers" (5.4.117–19, 128). And in *A*

Midsummer Night's Dream, the fairies' final procession, as they set out singing and dancing to bless the newlyweds and their issue, becomes an emblem of harmony. The reconciliation of Titania and Oberon, supernatural forces whose earlier strife had disrupted the weather, combines with the correct alignment of the earthly lovers to produce the right kind of dance.

> *With this field-dew consecrate,*
> *Every fairy takes his gait,*
> *And each several chamber bless,*
> *Through this palace, with sweet peace,*
> *And the owner of it blest*
> *Ever shall in safety rest.*

(5.1.415–20)

Notes

1. Degree and Rank in Elizabethan England

1. I have not used the term *social class* because for present-day readers the connotations are likely to be misleading. The idea of a "class" in the sense of a large and at least potentially allied segment of society, conscious of itself as such and especially conscious of its relationship to one or more other large segments in a drama of exploiters and exploitees, poised for imminent conflict, is not really applicable to the period we will examine here. In preindustrial England, people belonged to any of a large variety of different status groups and did not primarily concern themselves with the exercise of political power. As Charles Wilson has pointed out in *England's Apprenticeship 1603–1763* (London: Longman, 1965), "the social categories invented by nineteenth-century historians—feudal, bourgeois, working class—do not sit happily on such a society" (xiv).

2. A useful modern edition is that done by Georges Edelen in 1969 for the Folger Shakespeare Library, published by Cornell University Press. Edelen modernizes the spelling and includes corrections to F. J. Furnivall's edition of 1877–1908 for the New Shakspere Society [sic].

3. Ibid., 94.

4. Ibid., 102.

5. Ibid., 113–14. Joyce Youings in *Sixteenth-Century England* (Harmondsworth: Penguin, 1984), 321, points out that Harrison's wording here is close to that of a passage written by Sir Thomas Smith and published in 1584 in *De Republica Anglorum: The Manner of Government or Policy in the Realm of England.*

6. Harrison, 115.

7. Ibid., 117–18.

8. Ibid., 118.

9. King's figures are given in tabular form in Peter Laslett's *The World We Have Lost* (New York: Scribner's, 1965), 32–33. This version is based on that printed by Charles Davenant in his 1699 *Essay upon the Probable Methods of Making a People Gainers in the Balance of Trade.* Besides his experience in drawing up genealogies, King had served as secretary to several high government ministers and had access to many kinds of official tabulations. His figures are not based on actual census records of the kind familiar today, but as well-informed estimates they have won the respect of his contemporaries and also of present-day scholars equipped with more detailed, though fragmentary, data such as parish burial records. As Laslett puts it, "We have found . . . that King's figures are surprisingly accurate wherever we have been able to provide independent checks on them" (245).

10. G. R. Elton, *England under the Tudors,* 2d ed. (London: Methuen, 1974), 230. This three-and-a-half million applies to England only. Present-day Great Britain also includes Scotland and Wales (with the further addition of Northern Ireland in references to the United Kingdom), and figures on England by herself are, in fact, hard to come by as they lack official status. Nevertheless, William Harford Thomas, in the fifteenth-edition *Encyclopedia Britannica*'s article on "England," interprets figures from the 1981 census to give a population for England alone of 46,221,000. It would seem that when we create Elizabethan England in our mind's eye, we must imagine a much lonelier landscape than we see today.

11. The reader will recall that the title of baronet had been invented by James I in 1611. After eighty years, it appears to have eclipsed the knights, although, since knighthoods are created individually, the ratio is not at all stable. The middle of the twentieth century, for example, found the kingdom with 1,205 baronets and approximately 3,700 knights, a figure taken from the irreverent but factual *Bluff Your Way in Social Climbing* (London: Wolfe, 1967), by "John Walker, Gentleman," 10.

12. King's remaining subcategories among the wealth-increasers are 60,000 households headed by "artisans and handicrafts," 5,000 headed by naval officers, and 4,000 headed by military officers. It is difficult to estimate the degree of education or of interest in books typical of these groups, but one suspects that enthusiasm for the printed word was more an exception than a rule. The question of definition might raise its unruly head, however. It is easy to picture an artisan buying a broadside ballad or an almanac and not thinking of himself as doing anything unusual.

13. Thirty thousand vagrants seems a small number. Presumably it reflects the fact that parish relief, which Americans would call welfare, was organized territorially, and that the majority of persons in need of help would have been included among the 400,000 households headed by "Cottagers and Paupers." King gives the number of individuals in this subcategory as 1,300,000. Adding the 30,000 vagrants, we find that almost a fourth of the total population lived below or barely above the subsistence line.

2. The Tudor Dynasty

1. The present chapter gives a quite simplified view of the dynastic underpinnings of the Tudor throne. Among the many historical works ready to provide a sound continuation, along with much more comprehensive foldout genealogical charts, are the relevant volumes of the *Oxford History of England* (Oxford: Clarendon Press), ed. G. N. Clarke: J. D. Mackie, *The Earlier Tudors, 1485–1558* (1952); John B. Black, *The Reign of Elizabeth, 1558–1603,* 2d ed. (1959); Godfrey Davies, *The Early Stuarts, 1603–1660,* 2d ed. (1959).

2. The Elizabethans' ideas of kingship had evolved over a long period of time and were more complex than my necessarily simplified description may imply. Useful discussions can be found in Ernst H. Kantorowicz, *The King's Two Bodies: A Study in Mediaeval Political Theology* (Princeton: Princeton University Press, 1957), and John Neville Figgis, *The Divine Right of Kings* (1896; reprint ed., Gloucester, Mass.: Peter Smith, 1970).

3. The Genealogies of Shakespeare's Kings

1. Recent works treating the history plays in detail include Peter Saccio's *Shakespeare's English Kings* (Oxford: Oxford University Press, 1977), and H. R. Coursen's *The Leasing Out of England: Shakespeare's Second Henriad* (Washington, D.C.: University Press of America, 1982).

2. Robin Headlam Wells, *Shakespeare, Politics and the State* (London: Macmillan, 1986), 90. Headlam Wells musters a great deal of evidence for the variety of opinions held by the Elizabethans on political theory, pointing out that the official Tudor doctrine of unquestioning

obedience to the monarch was only one of several prevalent views of the subject, some of which supported the removal of a tyrannical king.

3. A. F. Pollard, "Stafford, Edward, third duke of Buckingham," *Dictionary of National Biography.*

4. Elizabethan Cosmology in Church and Government

1. A. O. Lovejoy's *The Great Chain of Being* (Cambridge, Mass.: Harvard University Press, 1936) and E. M. W. Tillyard's *The Elizabethan World Picture* (London: Chatto and Windus, 1952) provide accessible views of this way of thinking. Lovejoy's work traces the concept of the Great Chain, with some of its paradoxical implications, from Plato to nineteenth-century romanticism; Tillyard focuses on the place and time indicated by the title, with considerable attention to literary metaphors. The reader is cautioned against adopting either work as a source of instant push-button answers to the period's literary and philosophical complexities. Renaissance writers enjoyed controversy and paradox, and did not merely subscribe to an idealistic party line. Spenser's *Mutabilitie Cantos* supply an example; the principle of change may itself turn out to be part of an unchanging reality, but the reader is not meant to accept a pat formula as a substitute for the experience of the poem.

2. A. G. Dickens, *The English Reformation* (New York: Schocken, 1964), 46.

3. Paul Hair, ed., *Before the Bawdy Court: Selections from Church Court and Other Records Relating to the Correction of Moral Offenses in England, Scotland, and New England, 1300–1800* (New York: Barnes and Noble, 1972).

4. G. W. O. Woodward gives a detailed account of this undertaking in *The Dissolution of the Monasteries* (London: Blandford Press, 1966).

5. W. Broughton Carr, "Bee," *Encyclopedia Britannica*, 11th ed. (1910).

5. Elizabethan Money

1. Fischer provides an extensive glossary, listing individual coins, economic terms, jewels, and money-related objects such as various types of purses, as well as the economic connotations of words with non-economic primary meanings. References are provided to some eighty-

odd Renaissance plays, including Shakespeare's. Puns and metaphors are clarified, with particular attention, as the author points out, to "the application of economic value to the appraisal of individual human worth" (27).

2. James Mackay, *A History of Modern English Coinage, Henry VII to Elizabeth II* (London: Longman, 1984), 5.

3. Harrison, 298.

4. R. B. McKerrow, "Booksellers, Printers and the Stationers' Trade," in Sidney Lee and C. T. Onions, eds., *Shakespeare's England: An Account of the Life and Manners of His Age,* vol. 2 (Oxford: Clarendon Press, 1916), 229. McKerrow notes that this statement "should be received with caution, for it appears to rest on no more than a manuscript note cited by George Steevens as occurring in a copy then in the possession of Mssrs. White, booksellers in Fleet Street." McKerrow points out the scarcity of information on book prices; the Stationers' Register, for example, source of so many factual glimpses into the world of Elizabethan publishing, is silent on this matter.

5. McKerrow, 229.

6. In the sixteenth century there were still some local variations among what have since become standard weights and measures. The *Oxford English Dictionary* tells us that pound standards of different weights were used "for different articles, as bread, butter, cheese." The possibility of a difference does not seem worth worrying about for our present purpose.

7. Cited by Percy MacQuoid, "The Home," in *Shakespeare's England,* 2:135.

8. John Stow, *A Survey of London,* vol. 1 (Oxford: Clarendon Press, 1908), 126.

9. MacQuoid, 136.

10. Ibid., 138.

11. Of many possible references here I will give a sixteenth-century will cited by Rowland Parker in *The Common Stream* (London: Collins, 1975), 140, including "two horses the pryce of £6 bothe."

12. *Richmond Times-Dispatch* (Richmond, Va.), Oct. 23, 1988. The quarter horse is an American breed, originally developed to run races of a quarter mile, and valued for quickness and intelligence in working with cattle.

13. *Richmond Times-Dispatch,* Oct. 9, 1988. The Morgan, also an

American breed, originated as a stylish all-purpose horse for riding or driving.

14. Ibid.

15. Edwin Dampier Brickwood, "Horse," *Encyclopedia Britannica*, 11th ed. (1910); Clements Robert Markham, "Markham, Gervase," *Dictionary of National Biography*. Gervase Markham (1568?–1637) was the author of many books on horses, agriculture, and other matters.

16. C. E. Challis, *The Tudor Coinage* (Manchester: Manchester University Press, 1978), 97.

6. London

1. S. T. Bindoff, *Tudor England* (Harmondsworth: Penguin, 1950), 40; David M. Palliser, *The Age of Elizabeth: England under the Later Tudors, 1547–1603* (London: Longman, 1983), 213. These are conservative totals. Some writers suggest 300,000 for the year 1600.

2. Stow, 1:27–44.

3. John Earle, *Micro Cosmographie*, ed. Edward Arber (London: J. and W. Rider, 1869), 26–27.

4. J. E. Neale, *Queen Elizabeth I* (New York: Doubleday Anchor Books, 1957), 61–62.

5. George Unwin's *The Guilds and Companies of London* (London: Frank Cass, 1966) provides a useful survey of this field; William Herbert's *The History of the Twelve Great Livery Companies of London*, 2 vols. (London: published by the author for sale at the Library, Guildhall, 1837), goes into greater depth on the top twelve companies.

6. John Dover Wilson, in *Life in Shakespeare's England* (Cambridge: Cambridge University Press, 1911), assembles extracts from a variety of contemporary sources in his chapter on London.

7. Ann Jennalie Cook surveys estimates of the capacities of most of the London playhouses in *The Privileged Playgoers of Shakespeare's London, 1576–1642* (Princeton: Princeton University Press, 1981), 175–176.

8. Andrew Gurr, in *Playgoing in Shakespeare's London* (Cambridge: Cambridge University Press, 1987), gives a list of every individual person who can be identified through contemporary documents as having attended one or more plays between 1567 and 1642 (191–204). The total of 162 persons include lawyers, city gallants, merchants, and many other

categories and occupations, along with a number of apprentices and feltmakers whose documentation has to do with their involvement in "an affray at the Fortune," or similar misdoings. Ladies and aristocrats are most often recorded as attending private playhouses. The number of persons on the list seems remarkably small, but, of course, there was no mechanism for recording individuals at a theatrical performance— the equivalent of a present-day society columnist at an opening night, or a list of season-ticket subscribers.

7. Village and Countryside

1. The present-day reader seeking a sharper sense of preindustrial rural life may wish to go on from the minimal overview presented by this chapter into the realm of social history, where considerable illumination is taking place. Peter Laslett's *The World We Have Lost,* cited in chapter 1, above, and Rowland Parker's *The Common Stream,* cited in chapter 5, are highly readable examples of the methods and results of this scholarship. *The World We Have Lost* focuses on the seventeenth century; *The Common Stream* tells the story of a Cambridgeshire village from pre-Roman times to the present and moves through the centuries in a gripping fashion.

2. Palliser, 104.

3. R. E. Prothero, "Agriculture and Gardening," in *Shakespeare's England* 1:350.

4. Parker, 70.

5. Thomas Tusser, *Five Hundred Pointes of Good Husbandrie* (London: Trübner, 1878), chap. 53, stanza 22. This edition was published for the English Dialect Society and collates the editions of 1573, 1577, and 1580.

6. Harrison, 307.

8. Marriage Arrangements and Customs

1. Joel Hurstfield, in *The Queen's Wards: Wardship and Marriage under Elizabeth I* (London: Longman, 1958), gives a detailed account of the system.

2. Laslett, 83.

3. Anne Hathaway's age is calculated from the brass marker on her

gravestone; her death occurred in 1623, and the inscription gives her age as sixty-seven. Samuel Schoenbaum has pointed out that the engraver might have read a "1" in his script as a "7," thus adding the six years, in *William Shakespeare: A Documentary Life* (New York: Oxford University Press, 1975), 69.

4. Harrison, 131.

9. Education

1. Palliser, 359.

2. David Cressy, *Literacy and the Social Order: Reading and Writing in Tudor and Stuart London* (Cambridge: Cambridge University Press, 1980), 20.

3. Palliser, 359, citing Edmund Coote's *English Schoole Master.* Palliser points out that this work went through twenty-five editions between 1596 and 1625, an indication of the need it addressed.

4. Schoenbaum, 53.

5. Harrison, 70.

10. Literary Stereotypes: Religious, Occupational, and Regional

1. *The Works of Thomas Nashe,* ed. R. B. McKerrow (London: Sidgwick and Jackson, 1910), 2:315–16.

2. J. H. Baker, "Law and Legal Institutions," in John F. Andrews, ed., *William Shakespeare: His World, His Work, His Influence* (New York: Scribner's, 1985), 1:47. Montacute and Blickling, respectively, were built by Sir Edward Phelips and Sir Henry Hobart, high-ranking legal figures. Both houses are now in the care of the National Trust and may be visited by the public.

3. Stow, 1:78.

4. William Lambarde's *Eirenarcha: or Of the Office of the Justices of the Peace* appeared in ever-larger editions from the 1580s into the early decades of the seventeenth century. Here the justice might discover what fines to give first-offense poachers (twenty shillings for a pheasant, ten shillings for a partridge), and how to punish a person who has used witchcraft to find a treasure of gold or silver (four times in the pillory).

5. Earle, 62–63.

11. Outsiders: Witches, Criminals, and Vagabonds

1. Alan Macfarlane, *Witchcraft in Tudor and Stuart England* (New York: Harper & Row, 1970), 150–51.
2. Ibid., 16.
3. Reginald Scott, *Discoverie of Witchcraft,* ed. Brinsley Nicholson (London: Eliot Stock, 1886), 17. Nicholson reprints the first edition of 1584.
4. Scott, 29.
5. King James of England, *Daemonology,* ed. G. B. Harrison (New York: Dutton, 1924), 43–44. Harrison reprints the edition of 1597 and includes the anonymous *Newes from Scotland* (1591).
6. *Newes from Scotland,* 15.
7. Quoted by Alexander Gordon, *Dictionary of National Biography.* I have modernized the spelling. Gordon cites "Hutchinson's Historical Essay Concerning Witchcraft," 1720, as the source of the description of Hopkins's end. Its irony, though appealing, seems suspiciously pat.
8. John Bellamy, *The Tudor Law of Treason* (London: Routledge and Kegan Paul, 1979), 204.
9. Harrison, 188.
10. Sidney Lee, "Stubbs, John," *Dictionary of National Biography.* The judge was Robert Monson.
11. E. H. Miller, in *The Professional Writer in Elizabethan England* (Cambridge, Mass.: Harvard University Press, 1959), gives a tabulation of Greene's and Dekker's sources, 234–39.

12. Travel and Exploration

1. "Of Travel," in James Spedding, ed., *The Works of Francis Bacon* (London: Longman, 1870), 6:417–18.
2. *Moryson's Itinerary,* first written in Latin but translated by the author, was published in 1617. *Coryats Crudities Hastily Gobbled Up in Five Months Travels,* published in 1611, covers the author's first European journey. The word *crudity* here means a hard-to-digest food. On his later expeditions, Coryate wrote letters to his friends, some of which were published after his death.
3. Moryson, *An Itinerary* (Glasgow: University of Glasgow Press, 1907), 3:388–89.

13. The Military: Arrows, Cannon, and Sails

1. Especially readable modern studies of the Battle of Agincourt include John Keegan's *The Face of Battle* (New York: Vintage, 1977), 79–116; and Christopher Hibbert's *Agincourt* (London: Batsford, 1978). Both works are based on the earlier sources and deal with the discrepancies that occasionally occur in them. I have used the statistics that seem most generally agreed upon. Holinshed, one of these early sources, was much used by Shakespeare for this play as for others. Richard Hosley's edition, *Shakespeare's Holinshed* (New York: Capricorn Books, 1968), provides a conveniently arranged selection of the most pertinent passages.

2. Keegan goes into the logistics of killing large numbers of people in a short time, and concludes it was unlikely this order was fully carried out (110–11).

3. My dating here follows the Julian calendar that England was using in the sixteenth century. Spain had already switched to the Gregorian calendar; consequently, dates given by Spanish historians are some nine days later.

14. Life's Extras

1. Harrison, 200–201.

2. It can hardly be doubted that royal hunts were conducted with elaborate protocol, but it is difficult to determine exactly what that might have been. George Turberville's *The Noble Arte of Venerie,* published in 1576, contains many interesting details and is often cited as an authority on English hunting, but in fact Turberville was translating several French works and cannot be considered an accurate source on English customs.

3. An unsigned article on "Forest Law" in the *Encyclopedia Britannica,* 11th edition, gives a useful outline of the situation here.

4. Gervase Markham, *A Way to Get Wealth,* 6th ed. (London: John Harison, 1638), 158.

5. Nashe's dedication to Robert Greene's *Menaphon,* 1589, cited in the *Oxford English Dictionary.*

6. Included by Edward Arber in his 1895 edition of King James's *The Essays of a Prentice in the Divine Art of Poetry, and A Counterblaste*

to *Tobacco* (Westminster: Constable and Co., 1895). Arber cites evidence supporting both sides of the question.

7. King James, 112.

8. Joan Thirsk, *Economic Policy and Projects: The Development of a Consumer Society in Early Modern England* (Oxford: Clarendon Press, 1978), 84.

9. The word *gamut* has a number of musical meanings. The one most applicable here is that of hexachord, and the article by that name in *Grove's Dictionary of Music and Musicians* (fifth edition, 1954) provides an explanation of the teaching method, with a diagram of the "gamut" taken from Morley's book. The "hexachord" article in *The New Grove Dictionary of Music and Musicians* (1980), incidentally, is shorter and less clear.

10. Tillyard, 96.

11. Northrop Frye's *Anatomy of Criticism* (Princeton: Princeton University Press, 1957), 163–86, gives a cogent discussion of comedy in its larger-scale perspectives.

Bibliography

The following list contains works cited in the notes, and also a number of studies which have not been quoted but which are useful treatments of their specific topics. Most of these are immediately accessible to American readers in that they supply explanations of the less transferable details of British culture.

Andrews, John F., ed. *William Shakespeare: His World, His Work, His Influence.* 3 vols. New York: Scribner's, 1985.

Bellamy, John. *The Tudor Law of Treason.* London: Routledge and Kegan Paul, 1979.

Bindoff, S. T. *Tudor England.* Harmondsworth: Penguin, 1950.

Black, John B. *The Reign of Elizabeth, 1558–1603. The Oxford History of England,* 2d ed., vol. 8. Oxford: Clarendon Press, 1959.

Briggs, Julia. *This Stage-Play World: English Literature and Its Background, 1580–1625.* Oxford: Oxford University Press, 1983.

Byrne, Muriel St. Clare. *Elizabethan Life in Town and Country.* Rev. ed. London: Methuen, 1961.

Challis, C. E. *The Tudor Coinage.* Manchester: Manchester University Press, 1978.

Cook, Ann Jennalie. *The Privileged Playgoers of Shakespeare's London, 1576–1642.* Princeton: Princeton University Press, 1981.

Coursen, H. R. *The Leasing Out of England: Shakespeare's Second Henriad.* Washington, D.C.: University Press of America, 1982.

Cressy, David. *Literacy and the Social Order: Reading and Writing in Tudor and Stuart London.* Cambridge: Cambridge University Press, 1980.

Crofts, John. *Packhorse, Waggon and Post: Land Carriage and Com-*

munications under the Tudors and Stuarts. London: Routledge and Kegan Paul, 1967.

Cruikshank, C. G. *Elizabeth's Army.* 2d ed. Oxford: Oxford University Press, 1966.

Cunningham, Willet, et al. *A Dictionary of English Costume.* London: Adam and Charles Black, 1976.

Davies, Godfrey. *The Early Stuarts, 1603–1660. The Oxford History of England,* vol. 9, 2d ed. Oxford: Clarendon Press, 1959.

Dickens, A. G. *The English Reformation.* New York: Schocken, 1964.

Earle, John. *Micro Cosmographie.* Edward Arbor, ed. London: J. and W. Rider, 1869.

Elton, Geoffrey Rudolph. *England under the Tudors.* 2d ed. London: Methuen, 1974.

Figgis, John Neville. *The Divine Right of Kings.* 1896; reprint ed., Gloucester, Mass.: Peter Smith, 1970.

Fischer, Sandra K. *Econolingua: A Glossary of Coins and Economic Language in Renaissance Drama.* Newark, Del.: University of Delaware Press, 1985.

Frye, Northrop. *Anatomy of Criticism: Four Essays.* Princeton: Princeton University Press, 1957.

Gilkes, R. K. *The Tudor Parliament.* London: University of London Press, 1969.

Gleason, John Howes. *The Justices of the Peace in England, 1558–1640.* London: Clarendon Press, 1969.

Graham, Winston. *The Spanish Armadas.* New York: Doubleday, 1972.

Gurr, Andrew. *Playgoing in Shakespeare's London.* Cambridge: Cambridge University Press, 1987.

Hair, Paul, ed. *Before the Bawdy Courts: Selections from Church Court and Other Records Relating to the Correction of Moral Offenses in England, Scotland, and New England, 1300–1800.* New York: Barnes and Noble, 1972.

Harrison, William. *The Description of England.* Edited by Georges Edelen. Ithaca: for the Folger Shakespeare Library by the Cornell University Press, 1969.

Headlam Wells, Robin. *Shakespeare, Politics and the State.* London: Macmillan, 1986.

Herbert, William. *The History of the Twelve Great Livery Companies of London.* 2 vols. London: published by the author for sale at the Library, Guildhall, 1837.

Hibbert, Christopher. *Agincourt.* London: Batsford, 1978.

Hoskins, W. G. *The Age of Plunder: The England of Henry VIII, 1500–1547.* London: Longman, 1976.

Houlbrooke, Ralph. *Church Courts and the People during the English Reformation, 1520–1570.* Oxford: Oxford University Press, 1979.

Hurstfield, Joel. *The Queen's Wards: Wardship and Marriage under Elizabeth I.* London: Longman, 1958.

James I of England. *Daemonology.* Edited by G. B. Harrison. New York: Dutton, 1924. Includes anonymous *Newes from Scotland,* both first published 1597.

———. *The Essays of a Prentice in the Divine Art of Poesie and A Counterblaste to Tobacco.* Edited by Edward Arber. Westminster: Constable and Co., 1895.

Kantorowicz, Ernst H. *The King's Two Bodies: A Study in Mediaeval Political Theology.* Princeton: Princeton University Press, 1957.

Keegan, John. *The Face of Battle: A Study of Agincourt, Waterloo and the Somme.* New York: Vintage, 1977.

LaMar, Virginia A. *English Dress in the Age of Shakespeare.* Charlottesville: The University Press of Virginia for the Folger Shakespeare Library, 1958.

———. *Travel and Roads in England.* Charlottesville: The University Press of Virginia for the Folger Shakespeare Library, 1960.

Lambarde, William. *Eirenarcha, or Of the Office of the Justices of the Peace.* Rev. ed. London: Company of Stationers, 1619.

Laslett, Peter. *The World We Have Lost.* New York: Scribner's, 1965.

Lee, Sidney, and C. T. Onions, eds. *Shakespeare's England: An Account of the Life and Manners of His Age.* 2 vols. Oxford: Clarendon Press, 1916.

Lovejoy, A. O. *The Great Chain of Being.* Cambridge, Mass.: Harvard University Press, 1936.

Macfarlane, Alan. *Witchcraft in Tudor and Stuart England.* New York: Harper & Row, 1970.

Mackay, James. *A History of Modern English Coinage: Henry VII to Elizabeth II*. London: Longman, 1984.

Mackie, J. D. *The Earlier Tudors, 1485–1558. The Oxford History of England*, vol. 7. Oxford: Clarendon Press, 1952.

Markham, Gervase. *A Way to Get Wealth: Containing Six Principal Vocations or Callings, in Which Every Good Husband or Housewife May Lawfully Employ Themselves*. 6th ed. London: John Harrison, 1638.

Miller, Edwin Haviland. *The Professional Writer in Elizabethan England: A Study of Nondramatic Literature*. Cambridge, Mass.: Harvard University Press, 1959.

Moryson, Fines. *An Itinerary*. Glasgow: University of Glasgow Press, 1907.

Neale, John E. *The Elizabethan House of Commons*. London: Cape, 1963.

———. *Queen Elizabeth I: A Biography*. New York: Doubleday Anchor Books, 1957.

Palliser, David M. *The Age of Elizabeth: England under the Later Tudors, 1547–1603*. London: Longman, 1983.

Parker, Rowland. *The Common Stream*. London: Collins, 1975.

Pound, John. *Poverty and Vagrancy in Tudor England*. London: Longman, 1971.

Saccio, Peter. *Shakespeare's English Kings: History, Chronicle, and Drama*. Oxford: Oxford University Press, 1977.

Schoenbaum, Samuel. *William Shakespeare: A Documentary Life*. New York: Oxford University Press, 1975.

Scott, Reginald. *Discoverie of Witchcraft*. Edited by Brinsley Nicholson. London: Eliot Stock, 1886. Reprints the first edition of 1584.

Slavin, Arthur J. *The Tudor Age and Beyond: England from the Black Death to the End of the Age of Elizabeth*. Malabar, Fla.: Krieger, 1987.

Smith, Lacey Baldwin. *The Horizon Book of the Elizabethan World*. New York: American Heritage, 1967.

Stow, John. *A Survey of London*. 2 vols. Oxford: Clarendon Press, 1908.

Thirsk, Joan. *Economic Policy and Projects: The Development of a Consumer Society in Early Modern England*. Oxford: Clarendon Press, 1978.

Thomas, Keith. *Religion and the Decline of Magic: Studies in Popular Beliefs in Sixteenth and Seventeenth Century England*. London: Weidenfeld and Nicolson, 1971.

Tillyard, E. M. W. *The Elizabethan World Picture*. London: Chatto and Windus, 1952.

Tusser, Thomas. *Five Hundred Pointes of Good Husbandrie*. Edited by W. Paune and S. J. Herritage. London: Trübner, 1878.

Unwin, George. *The Guilds and Companies of London*. London: Frank Cass, 1966.

Walker, John. *Bluff Your Way in Social Climbing*. London: Wolfe, 1967.

Williams, Penry. *Life in Tudor England*. New York: Putnam, 1964.

Wilson, Charles. *England's Apprenticeship 1603–1763*. London: Longman, 1965.

Wilson, John Dover, ed. *Life in Shakespeare's England: A Book of Elizabethan Prose*. Cambridge: Cambridge University Press, 1911.

Woodward, George William Otway. *The Dissolution of the Monasteries*. London: Blandford Press, 1966.

Youings, Joyce. *Sixteenth-Century England*. Harmondsworth: Penguin, 1984.

Index